THE ALL NEW GO GUIDE

Pittsburgh Post-Gazette

About the authors

JAYNE CLARK has been a newspaper reporter and editor in Los Angeles, Phoenix, and Pittsburgh. She is travel editor of the Pittsburgh Post-Gazette.

GERRY WINGENBACH is a long-time free-lance writer whose articles have appeared in U.S. and foreign publications. He is the author of a book on the Rocky Mountains.

THE ALL NEW GO GUIDE

TWO-DAY GETAWAYS FROM PITTSBURGH

by **JAYNE CLARK**
and **GERRY WINGENBACH**

𝔓𝔦𝔱𝔱𝔰𝔟𝔲𝔯𝔤𝔥 𝔓𝔬𝔰𝔱-𝔊𝔞𝔷𝔢𝔱𝔱𝔢

THE ALL NEW GO GUIDE

**BY JAYNE CLARK
AND GERRY WINGENBACH**

Pittsburgh Post-Gazette

34 Boulevard of the Allies
Pittsburgh, PA 15222
(412) 263-1100
(412) 263-2014 (fax)

The Pittsburgh Post-Gazette and PG Publishing Co. are divisions of Blade Communications Inc., Toledo, Ohio.

Copyright © 1997 by the Pittsburgh Post-Gazette

Editor: Woodene Merriman
Editing assistants: Karen Carlin, Patt Risher
Cover design and illustration: Stacy Innerst
Interior design and production: Tracy A. Collins
Back cover photography: (From top) Courtesy of the Rock and Roll Hall of Fame Museum; and Robert J. Pavuchak and Tony Tye, Pittsburgh Post-Gazette

NOTICE OF RIGHTS

All rights reserved. No part of this book may be reproduced or transmitted in any form by any means, electronic, mechanical, photocopying, recording, or otherwise, without the prior written permission of the publisher. For information on getting permission for reprints and excerpts, contact Matthew Kennedy at the Pittsburgh Post-Gazette.

ISBN 0-9657325-0-9

Printed and bound in the United States of America.

Table of contents

Introduction vi

NORTH

ERIC AND PRESQUE ISLE 2-15
ALLEGHENY FOREST 16-29
CLEVELAND... 30-42
OIL COUNTRY 43-52
COOK FOREST 53-67
HISTORIC SMALL TOWNS 68-78

FINDING FALL'S FOLIAGE 79-82

SOUTH

NORTHERN W.VA. 84-97
WESTERN MARYLAND.. 98-110

BED AND BREAKFASTS..................................... 111-112

EAST

NATIONAL HIGHWAY 114-127
LINCOLN HIGHWAY 128-144

VISITORS BUREAUS... 145-147

WEST

W.VA. PANHANDLE 149-161
OHIO AMISH COUNTRY..................................... 162-177
MARIETTA, OHIO 178-188

STATE PARKS 189-193

INDEX 194-205

WELCOME TO THE GO GUIDE

Western Pennsylvanians looking for diversions can consider themselves lucky. Within three hours or less of Pittsburgh lie an amazing number of travel opportunities ranging from experiencing unsullied wilderness, to delving into history to shopping for bargains.

And it's all in some of the prettiest country anywhere.

This guide outlines 13 itineraries within 175 miles or less (one way) of Pittsburgh. The trips are presented as complete itineraries, usually taking a circular route to avoid too much backtracking. Some of the routes take in a relatively small amount of territory and can comfortably be traveled in a day. Others cover a wider swath and require more time to adequately experience all there is to see and do. Or you can select particular attractions that appeal to you and break the itineraries into shorter trips.

Directions and approximate mileage are plotted from Pittsburgh. The routes we've chosen aren't always the fastest ones, but we believe when it comes to road trips, getting there should be as enjoyable as the destination.

We've tried to provide specifics on major points of interest along each route, but the information included in this guide is not intended to be an encyclopedic listing of every attraction, inn or other commercial enterprise in the areas covered. Phone numbers and addresses for the appropriate tourist organizations are given following each narrative. These agencies are generally an excellent source of information on events, lodgings and other attractions.

We've attempted to make the Go Guide as current as possible. But businesses come and go; prices change; and the timing of events is sometimes altered. If you're intent on attending a particular festival or staying in a particular lodging, for instance, we strongly recommend you call ahead to check rates and availability.

Included in the guide are several appendixes with other sources and tips for traveling around the region. One is a comprehensive list of tourist information contacts in areas of Pennsylvania, Ohio, West Virginia and Maryland. One offers some suggestions on ideal places to view fall foliage. Another supplies tips on choosing bed and breakfast inns, along with information on where to find them. A complete list of state parks in the four-state region also is included.

These points noted, we hope you'll enjoy your travels as much as we enjoyed ours.

—*Jayne Clark and Gerry Wingenbach*

GO

NORTH

GO to Erie & Presque Isle

A windsurfer shares the lake on a beautiful day off Presque Isle.

TONY TYE/PITTSBURGH POST-GAZETTE

Erie & Presque Isle

GREAT LAKESIDE VIEW OF NATURE, HISTORY

Pennsylvania's third-largest city might be a step or two behind its big city neighbors of Pittsburgh, Buffalo and Cleveland, but that's part of its charm. Here you'll find a mid-size, unhurried city with plenty of family-oriented attractions, bordered by the closest thing the state has to a seashore, plus miles of pastoral wine-growing country.

Erie celebrated its 200th birthday in 1995 and treated itself to a new 6,000-seat ball park. It also dressed up its downtown waterfront. Dobbins Landing, the public dock area at the foot of State Street, is the site of a refurbished pier, a 15-story observation tower and several waterview restaurants that are squeezing out the old bait shops. Also new on the bayfront is a library and the state-operated Erie Maritime Museum, with a new berth for the U.S. Brig Niagara, Commodore Oliver Hazard Perry's reconstructed War of 1812 flagship. It is the tallest ship on the Great Lakes and is the official flagship of Pennsylvania. Tours are offered when it's in port.

DISCOVERY SQUARE

Near the bayfront on State Street, visitors can view regional art and explore Erie's history at Discovery Square, which includes the Erie Art Museum and the Erie History Center. The Erie Art Museum is housed in a beautiful Greek Revival building known as the Old Customs House (411 State St.) and offers a year-round schedule of art exhibits, jazz concerts and special events.

The Erie History Center occupies an 1840 commercial building. Also part of the complex is the new ExpERIEnce Children's Museum, with two floors of hands-on exhibits devoted to the wonders of science and designed to promote learning as fun for ages 2 through 12.

CITY CENTER

Downtown Erie packs in crowds on game days, thanks to the new Jerry Uht Baseball Field, home of the Pittsburgh franchise Erie SeaWolves professional Class A baseball team, and the Tullio Convention Center, home of the Erie professional hockey team. Both facilities are part of the Erie Civic Center complex, which also houses cultural attractions. They include the Warner Theatre, a restored 1931 jewel that was originally commissioned by the movie-making Warner brothers. The landmark theater now houses the Erie Philharmonic Orchestra and is a year-round venue for concerts, plays, special movie showings and more. Two blocks south is the Erie Playhouse, designated as one of America's 10 best community theaters. It features musicals, comedies and dramas all year.

PERRY HOUSE AND DICKSON TAVERN

Also worth a visit is the restored Perry Memorial House and Dickson Tavern (201 French St.), one of the oldest surviving structures in the city. Dating back to the early 1800s, it now serves as a museum with period furnishings. Dickson Tavern is contained in the lower part of the house. It was a stop on the Civil War-era "Underground Railroad" offering refuge to escaping slaves. The house is open to view on summer weekends free of charge.

MILLIONAIRE'S ROW

The Erie Historical Society has outlined walking and driving tours that pass stately homes and other noteworthy architecture in the area. West Sixth Street, with its particularly fine collection of homes, is the city's historic Millionaire's Row and the site of the Romanesque-style Erie Historical Museum and Planetarium.

PRESQUE ISLE BAY

In summer, Erie residents relish their lakeside location. More than 3,500 boats are berthed in bay marinas, and on weekends a steady pa-

GO to Erie & Presque Isle

rade of watercraft passes through Presque Isle Bay headed for the boundless waters of Lake Erie. Land-locked visitors can join the flotilla by boarding the "Little Toot," which departs Dobbins Landing on regularly scheduled narrated tours. Ferry service to Presque Isle also departs from the landing.

DOBBINS LANDING/ BICENTENNIAL TOWER

At the foot of State Street, local youth have been "cruising the dock" for generations. Erie's main public dock, Dobbins Landing, is a favorite spot for bay views, fishing or romantic rendezvous. Dobbins Landing was rebuilt in 1996 and a 187-foot observation tower, the Bicentennial Tower, was added at the end of the dock offering spectacular views of Lake Erie.

ZOO AND BOTANICAL GARDENS

Erie's Zoological Park and Botanical Gardens of Northwestern Pennsylvania is home to more than 300 animals from around the world, including giraffes, elephants, camels and even a white Bengal tiger. Most of the animals are in simulated natural environments and the 15-acre facility is manageable on foot with children in tow. Zoo memberships from Pittsburgh and many other cities are honored.

WALDAMEER PARK

Another popular family spot is Waldameer Park and Waterland, near the entrance to Presque Isle State Park. The park has water slides, thrill rides and a 10-story Ferris wheel offering a bird's eye view of Presque Isle. It is one of the largest water parks in the nation.

PRESQUE ISLE

The attraction that draws most leisure travelers to Erie is Presque Isle, a seven-mile hook of land that juts into Lake Erie on the western edge of the city. It is Pennsylvania's most visited state park, with more than 4 million visitors annually. But some regulars who know the depth of the diversity in the unique park believe it's still one of the best-kept secrets around.

In summer, Presque Isle's main attraction is its beaches. With broad expanses of sand and the seemingly endless waters of Lake Erie beyond, it feels like the seashore. There are even calm, shallow children's beaches, and a boardwalk beach for wheelchairs. Another lure is the park's scenic six-mile paved trail that weaves along Presque Isle Bay, attracting walkers, runners, in-line skaters and cyclists. For serious nature watchers, the park operates free pontoon rides on Big Pond, an ecologically rich waterway in the heart of the peninsula. (Sign up in advance at the park's interpretive center; space is limited.)

At the end of a long summer day, the perfect place to position yourself is

**GO to
Erie & Presque Isle**

GERRY WINGENBACH
Relishing the warmth of the sun and the cool Lake Erie breeze on Presque Isle's beaches.

out at Sunset Point on Budny Beach. Pull up a piece of driftwood and settle down for the daily finale as the sun slips into Lake Erie, leaving only the burning embers of clouds above.

In winter, ice fishing huts dot the surrounding waters and cold-weather sports enthusiasts enjoy ice skating, ice sailing and cross-country skiing in the park.

BIRD WATCHING

In spring and fall, Presque Isle is one of the best spots in the nation for bird watching. Located on the Atlantic Flyway, the peninsula is what ornithologists call a "migrant trap," a natural stopover for hungry and exhausted birds that have made the long flight over the lake. More than 300 bird species have been spotted here. Mid-September through mid- to late-October is an ideal time to see warblers, sparrows and other perching birds. The best places to spot them are on the east ends of the Pine Tree and Dead Pond trails, on the Sidewalk Trail and at Fry's Landing near the tip of the peninsula.

Waterfowl make themselves at home from around mid-October into December, until the lake freezes. An observation platform accessible from the Gull Point Trail (at the east end of the Beach 10 parking lot) offers a great vantage point from which to see sandpipers and other shorebirds. Gull Point, at the tip of the peninsula, is a nesting area closed to the public from April

**GO to
Erie & Presque Isle**

THE FRUITS OF FALL'S HARVEST

Inside a 165-year-old cattle barn, Theresa Pekelnicky was delivering a machine-gun-rapid pitch that was impossible to dodge.

"Sweets are at this end. Drys at the other. Mulls in the crock pot," she said, indicating a row of 32 precisely placed bottles on the counter. A jar of pretzels and a stack of little white cups sat nearby.

"Now, designate a driver and party!"

A similar, if not quite as exuberant, scene is played out almost daily in the wine-tasting rooms of the wineries in North East, 15 miles east of Erie.

That grape-growing is big business here is evident. Even non-agricultural enterprises have adopted the purple moniker — there's the Grape City Beer Co., the Grape Arbor Inn, and the local high school's athletic teams are The Grape Pickers.

Most everyone agrees that the fall harvest is an ideal time to visit the area. The pungent aroma of grapes hangs in the air and roadside stands heave with fat bunches of Concords. Local wineries grind into action and trucks rumble back and forth from the fields to the processing plants.

Welch's, the biggest of the bunch, processes a mind-boggling 100 tons or more of grapes every hour, 24 hours a day, seven days a week, during the four- to six-week harvest.

One caveat: "Wear tennis shoes. There's wine and water everywhere," warned Pekelnicky. "You're in here long enough, your shoes get drunk. It's the nature of the beast."

through November.

WINE COUNTRY

Just east of Erie lies some of Pennsylvania's finest grape-growing country. Surrounding the town of North East, 15 miles from Erie, acres and acres of vineyards stretch to the lakeshore. About 85 percent of the grapes grown in the region are Concord, the sugar-rich grapes used in jam, jelly and juice. Most of the grapes are destined for the nearby Welch's processing plant. Vineyards thrive here because Lake Erie creates a cozy microclimate that extends the growing season. The first frost generally doesn't hit until early November in a 60-mile-long, three-mile-wide swath along the lake.

Preparing for visitors at Heritage Wine Cellars in Erie wine country, east of Erie.

During the summer, lake winds circulate through the vines, keeping deadly diseases away.

But the climate is equally kind to vitis vinifera, the European varietal grape used in wine making. More popular among local growers, however, are French-American hybrids, disease-resistant wine grapes developed by scientists at Cornell University.

Vineyards first took root along the lake more than a century before the current crop of wineries sprouted up. In 1850, two growers planted the first wine grapes and the first winery opened in 1869. Others followed, only to be shut down in 1919 by Prohibition. None would reopen until half a century later with the passage of Pennsylvania's Limited Winery Act, which allowed wine producers to once again ply their craft.

Today, 15 wineries operate near the shore between Dunkirk, N.Y., south of Buffalo, and the Lake Erie islands, west of Cleveland. Four of the wineries are clustered around North East, population about 6,000, and are open to the public year round. But the best time to visit is in the fall, during the annual grape crush, when wineries buzz with activity.

HARVEST FESTIVAL

Depending on the weather, the harvest can fall as early as late August and as late as early October.

**GO to
Erie & Presque Isle**

A canoe is a great way to get around Big Pond on Presque Isle.

GERRY WINGENBACH

Picking usually begins around the last week of September, which coincides perfectly with North East's annual Wine Country Harvest Festival on the last weekend in September.

WINERY TOURS

Of the four local wineries, Heritage Wine Cellars has the most extensive facilities for visitors. The owners recently added a 200-seat restaurant in the loft of its rustic barn-turned-tasting room. Owner Robert Bostwick, a fifth-generation winemaker, started the current family enterprise in 1977. Decades earlier, his great-grandfather operated a winery about a mile away that closed during Prohibition. The winery produces about 60,000 gallons of wine a year, with about 38 varieties.

North East's other three wineries also have tasting rooms. And though they all make a number of varieties, each has its specialties.

At Mazza Vineyards, where about 50,000 gallons are produced yearly, ice wine is a best-seller. It's a sweet dessert wine made from vidal blanc grapes that are harvested after the first freeze, when sugar content is at its peak. Its price reflects its scarcity: a half bottle goes for about $16.

A canopy of grapes shelters the entrance to the winery at Penn Shore Vineyards. Inside, a quote from Thomas Jefferson advises that "No nation is drunken where wine is cheap." Among the 20,000 gallons of wine produced here annually, the specialty is kir, a semi-sweet dessert wine made with black currants.

Presque Isle Wine Cellars produces 3,000 to 5,000 gallons a year. The bulk of its business is in selling wine-making equipment, though its cabernet sauvignon and chardonnay are popular.

MEADVILLE

A couple of detours off I-79 on the way to or from Erie make for pleasant diversions, or day trips in their own right. Meadville, 30 miles south of Erie and 75 miles north of Pittsburgh, has a couple of interesting stops in its downtown historical area. They include the old Market House, an 1870 farmers market that was renovated in 1970. Small vendors sell homemade products, including crafts, cheeses and produce six days a week. It's also a popular local breakfast spot. The market's second floor houses an art gallery and small theater. Call for performance schedules. Nearby on Chestnut Street is the Academy Theatre, designed in 1885 to be a "new and beautiful Temple of Amusement." It remains so to this day, with a variety of performances staged throughout the year.

Another wonderfully preserved building is the Baldwin-Reynolds House Museum, former home of a U.S. Supreme Court Justice. The four-story, 19th-century house is filled with period antiques. Outside is an ice house and tannery on three acres of beautifully landscaped gardens.

Considerably more humble is the David Mead Log Cabin, a replica of the cabin built in 1787 by brothers David and John Mead, the area's first settlers. It's on the banks of French Creek in Kenneth A. Beers Jr. Bicentennial Park, and is furnished on one side as David Mead's home may have looked; the other side replicates a schoolhouse of the era.

CONNEAUT LAKE

About 12 miles west of Meadville is Conneaut Lake, Pennsylvania's largest natural lake. Tourism slowed after the 1994 closure of Conneaut Lake Park, an amusement park and hotel that had been a lakeshore fixture for more than a century. But the park reopened mid-summer in 1996. The 155-room lakefront hotel built in 1902 reopened as well.

The three-mile-long, 1½-mile-wide lake continues to attract boaters, fishers and those who just want to relax by the shore. Privately owned houses ring the lake, along with several public campgrounds, rental cottages and motels. There's a free state-run boat launch on N. Comstock Street off Route 618 near Conneaut Lake Park. Or board the stern-wheeler Barbara J. for narrated sightseeing cruises. A number of restaurants and other family-style amusements lie on

A father and son enjoy a day of fishing on Lake Erie.

the west side of the lake.

LINESVILLE

Continue west on Route 6 about six miles to Linesville, where a fish culture station operated by the Pennsylvania Fish Commission on Hartstown Road just south of the center of town is an interesting stop, particularly for children. Eight fish species are raised in outdoor ponds for later release into steams and lakes. Inside the visitors center is a circular, two-story aquarium that brings you face-to-face with the fish.

A half mile south of here the Pymatuning Visitors Center features a wildlife museum with interpretive displays along with more than 250 specimens, including birds, a bobcat and a black bear cub. Outside is a quarter-mile-long wheelchair-accessible nature trail.

Continuing south a half mile on Hartstown Road is a spillway billed as "where the ducks walk on the fishes' backs." On summer weekends, spectators gather at the spillway to throw bread and other food and watch thousands of fat carp engaging in a spirited food fight. It is a remarkable sight.

PYMATUNING STATE PARK

The Pymatuning Reservoir, created in the 1930s to provide water to area communities, is also an ideal bird-watching area. Like Presque Isle to the north, the reservoir is on the Atlantic Flyway and several hundred thousand

GO to
Erie & Presque Isle

waterfowl visit the refuge during the annual spring and fall migrations. Late September is prime time for waterfowl. In early February and March, you might spot bald eagles.

The 21,000-acre Pymatuning State Park (more than half of the acreage is water) has beach areas, picnic pavilions, fishing and boat rentals in summer, and cross-country skiing, ice skating and snowmobiling in winter.

The huge park sports more than 800 campsites in three campgrounds, and 20 modern cabins for rent. Most of the facilities, including the park office, cabins, major campgrounds and restaurant are at the southern tip of the lake just northwest of Jamestown.

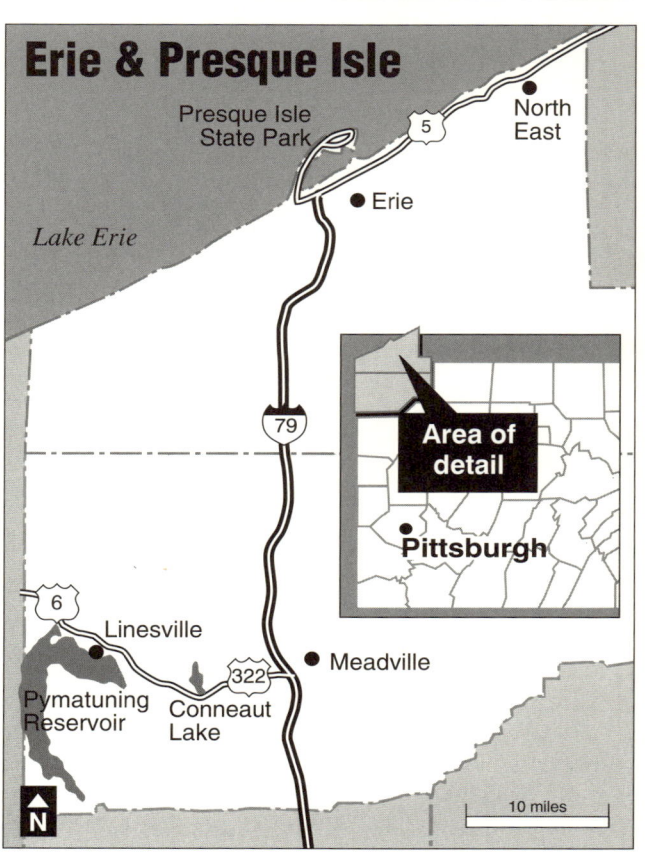

THE ROUTE

Erie & Presque Isle

From Pittsburgh take I-79 north, which goes right into the Bayfront Parkway at Erie. North East is 15 miles east of Erie. **Round-trip mileage: 270.**

To reach Conneaut Lake take exit 36B off I-79 and head west on Rt. 322. Linesville is 6 miles from the west side of the lake via Rt. 6.

GO to Erie & Presque Isle

MORE INFORMATION

➥ **Erie Area Convention & Visitors Bureau,** 1006 State St., Erie, PA 16501; (814) 454-7191

➥ **Presque Isle State Park,** Department of Conservation and Natural Resources, Box 8510, Erie, PA 16505; (814) 833-7424

➥ **North East Area Chamber of Commerce,** 21 S. Lake St., North East, PA 16428; (814) 725-4262

➥ **Crawford County Tourist Association** (Meadville and Conneaut Lake area), 242 Chestnut Ave., Meadville, PA 16335; (800) 332-2338 or (814) 333-1258

➥ **Pymatuning State Park,** Box 425, Jamestown, PA 16134; (412) 932-3141

THINGS TO DO, PLACES TO SEE

ERIE

➥ **Bicentennial Tower,** foot of State St.; (814) 455-7557. Hours: 10—6 daily. Admission: $2 adults; $1 ages 6—12; free on Tues. Observation deck at the 138-foot level of tower sits at end of the pier for great lake views. Concessions and elevator.

➥ **Erie Art Museum,** 411 State St.; (814) 459-5477. Hours: 11—5 Tues.—Sat.; 1—5 Sun. Admission: $1.50 adults; 75 cents seniors and students; 50 cents under 12; free admission Wed. Exhibits, workshops and lectures related to art and history of the region.

➥ **Erie Historical Museum and Planetarium,** 356 W. 6th St.; (814) 871-5790. Hours: June—Aug., 10—5 Tues.—Fri.; 1—5 Sat., Sun.; Sept.—May, 1—5 Tues.—Sun. Planetarium shows 2 p.m. and 3 p.m. Sun. Admission: $2 adults; $1 ages 2—12. Half-price Tues. Regional exhibits and period rooms in century-old mansion.

➥ **ExpERIEnce Children's Museum,** 420 French St.; (814) 453-3743. Hours: July and Aug., 10—4 Tues.—Sat.; 1—4 Sun.; other times of year, 10—4 Wed.—Sat.; 1—4 Sun. Admission: $3.50; free under 2.

➥ **Firefighters Historical Museum,** 428 Chestnut St.; (814) 456-5969. Hours: May—Aug., 10—5 Sat.; 1—5 Sun. Fire-fighting memorabilia housed in old #4 Erie firehouse.

➥ **Flagship Niagara,** foot of Holland St.; (814) 871-4596. Hours: May—Sept., 9—6 Tues.—Sat.; also Sun. and Mon. May—mid-June. Admission: $4 adults; $3.50 seniors; $2 ages 6-12. A reconstruction of Commodore Perry's ship from the War of 1812.

➥ **Little Toot,** Dobbins Landing at the foot of State St.; (814) 455-5892. Tours depart at regular intervals. Fare: $6 adults; $3 children. 45-minute narrated tours of the Lake Erie harbor.

➥ **Best of All Tours,** near Perry monument, Presque Isle State Park; (814) 836-0201. Hours: June 15—Labor Day, 11 a.m., 1 p.m., 3 p.m., 5 p.m.; May 1—June 15 and Labor Day—Oct. 31, Sat., Sun. 11 a.m., 1 p.m., 3:30 p.m. Fare: $10 adults; $7 ages 12—5; free under 5.

GO to Erie & Presque Isle

Narrated tours include Presque Isle Bay and Lake Erie on 49-passenger Lady Kate.

➡ **Presque Isle State Park.** Hours: Memorial Day—Labor Day, 5 a.m.—11 p.m.; 5 a.m.—9 p.m. off season. Day shelters can be rented through the park office; no overnight camping allowed. Several private campgrounds are near the park entrance.

➡ **Waldameer Park & Water World,** 220 Peninsula Dr.; (814) 838-3591. Park hours: mid-June—Labor Day, 1—10 p.m. Tues.—Sun. (closed Mon. except holidays); limited hours May—mid-June. Water World hours: 11—7 weekdays; until 7:30 weekends. Admission: $14 all-day pass; $9.75 if under 42 inches tall. Free admission to park grounds. Outdoor, water-themed amusement park.

NORTH EAST

➡ **Lake Shore Railway Museum,** 31 Wall St.; (814) 825-2724. Hours: Memorial Day—Labor Day, 1—5 Wed.—Sat.; weekends only in Sept. Admission: free. Railroad memorabilia. Also, several antique locomotives on the tracks outside, plus a view of 60-plus modern trains that pass by daily.

➡ **Lake Country Bike,** 21 E. Main St.; (814) 725-1338. Bicycle rentals and route information for touring nearby wine country.

➡ **Heritage Wine Cellars,** 12162 E. Main Rd.; (800) 747-0083 or (814) 725-8015. Hours: 9—6 daily; 9—5 in winter.

➡ **Mazza Vineyards,** 11815 E. Lake Rd.; (800) 796-9463 or (814) 725-8695. Hours: July—Aug., 9—8 Mon.—Sat.; 11—4:30 Sun.; Sept.—June, 9—5:30 Mon.—Sat.; 11—4:30 Sun.

➡ **Penn Shore Vineyards,** 10225 E. Lake Rd.; (814) 725-8688. Hours: July—Aug., 9—8 Mon.—Sat.; 11—5 Sun.; Sept.—June, 9—5:30 Mon.—Sat.; 11—5 Sun.

➡ **Presque Isle Wine Cellars,** 9440 Buffalo Rd.; (814) 725-1314. Hours: 8—5 Mon.—Sat. During grape harvest (mid-Sept.—Oct.) 8—6:30 Mon.—Sat.; 8—3 Sun.

MEADVILLE

➡ **Meadville Market House,** 910 Market St.; (814) 336-2056 or (814) 337-8023. Hours: Mar.—Dec., 8—5 daily; Jan.—Feb., 8—3 Mon.—Thurs.; 8—5 Fri.; 7—3 Sat. Vendors sell food and craft items in 1870s market.

➡ **Baldwin-Reynolds House Museum,** 631 Terrace St.; (814) 724-6080. Hours: Memorial Day—Labor Day, 1—5 Wed., Sat., Sun. Admission: $3 adults; $2 seniors; $1 ages 5—12.

➡ **David Mead Log Cabin,** Kenneth A. Beers Jr. Bicentennial Park; (800) 332-2338. Hours: Memorial Day—Aug., 1—4 Sat.—Sun. Admission: free.

➡ **Academy Theatre,** 275 Chestnut St.; (814) 337-8000. Box office hours: 11—4 Wed.—Sat. Variety of performances in 19th-century theater.

CONNEAUT LAKE

➡ **Conneaut Lake Park and Hotel,** off Rt. 618 west side of Conneaut Lake; (814) 382-5115. Hours: weekends only late May—mid-June, then daily through Labor Day, noon—9 Sun.—Thurs. and noon—10 Fri.—Sat. Water park hours: noon—dusk daily. Admission: free entry to park; $10—$13 amusement-ride tickets. Water park admission: $6. Old-fashioned lakefront amusement park with thrill rides, water park, beach and other diversions. Rates at 155-room hotel built in 1902: $69—$79; suites $110.

➡ **Barbara J. Stern-Wheeler excursions,** departures from waterfront at Conneaut Lake Park; (888) 802-3301 or (814) 382-7472. 45-minute narrated tours depart hourly Memorial Day—

GO to Erie & Presque Isle

Labor Day, noon—8. Call for days of operation.

↪ **Conneaut Cellars Winery,** Rt. 322, Conneaut Lake (exit 36 B off I-79); (814) 382-3999. Hours: 10—6 daily. Closed Mon., Jan.—Mar. Winery tours and tastings.

PYMATUNING/LINESVILLE

↪ **Pymatuning State Park,** Rt. 322, Jamestown; (412) 932-3141. Campgrounds, cabins, beaches, boat rentals and more. Camping, 2nd weekend in Apr.—3rd weekend in Oct. Campsites, cabins available on first-come basis, except on summer holiday weekends, when reservations are accepted.

↪ **Pymatuning Visitors Center,** 12590 Hartstown Rd., Linesville; (800) 533-6764 or (814) 683-5545. Hours: Mid-Mar.—Oct., 8—4 Mon.—Fri.; 9—5 weekends (till 8 p.m. Sat. Memorial Day—Labor Day). Wildlife museum and wheelchair-accessible nature trail. Call for information on special programs.

↪ **Pennsylvania Fish and Boat Commission's Linesville Fish Culture Station,** 13300 Hartstown Rd., Linesville; (814) 683-4451. Hours: 8—4 daily. Free admission. Fish hatchery is one of world's largest with about 100 rearing ponds. Visitors center has stocked 10,000-gallon aquarium early Apr.—early Oct.

ACCOMMODATIONS

↪ Numerous older, independently owned motels line Alt. Rt. 5 between Erie and Presque Isle.

Also, a good selection of chain lodgings are located along interstates 79 and 90. For information on motels and cabin rentals around Conneaut Lake, contact the Crawford County Tourist Association.

↪ **Avalon Hotel,** 16 W. 10th St., Erie;
(800) 822-5011 or (814) 459-2220. Rates: $74—$89, depending on season. A full-service hotel in the center of downtown.

↪ **Bel Aire Hotel,** 2800 W. 8th St., Erie; (800) 888-8781 or (814) 833-1116. Rates: $85—$105, depending on season. Large, full-service hotel near Presque Isle State Park.

↪ **Hampton Inn,** 3041 W. 12th St., Erie (exit 44B off I-79); (800) 426-7866 or (814) 835-4200. Rates: $74—$99, depending on season. Includes breakfast.

↪ **Spencer House Bed & Breakfast,** 519 W. 6th St., Erie; (800) 890-7263 or (814) 454-5984. Rates: $75—$95. A stately 1876 Victorian close to Presque Isle and the Erie waterfront; 5 guest rooms all w/private bath.

↪ **Glass House Inn,** 3202 W. 26th St., Erie; (814) 833-7751. Rates: Late May—late June, $55—$90; late June—Aug., $63—$97; Sept.—May, $47—$77. 30-room inn w/ swimming pool 2 miles from Presque Isle State Park. Rates include breakfast.

↪ **Grape Arbor Inn,** 51 E. Main St., North East; (814) 725-5522. Rates: $85—$150. Handsome 1832 Federal-style house near the town's Victorian center. 2 rooms, 4 suites, all w/ private bath.

RESTAURANTS

↪ **Pie in the Sky,** 463 W. 8th St.; (814) 459-8638. Hours: 7:30 a.m.—10:45 a.m. and 11:30—2 Mon.—Fri. for breakfast and lunch; 5:30—9 Fri.—Sat. for dinner. Dinner menu changes weekly, includes imaginative specialties. Entrees including dessert, $11—$17. Lunch menu has California pizzas, sandwiches and salads, $4—$8.

↪ **Hopper's Brewpub,** 123 W. 14th St. (in Union Station); (814) 452-2787. Hours: 11:30—11 Fri., Sat.; 11:30—9:30 Mon.—

Thurs.; 12:30—4 Sun. Several microbrews on tap with good pub menu, including that regional favorite beef on 'weck. Lunch, $5; dinner, from $9.

➡ **Walnut Creek Grill,** 6590 West Lake Rd., Fairview (5 miles west of Erie); (814) 474-3304. Hours: 5—9 Mon.—Thurs.; 5—10 Fri.—Sat. Casual gourmet. Specialties include char-grilled ostrich. Entrees, $6—$18.

➡ **Chuck and Ginny's,** 1064 Raspberry (6 blocks west of downtown); (814) 455-0000. Hours: 11:30—2 and 5—9 Mon.—Thurs.; 11:30—2 and 4—10 Fri; 11:30—10 Sat. Small, casual Italian restaurant and bar. Generous helpings of homemade Italian food. Dinners, $5—$9.

➡ **George's Restaurant,** 2614 Glenwood Park Ave. (near 26th and State St); (814) 455-0860. Hours: 7 a.m.—8 p.m., Mon.—Fri.; 7—3 Sat. Ethnic and comfort foods like real Hungarian goulash and pierogies from scratch. Lunch, about $6; dinner, about $8.

➡ **Ali Baba,** 3602 West Lake Rd.; (814) 838-7197. Hours: 11—9:30 Mon.—Thurs.; 11—10 Fri.—Sat. Middle Eastern food; large vegetarian menu. Lunches, $5 range; dinners, about $9.

➡ **The Grapevine Cafe,** 26 S. Lake St., North East; (814) 725-2435. Hours: 7—7 Mon., Wed.; 7—3 Tues.; 7 a.m.—9 p.m. Thurs.—Sat. Attractive little cafe just off the main drag. Salads and sandwiches about $5; dinner, mainly pastas and seafood, $6—$11.

➡ **Elephant Bar & Restaurant,** 2826 W. 8th St.; (814) 838-3613. Hours: 11—10 Mon.—Thurs.; 11—11 Fri.—Sat.; 10—10 Sun. American food; casual dining 1 block from Presque Isle. Lunch, $5; dinner, $10.

BIG EVENTS

➡ **Erie Summer Festival of the Arts,** end of June on the Villa Maria campus, Erie. (814) 833-0812.

➡ **Discover Presque Isle,** last weekend in July at state park. Music, crafts, sand sculpture, food and more. (814) 833-7424.

➡ **Cherry Festival,** five days in early July in North East. Midway rides, food, crafts and music. (814) 725-4262.

➡ **"We Love Erie Days,"** four days around third weekend in Aug., Perry Square and the bayfront. Entertainment, ethnic foods, fireworks, boat races, craft show, historical tours. (814) 454-7191.

➡ **Wine Country Harvest Festival,** last weekend in Sept. in North East; (814) 725-4262. Antiques, classic car and art shows, plus grape-stomping contests, children's activities and farmers market.

GO to Allegheny Forest

Allegheny National Forest has many places to stop and enjoy the view, including this vista of a bend in the Allegheny River.

GERRY WINGENBACH

Allegheny Forest

ONE OF NATURE'S GREAT SHOWCASES

Finding a spot to call your own in Pennsylvania's only national forest is a breeze. Even at the height of summer when hikers flock to the back country and boaters hit the blue waters of the Allegheny Reservoir. Even in fall when tourists come to feast their eyes on the dazzling reds and yellows that light up the forest. Even in spring when the first blush of warm weather spawns fresh growth and wild flowers. And even in winter when cross-country skiers and snowmobilers take to the trails.

Perhaps the dearth of crowds is due to the sparsely populated surrounding area. (Forest County, one of four counties that share the forest, boasts that it has no traffic lights, no daily newspaper and no radio station.) Or possibly, the vastness of this half-million acre forest guarantees its isolation.

Whatever the reason, the Allegheny National Forest seems largely undiscovered — even if it's not. It

GO to Allegheny Forest

appears on the map as a large green splotch that seeps into Forest, Elk, Warren and McKean counties in northwestern Pennsylvania. With year-round recreational possibilities, along with some unexpected sights like old rock Indian shelters, a free-roaming elk herd and a steam railroad, it's a perfect spot for those who prefer their outdoors experiences without crowds.

Logging was a major industry here in the late 1800s and early into this century. As a result, most of the black cherry, white and red oak, birch, maple and aspen are second- and third-growth forest. Remnants of dozens of lumber towns that died after the forests were logged out are evident. Some old-growth forest remains, however, including the Heart's Content National Scenic Area south of Warren, and Tionesta Scenic Area south of Route 6 near Sheffield, where 400-year-old white pine, hemlock and beech trees stand tall.

MARIENVILLE

The more than 500,000 acres were designated national forest land in 1923. In the southern portion near Marienville, in Forest County, 40 miles of trails have been developed for all-terrain vehicles and snowmobiles. If you're not into either, it's best to steer clear of this area. At the northern edge of the forest, the Allegheny Reservoir has 95 miles of shoreline. Elsewhere lies an immense spider's web of trails — more than 600 miles total — where you're unlikely to meet another soul.

Approaching from the south on Route 36, the forest pops up unexpectedly. One moment you're rolling along through open farmland and settlements too small to be called towns, and suddenly you're among towering stands of hardwood so thickly jammed together, the forest is in perpetual dusk. The rangers' station off Route 66, a mile north of Marienville, is a good spot to pick up detailed maps and other information. Other forest service offices are in Warren, Bradford and Ridgway.

KNOX & KANE RAILROAD

Marienville also is the originating point of the Knox & Kane Railroad, a scenic train route that hauls visitors to the Kinzua Viaduct. The round-trip ride takes eight hours. To cut the trip in half, board the train at the depot in Kane. The bridge was billed as the eighth wonder of the world when it was built in 1882. That ranking may have since been stripped by greater engineering feats, but it retains status as the nation's second highest railroad bridge. Its 2,100-foot span is a spectacular sight that rises more than 300 feet from the valley below. The best time to visit is at the peak of autumn, when the bridge overlooks a sea of brilliant foliage.

GO to Allegheny Forest

The Knox & Kane Railroad takes a scenic route to the Kinzua Viaduct. The round-trip ride is eight hours.

GERRY WINGENBACH

Several campgrounds and bed and breakfast inns are in the Marienville area. A few miles southeast of town, the Loleta camping area, the namesake of an old logging town, sports a handsome 1933 bathhouse (now closed) constructed by the Civilian Conservation Corps. The swimming area is a nice spot to picnic, even when the water's too cold for swimming. Unpaved Route 2005, which leads to Loleta and eventually winds down to the Clarion River, is a good fall foliage drive.

GO to Allegheny Forest

Some visitors cut the rail trip in half by boarding the train at Kane.

GERRY WINGENBACH

RUSSELL CITY

Back on paved terrain, Route 66 leads north out of Marienville and into Russell City: population 40. It's a tiny speck of a settlement in the forest, where the sole bit of commerce is a classic 1929 general store. Here, owner Ted Lutz fills gas tanks from pumps that look old enough to qualify as antiques. Inside, the store has a suitably eclectic inventory ranging from Elvis on velvet to hip-waders, plus plenty of tourist information.

KANE

The first community of any size is Kane, which bills itself as the Black Cherry Capital of the World. The town has a frontier feel to it. Streets are wide and many of the storefronts sport Western facades. Worth a stop is the Thomas L. Kane Memorial Chapel, a stone building with a soaring black cherry ceiling, stained glass windows and a pipe organ. The chapel houses a small museum dedicated to Kane and other family members. Kane is also the home of Holgate, manufacturer of wooden toys. Its factory store and museum are open to the public. Visitors also can watch toys being assembled in the factory.

KINZUA BRIDGE STATE PARK

To reach Kinzua Bridge State Park pick up Route 6 heading east toward Mount Jewett and follow the signs through town. The highlight here is the Kinzua Viaduct, the dizzying, 2,100-foot-long span that

GO to Allegheny Forest

A visitors center at a scenic point of Allegheny Reservoir.
GERRY WINGENBACH

you can walk across. (A railroad employee clears the tracks of pedestrians in plenty of time before the train rolls through.) Other lookout points within the park offer excellent views of the bridge, for those who don't want to venture out onto it.

BRADFORD

Heading back west from the state park to Route 219 north leads into Bradford. The Crook Farm, a restored 19th-century farm, home and schoolhouse is on the northern edge of town. For an overview of the region's oil history, stop at the Penn-Brad Historical Oil Well Park. You can't miss it; just look for the 72-foot drilling rig, believed to be the last of its kind in the country. Inside the museum, the story of the world's first billion-dollar oil field, which was drilled in this area, is told through artifacts and exhibits.

Another slice of Americana in Bradford, birthplace of the Zippo lighter, is at the Zippo Family Store & Museum. On display are more than 300 cigarette lighters and other Zippo artifacts. The company planned to open a new, expanded museum in the summer of 1997. Glass display cases are filled with testimonials from loyal customers along with vintage lighters. Other Zippos here are beyond hope, like the one returned by a Turtle Creek man who wrote: "Dear Sirs, I am returning my Zippo for repair. It got mixed up with a 6,000-ton press and will no longer serve me efficiently." A nugget of gray metal, all that re-

GO to Allegheny Forest

mains of the mangled Zippo, hangs in tribute.

ALLEGHENY RESERVOIR

Traveling west on Route 59 toward Warren are several spots with easy access to spectacular views of the Allegheny Reservoir. Created by the construction of the Kinzua Dam in 1965, the 25-mile-long waterway is a popular boating and fishing spot. It's also possible to walk across the entire dam. To learn more about its more serious functions of flood control and power generation, drop by the visitors center just downstream from the dam on Route 59.

Rimrock Overlook, off Route 59, 14 miles east of Warren, is a shady haven of ferns and moss-covered boulders. Stairs made of foundation stones from houses in villages that were flooded by the dam snake down through narrow passages surrounded by monolithic boulders to a ledge overlooking the reservoir. It's narrow, but the descent is relatively easy. At one spot along the way, cold air billows up even on the hottest summer days from cracks deep in the rocks that shelter a natural ice mine. Rimrock Overlook is also a good place to watch bald eagles floating on the wind currents.

JAKES ROCKS

A turnoff on the west side of the Cornplanter Bridge, which spans the reservoir on Route 59, leads to stunning views from Jakes Rocks that require minimal physical effort to enjoy. Paved trails wind to an area of rocky outcrops once used as shelter by the Seneca Indians. Some vantage points are accessible by car. The start of the Longhouse National Scenic Byway, a 29-mile drive that follows the Kinzua arm of the reservoir, also is on the turnoff to Jakes Rocks. If you have more time, a 95-mile route around the reservoir leads across the New York state line into Allegheny State Park. The drive is particularly beautiful in the fall.

KINZUA BEACH

Kinzua Beach, on the east side of the Cornplanter Bridge, has a well-maintained picnic and swimming area. Plenty of tables are set along a wide lawn that slopes down to the water. An area is roped off for swimming, plus there are charcoal grills, volleyball nets and a bathhouse.

WATER RECREATION

For a more complete water experience, consider renting a boat at the Kinzua-Wolf Run Marina on the Allegheny Reservoir located across Route 59 from Kinzua Beach. Boat rentals are seasonal.

A different sort of water experience comes from renting a canoe and paddling down the Allegheny River. A number of outfitters, including Allegheny Outfitters in Warren, rent canoes seasonally. Depending on water releases and the weather, rentals continue through October.

GO to Allegheny Forest

MUSEUM IS ALL THINGS LUCY

The principal players are gone and the last episode was filmed in 1960. But clearly, a lot of people still love Lucy.

Ask the Michigan woman who blew $100 and change on Lucy souvenirs. A Lucy teapot. A Lucy bank. A Lucy T-shirt. Lucy books.

Or the 9-year-old boy who spent two solid days knocking around old Lucy haunts.

Or the family who gathered around the rack of Lucy postcards acting out scenes depicted on them.

Or the Japanese visitors who put on their best Cuban-American accents to spontaneously warn, "Luuuuucy. You got some 'splainin' to do."

They all love Lucille Ball, and to a lesser extent, perhaps, Desi Arnaz (Ricky), William Frawley (Fred) and Vivian Vance (Ethel).

So does Jamestown, N.Y., which pays affectionate homage to its most famous native with a comedy festival every September. A more permanent tribute, the Lucy-Desi Museum, opened in 1996. Attendance quickly exceeded expectations.

The Arts Council for Chautauqua County first began making Lucy an annual thing in Jamestown in 1990, when it staged a comedy festival in her honor. Ball died in 1989, but her daughter, Lucie Arnaz, gave the museum permanent loan of hundreds of Ball's belongings. Lucky for them, the actress never threw anything out, and rooms full of all things Lucy are in storage for placement in rotating exhibits.

Clothing and photographs are displayed in the 2,100-square-foot museum, along with taped reminiscences by girlhood friends, videos and interactive exhibits that trace the history of

continued on next page

The stretch of river just below the Kinzua Dam to Warren is an excellent place to spot bald eagles.

WARREN

The town of Warren lies west of the dam along the Allegheny River. The initial approach from the east doesn't reveal the town's best side. Oil refinery tanks and smokestacks rise like giant birthday cakes. But beyond the refinery, the town's wide streets are lined with stately old homes, the legacy of timber and oil money from the last century. Pleasant park land skirts the Allegheny

GO to Allegheny Forest

GERRY WINGENBACH
A visitor takes in the Lucy lore at the Lucy-Desi Museum in Jamestown, N.Y., which pays homage to comedian Lucille Ball and her husband, Desi Arnaz.

comedy. The most curious Lucy artifacts: two red wiglets arranged with a collection of hair products — Mexican henna, little bottles of dye, rubber gloves, a dangerous-looking steel-toothed comb (a chunk of its teeth missing) and a hairbrush sprouting a tuft of carrot-colored strands. Exhibits follow the evolution of the 1948 radio show, "My Favorite Husband," in which Ball played a "silly, scheming middle-class wife," to the 1951 premiere of "I Love Lucy," about a Cuban bandleader's wife whose relentless attempts to break into show busi-

continued on next page

River as it flows through town. Warren also has the greatest number of lodging options along this route.

WILDERNESS AREAS

Continuing out of Warren back toward Pittsburgh, Route 62 runs near the Hearts Content National Scenic Area and the Hickory Creek Wilderness, at the national forest's western edge. The Allegheny River sidles along on the other side, undisturbed for a while at least, by commerce or community or anything other than the occasional fisher or hiker, out for a solitary day on the river or in the woods.

ness are constantly foiled. The show was an unbeatable Monday night fixture in American homes during its nine-year run. Its ratings even topped the inauguration of Dwight D. Eisenhower and the coronation of Queen Elizabeth.

The museum has less to say about Desi, although you learn he was from a prominent Cuban family that moved to Miami in 1934, and that he was discovered by band leader Xavier Cugat before forming his own band in 1937. There's nary a mention of the other "I Love Lucy'" players. But the museum, after all, is about Lucy, not just the show.

Though she was born in Jamestown in 1911, Ball actually grew up in her grandparents' home in the nearby town of Celeron, where she was sent after her factory-worker father died of tuberculosis. At age 15, she quit high school and headed for drama school in New York City. She dropped out a year later and did some modeling, shuttling between the city and Jamestown.

By the early '30s, Ball was landing roles in Hollywood and sent for members of her Jamestown family. Museum employees aren't aware of any close Ball relatives still living in the area, though they do get a number of MacGillicuddys wandering into the museum. In "I Love Lucy," Ball often made reference to real people and events from her Jamestown childhood. MacGillicuddy, her maiden name in the television show, was not one of them, however.

"People always come in and say, 'She was a cousin of mine. My name is MacGillicuddy,'" said an employee. "A lot of people have a hard time distinguishing between TV and reality."

Similarly, some visitors believe the actor who played Little Ricky was Lucy's and Desi's real-life son. And they express dismay that the couple, who seemed so happy on television, divorced in 1960.

After the show and the marriage ended, Ball went on to do her own, less-celebrated series.

But in the minds of many — no small thanks to endless reruns on cable television — Lucille Ball and Desi Arnaz will always be an ageless Lucy and Ricky Ricardo. Fred and Ethel Mertz will live on as their faithful sidekicks. Little Ricky will always be little.

And they'll always, always love Lucy.

➡ **The Lucy-Desi Museum,** 212 Pine St., Jamestown, NY (about 15 miles north of Warren); (716) 484-7070. Hours: Apr.—Sept., 10:30—5:30 Mon.—Sat.; 1—5 Sun.; Oct.—Mar., 10—5:30 Sat.; 1—5 Sun. Admission: $5 adults; $3.50 seniors; $15 families.

GO to Allegheny Forest

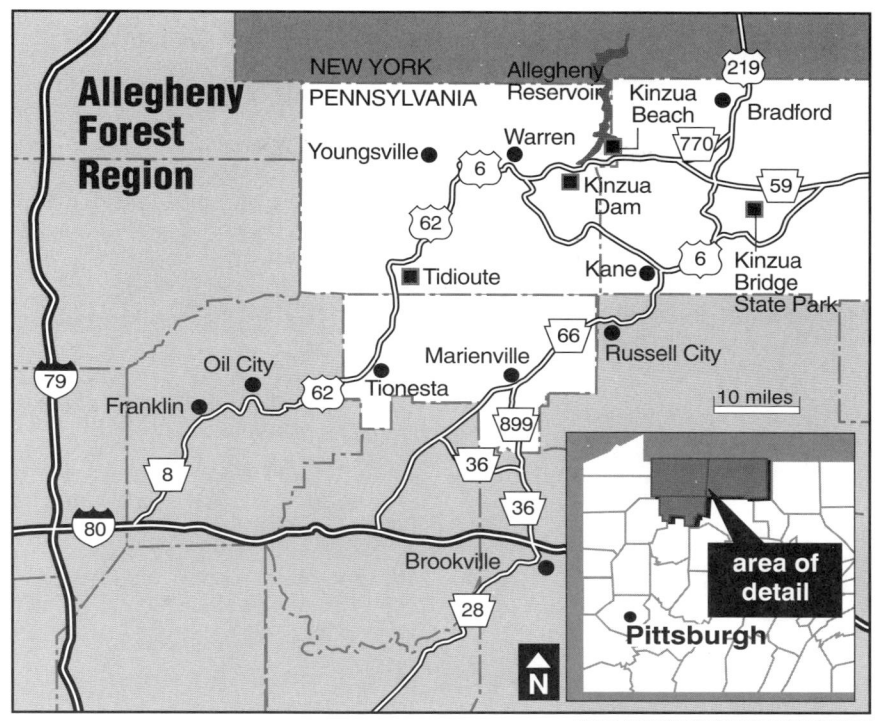

DIANE JURAVICH/PITTSBURGH POST-GAZETTE

THE ROUTE

Take Rt. 28 north to Brookville and continue north on Rt. 36 to Rt. 899. At Marienville, take Rt. 66 north to Kane. Head out of Kane on Rt. 6 east, then take Rt. 219 north to Bradford. Returning from Bradford, take Rt. 770 to Rt. 59 west, which joins Rt. 6 at Warren. Take Rt. 6 west to Rt. 62 south. Pick up Rt. 8 south at Franklin to I-80.
Approximate round-trip mileage: 320

MORE INFORMATION

➥ For general tourist information, plus maps outlining several scenic fall driving tours within the four-county area, contact any one of the agencies below.

➥ **Northern Allegheny National Forest Vacation Region** (Forest and Warren counties), Box 608, Tionesta, PA 16353; (800) 624-7802 or (814) 354-6332

➥ **Elk County Visitors Bureau,** Box 838, Saint Marys, PA 15857; (814) 834-3723

➥ **Allegheny National Forest Vacation Bureau** (McKean County), 10 E. Warren Rd., Custer City, PA 16725; (814) 368-9370

➥ **Allegheny National Forest,** 222 Liberty St., Warren, PA 16365; (814) 723-5150. Maps, camping, hiking and other information is available there and at three additional forest service offices in Bradford, Marienville and Ridgway.

GO to Allegheny Forest

THINGS TO DO, PLACES TO SEE

➡ **The Knox & Kane Railroad** runs June—Oct. to the Kinzua Bridge from 2 departure points — Marienville and Kane. Call for schedules. Fare on the 96-mile Marienville run is $20 adults; $13 ages 3—12. Cost for the 32-mile trip from Kane to the bridge is $14 adults; $8 children. Tickets and box lunches can be ordered and paid for in advance by writing Knox & Kane Railroad, Box 422, Marienville, PA 16239; (814) 927-6621.

➡ **Holgate Factory Toy Store and Museum,** Wetmore Ave., Kane; (800) 499-1929. Hours: 10—5 Mon.—Fri.; 10—3 Sat. Discounts of 10—60 percent on wooden toys; also, an antique toy museum.

➡ **Kinzua Bridge State Park,** south of Bradford near Mount Jewett off Rt. 6. Highlight is the Kinzua Viaduct, built in 1882 and still the second-highest railroad bridge in the nation.

➡ **Crook Farm,** Rt. 219 and Seward Ave. Extension, Bradford; (814) 362-6730. Hours: May—Oct., 10—4 Wed.—Sun. A restored 1848 farm, with outbuildings, farmhouse and one-room schoolhouse.

➡ **Penn-Brad Historical Oil Well Park,** south of Bradford on Rt. 219 in Custer City; (814) 362-1955. Hours: Memorial Day—Labor Day, 10—4 Mon.—Sat.; noon—5 Sun.; and by arrangement at other times. Oil exhibits and artifacts, including a rare 72-foot drilling rig. Admission: $4; children under 12 free.

➡ **Zippo/Case Visitors Center,** 1932 Zippo Dr., Bradford (1 block north of Zippo factory at 397 Congress St.);

(888) 442-1932 or (814) 368-2863. Hours: 9—5 Mon.—Fri.; seasonal Sat. hours. A collection of cigarette lighters from 1932 to the present in the town where Zippo was born.

➡ **Singer's Country Store,** jct. Rts. 219 and 770, Custer City; (800) 345-6639 or (814) 368-6151. Hours: 11—5 daily; closed Sun. Feb.—Apr. Old-fashioned country store sells candy, pickles from the barrel, food and gifts.

➡ **Kinzua Dam Visitors Center** on Rt. 59, about 10 miles east of Warren; (814) 726-0661. Hours: Memorial Day—Labor Day, noon—4 weekdays; 10—5 weekends and holidays. Call for hours other times of year. Highlights the nuts and bolts of the dam and its power plant.

➡ **Kinzua Boat Rentals & Marina,** Rt. 59, 10 miles east of Warren; (814) 726-1650. Canoes, pontoons and motor boat rentals. Open mid-May—Sept.

➡ **Allegheny Outfitters,** 2101 Pennsylvania Ave. E., Warren; (814) 723-4868. Canoe rentals ($24 for 1st canoe,

TONY TYE/PITTSBURGH POST-GAZETTE
Fall's foliage is always the forest's greatest attraction.

$20 for additional canoes); mountain bike trips, including rentals through Oct. Also, guided hikes and educational "eco-tours."

➡ **Scenic River Canoe Rentals,** Star Rt. 50, Irvine, (3 miles south of Rt. 6 on Rt. 62); (814) 563-9795. Canoe rentals May—Oct. on the Allegheny River from Kinzua Dam to Tionesta. Rates: $15—$30, depending on distance. Escorted trips also available.

➡ **Indian Waters Canoe Rentals,** Rt. 62, Tidioute (5 miles north of Tidioute Bridge); (814) 484-3252. Canoe rentals; day and overnight trips. $20 for 10-mile day trip.

ACCOMMODATIONS

➡ Fall foliage is usually at its peak in the Allegheny National Forest around the second week in October, though the leaves begin changing as early as late September. If you're planning an overnight trip during autumn, it's wise to make reservations in advance, especially on weekends. A statewide fall foliage hotline (800) 325-5467 gives updated leaf reports.

➡ Chain lodgings are clustered around Rt. 6 in Warren. Among them are Holiday Inn (814-726-3000) and Super 8 (800-800-8000 or 814-723-8881). Bradford has a Howard Johnson Motor Lodge (800-344-4656 or 814-362-4501).

Other choices include:

➡ **Pioneer Lodge,** Box 447, Marienville, 16239; (814) 927-6654. Rates: $65. The 1833 farmhouse of Marienville's founder, Cyrus Blood, has been extensively remodeled and sits on 200 acres. Broad porches, outdoor pool and massive stone fireplace are nice touches. 4 guest rooms w/ shared bath.

➡ **Russell City Lodge,** Rts. 66 and 948, Russell City; (814) 968-4415. Rates: $169 for the weekend (4 p.m. Fri.—4 p.m. Sun.); $499 weekly (4 p.m. Sun.—10 a.m following Sun.). 5-bedroom, 2-bath, wood-frame house on Russell City's short main drag isn't fancy, but it's roomy and has a full kitchen, family room and deck in the back. Located next to the national forest.

➡ **Kane Manor Country Inn,** 230 Clay St., Kane; (814) 837-6522. Rates: $99 w/ private bath; $89 shared bath. 10 guest rooms, 6 w/ private bath. Historic home has been an inn since the 1940s. Grand double staircase leads to eclectically furnished rooms.

➡ **Faircroft Bed and Breakfast,** Montmorenci Rd. (Rt. 948, 2 miles off Rt. 219), Ridgway; (814) 776-2539. Rates: $50. Restored homestead on former 75-acre dairy farm; 3 guest rooms, all w/ private bath, are furnished w/ antiques.

➡ **The Fisher Inn,** 253 E. Main St., Bradford; (814) 368-3428. Rates: $60-$80. 1847 restored farmhouse has 8 guest rooms, all w/ private bath. Located on neighborhood street away from the center of town.

➡ **Glendorn,** 1032 W. Corydon St., Bradford; (814) 362-6511. Rates: $345—$545 per night. Lovely resort built as a private, summer retreat has 2 suites and 2 guest rooms in stately 1929 main house, plus 7 cabins on 1,200 acres. All-inclusive rates include meals, drinks, skeet and trap shooting, tennis, fishing in stocked ponds, canoeing, biking and other recreational activities.

➡ **The Jefferson House,** 119 Market St., Warren; (814) 723-2268. Rates: $80. Restored Victorian B&B has 2 guest rooms, w/ shared bath.

➡ **Hickory Creek Wilderness Ranch,** Rt. 337 (4 miles off Rt. 62), Tidioute; (814) 484-7520. Rates: Furnished cabin (sleeps up to 10), $525 weekly; $275 weekends; $75 additional nights. Plus 2 no-frills bunkhouses (w/ outdoor privy and shower). Small bunk house (sleeps

GO to Allegheny Forest

up to 3), $175 weekly; $90 weekends; $25 weekdays. Larger bunkhouse (sleeps up to 6), $295 weekly; $125 weekends; $45 a night during the week. 105-acre horse ranch adjoining the Allegheny National Forest. The ranch also offers bed and breakfast packages and overnight pack trips into the forest. Day trips also can be arranged.

➡ **Flying W Ranch,** Rt. 666, 12 miles northeast of Tionesta; (814) 463-7663. 600-acre dude ranch has 7 cabins w/ full kitchens and baths, sleep 4 to 6. Rates: lodging only, $80 in-season; $59 off-season. Also, horseback riding packages available Apr.—Oct. Basic cowboy package includes 2 nights lodging, 6 meals and 6 hours of guided rides, $249 per person. Overnight pack trips also offered.

➡ For reservations at campgrounds operated within the Allegheny National Forest, call (800) 280-2267.

➡ For a list of privately run campgrounds in the Allegheny National Forest area, contact the U.S. Forest Service office in Warren, (814) 723-5150.

RESTAURANTS

➡ **The Jefferson House,** 119 Market St., Warren; (814) 723-2268. Hours: 11:30—2 and 5:30—9 Tues.—Sat. Mesquite-grilled seafood and ribs. Lunch, $5—$7; dinner, $11—$18.

➡ **Papa Nick's,** 316 Chase St., Kane; (814) 837-6652. Hours: 11—9 Mon.—Thurs.; 11—10 Fri.—Sat.; 11:30—9 Sun. American-Italian. Lunch, $2—$5; dinner, $6—$14.

➡ **Limberlost,** Kane Rd., Sheffield (on Rt. 6, 15 miles west of Kane); (814) 968-5204. Hours: 4—9:30 Mon.—Sat.; noon—7 Sun. Fine-dining steak restaurant. Dinners, $9—$17.

➡ **Docksider's Cafe,** Rt. 59 (4 miles east of the Kinzua Dam); (814) 726-9645. Hours: Memorial Day—Labor Day. 11—9 Mon.—Thurs.; 11—10 Fri.; 8 a.m.—10 p.m. Sat.; 8 a.m.—9 p.m. Sun. Casual restaurant overlooks Wolf Run Bay on the Allegheny Reservoir. Lunch, $4—$8; dinner, $8—$15.

BIG EVENTS

➡ **Bell Atlantic Mobile Sled Dog Race,** 2nd weekend in Feb., Westline and Mount Jewett. Sled dog races, winter carnival, children's activities.

➡ **Forest Fest,** 2nd weekend in June, various locations in the Allegheny National Forest. An open-house showcasing behind-the-scenes workings at a number of forest service facilities, including the federal fish hatchery and the Kinzua Dam. (814) 368-9370.

➡ **Black Cherry Festival,** 2nd weekend in July, Kane. Art show, street carnival, live music.

➡ **Zippo/Case Swap Meet,** 3rd weekend in July, Bradford. Thousands of collectors of cigarette lighters and knives converge on the town. Street dance, farmers market, sidewalk sales. (814) 368-9370.

➡ **Crook Farm County Fair,** last weekend in Aug., Bradford. Juried arts and crafts show; also traditional crafts demonstrations. (814) 362-6730.

➡ **Native American Festival,** weekend after Labor Day, Ludlow. Native American competition dancing, arts and crafts and storytelling. (814) 368-9370.

➡ **Wild Wind Folk Festival,** weekend after Labor Day, Warren County Fairgrounds, Rt. 6, Pittsfield (10 miles west of Warren); (814) 723-2610. Juried crafts show attracts more than 100 artisans. (814) 723-2610.

GO to Allegheny Forest

ALSO IN THE AREA

➡ A herd of about 250 elk roam free in the appropriately named Elk County. Best sighting spots: near the airport at Saint Marys, or in the Benezette area.

➡ **Jamestown Audubon Nature Center,** 1600 Riverside Road, Jamestown, NY; (716) 569-2345. Hours: summer, 10—5 Tues.—Sat.; 1—5 Sun. Nov.—Mar., 10—4 Tues.—Sat.; 1—4 Sun. Trails open dawn to dusk. An easy 15-mile drive north of Warren on Rt. 62, just a mile north of the state line is the 600-acre Burgeson Wildlife Sanctuary, part of the Jamestown Audubon Nature Center. A variety of habitats, plus an abundance of food, make this a prime bird-watching spot. The sanctuary has 9 distinct habitats ranging from pine forests to swamp land that attract a large number of bird species. The fall migration in mid-Aug. and Sept. brings shorebirds — swans, geese, ducks, warblers, blue herons and an occasional eagle.

Five miles of maintained trails and boardwalks make it easy to get out into the forests and marshes. Inside the Roger Tory Peterson Nature Interpretive Building is a discovery room where kids are encouraged to touch shells, skulls, stuffed waterfowl and more. A collection of more than 200 stuffed birds (3 of them now extinct) are in an adjoining room. The collection, from the early 1920s, is an example of the "shotgun school of ornithology." These days, birds are studied by temporarily netting or trapping them, then banding them, so birders can monitor their migratory habits, population density and lifespan.

GO to Cleveland, Ohio

GERRY WINGENBACH

The Cuyahoga River has been cleaned up and now lures recreational boaters.

GO to Cleveland, Ohio

Cleveland

NO MISTAKING ITS GLORY BY THE LAKE

For many Clevelanders, the most dramatic change in recent times was the departure of their beloved NFL Browns. For visitors, the changes are more visual. And they are particularly evident along the city's riverfront areas and on the shoreline of Lake Erie, where the Rock and Roll Hall of Fame and Museum has added a new dimension to the city's skyline.

Housed in a stunning $92-million I.M. Pei-designed seven-story building, the hall of fame attracted more than 1 million visitors in its first year of operation.

But there's much more to Cleveland. The city has been undergoing a quiet renaissance in recent years, and the Labor Day 1995 Rock and Roll Hall of Fame opening ceremony was, in a sense, a coming-out party for the revamped Cleveland. With a new downtown baseball stadium, a new science center, tony downtown shopping centers and a world-renowned art gallery, the former Rodney Dangerfield of cities is beginning to get some respect as a destination.

In 1870, Cleveland became America's oil capital when John D. Rockefeller founded the Standard Oil Co. here. The city prospered and in the first half of the 1900s it was one of the great engines that fueled American industrialism. But when the engine rusted and the downturn of the industrial heartland hit bottom in the 1970s, the city's prospects were bleak. The "Mistake by the Lake" moniker hung over Cleveland like a layer of smog. Even the Cuyahoga River caught fire. Then in the

GERRY WINGENBACH
A vibrant boardwalk area draws fun seekers.

GO to Cleveland, Ohio

1980s, plans for the city's transformation were put into action.

TERMINAL TOWER

Despite all the recent changes, the dominant feature of downtown remains the 52-story Terminal Tower, built in the 1920s. A good way to get oriented before touring the area is to take the elevator to the observation area on the 42nd floor. You'll get a hawk's-eye view of much of the city and the Lake Erie shore. At the base of Terminal Tower is the refurbished 35-acre Terminal City Center, with three levels of retail stores that form downtown Cleveland's main shopping complex.

PUBLIC SQUARE

The entrance to Terminal Tower faces Public Square, the heart of the city and a logical place to embark on a walking tour. Anchored in the square is a statue of Gen. Moses Cleaveland, who founded the city in 1796. (Apparently the "a" in the general's name was dropped so an early newspaper could fit the town's name on its masthead.) On the southeast quadrant of the square is the 1894 Soldiers' and Sailors' Monument depicting scenes from the Civil War. Facing the square, on the north side across from Terminal Tower, is the Old Stone Church at 91 Public Square. The 1855 church is decorated with some of the finest Tiffany stained-glass windows in the country. Inside, the wooden barrel-vaulted ceiling, golden oak interior paneling and massive pipe organ are worth a look.

Next to the Old Stone Church is a replica of the original arc lamps that were installed along the square in 1879, the first electric streetlights in the United States.

Heading east from Public Square along Superior Avenue is the Old Federal Building (201 Superior N.E.), built between 1905 and 1911, and the Cleveland Public Library (325 Superior N.E.), which is reportedly the largest lending library in the world. Its rooms house more than 50 miles of shelves. A tranquil garden is also part of the complex.

THE ARCADE

A block south of the library at 401 Euclid is the Arcade, a spectacular four-level 1890s Romanesque Revival building that was the country's first enclosed shopping mall. The Arcade might be past its prime as far as serious shoppers are concerned, but it's worth a stroll through or a stop at one of its cafes to take in the mosaic floors and Old World splendor. Additional downtown shopping is in the 60-plus shops of the glass-enclosed Galleria at Erieview (East Ninth Street and St. Clair), a few blocks east and north of Public Square.

THE MALL

A block north of the library, to the east of the Convention Center, is a

GO to Cleveland, Ohio

sweeping public space known simply as the Mall. The immense open plaza offers a sweeping view of Lake Erie and the new North Coast Harbor development. The latter is dominated by the Rock and Roll Hall of Fame and Museum. Anchored on the lake's shore is The Steamship William G. Mather Maritime Museum, a restored 1925 Great Lakes freighter.

NORTH COAST HARBOR

The North Coast Harbor is evolving as Cleveland's major attraction. In the summer of 1996, the Great Lakes Science Center opened next to the Rock and Roll Hall of Fame. The $55-million facility houses a six-story Omnimax Theater and hands-on exhibits relating to the environment of the Great Lakes.

Also new in 1996 was the Waterfront Line, an extension of Cleveland's light rail transportation system that connects Public Square, North Coast Harbor and the Flats, a riverfront entertainment area on the western border of downtown.

GERRY WINGENBACH
The Thinker ponders life outside the Cleveland Museum of Art.

WATER VIEWS

For a water-level view of the city, the 1,000-passenger Goodtime III offers sightseeing and entertainment cruises on the Cuyahoga River and Lake Erie. The Nautica Queen, a smaller cruise and restaurant vessel

GO to Cleveland, Ohio

IN CLOSE PROXIMITY TO FAME

The stretch of I-77 between Cleveland, Akron and Canton has been dubbed the Hall of Fame Connection, since it takes in three monuments to human achievement all within an hour's drive of one another.

Start in Cleveland at the Rock and Roll Hall of Fame, continue south to Inventure Place, the National Inventors Hall of Fame, and end in Canton at the Pro Football Hall of Fame. The undertaking is bound to leave you bleary-eyed and brimming with newly discovered facts as disparate as drummer Keith Moon's school grades (A- in music, D in art); the meaning of tetrafluoroethylene polymers (Teflon); and the size of William "The Refrigerator" Perry's Super Bowl ring finger (really big).

Should you decide to tackle all of the museums, here's a brief look at three very different halls of fame.

GERRY WINGENBACH
I.M. Pei's impeccable creation, the Rock and Roll Hall of Fame and Museum.

ROCK AND ROLL HALL OF FAME

THE PARTICULARS: 1 Key Plaza, Cleveland; (216) 781-7625. Hours: Memorial Day—Labor Day, 10—5:30 Sun.—

continued on next page

---

that holds 400 passengers, also sails the lake and river. Both ships operate seasonally from the Flats.

THE FLATS

The Flats is a vibrant mix of old and new — industry, entertainment and housing — located along the winding banks of the Cuyahoga River. The river is one of the nation's busiest industrial waterways, a trait that makes it a dramatic backdrop for most of Cleveland's nightlife. Ocean-going freighters drift up and down the river a stone's throw from patrons dining and drinking at boardwalk restaurants and nightclubs.

Anchoring the west bank of the Flats is the Nautica Entertainment Complex, which includes an am-

GO to Cleveland, Ohio

Tues. and 10—9 Wed.—Sat.; Labor Day—Memorial Day, 10—5:30 Thurs.—Tues. and 10—9 Wed. Admission: $12.95 adults; $9.50 ages 4—11 and over 55.

IN A NUTSHELL: More than 100,000 objects chronicling all things rock 'n' roll. The treatment is audio and visual from the stereo speakers disguised as rocks in the garden out front to MTV-style clips and sound bites throughout.

THE VENUE: A striking, seven-story triangular "tent" perched on the edge of Lake Erie. The $92-million, skyline-transforming building was designed by I.M. Pei.

FUN FACT: The term "rock 'n' roll" was coined by Cleveland disc jockey Alan Freed in 1952 to describe music formerly called rhythm and blues.

QUOTABLE: *"Whatever you do, don't try to grow old gracefully."* — The Who's Pete Townsend

INVENTURE PLACE — THE NATIONAL INVENTORS HALL OF FAME

THE PARTICULARS: 221 S. Broadway St., Akron; (800) 968-4332 or (330) 762-6565. Hours: Mar.—Labor Day, 9—5. Mon.—Sat and noon—5 Sun; Labor Day—end of Mar., 9—5 Wed.—Sat. and noon—5 Sun. Admission: $7.50 adults; $6 ages 3—17 and over 55.

IN A NUTSHELL: A monument to people who wake up in the middle of the night and look for something to fix. Explanations of how John Deere built a better plow by cutting the teeth off a saw blade; how Eli Whitney's cotton gin began with some wires from an old bird cage; how Elisha Graves Otis made an elevator safety brake from a wagon spring, and hundreds of other inventions dreamed up by familiar

continued on next page

---

phitheater, restaurants and the Powerhouse. Built in 1892 to supply power to street car lines, the Powerhouse now houses restaurants, a comedy club and the Rock Bottom Brewery.

TROLLEY TOUR

If your feet need a rest, hop on board Lolly the Trolley, which departs from the Powerhouse at Nautica off Elm Street on the west bank of the Flats. One- and two-hour tours are offered. The longer tour prowls 20 miles of city streets while highlighting more than 100 points of interest. The driver delivers a colorful narrative, making the tour an informative introduction to the sights, history and present-day concerns of Cleveland. The trolley also picks up passengers

GO to Cleveland, Ohio

and not-so-familiar names.

THE VENUE: A five-story building shrouded on one side by a 10-story stainless-steel sail in downtown Akron. The ground floor houses "The Inventors Workshop," an indoor playground where kids can mess around with computers, microscopes, lasers, magnets and other serious stuff that's so entertaining they'll never guess they just might be learning something.

FUN FACT: Thomas Edison took out 1,093 U.S. patents ranging from the phonograph to the telephone.

QUOTABLE: *"A mind stretched by a new idea can never go back to its original dimension."*
— Oliver Wendell Holmes

PRO FOOTBALL HALL OF FAME

THE PARTICULARS: 2121 George Halas Drive N.W., Canton; (330) 456-8207. Hours: Memorial Day—Labor Day, 9—8 daily; rest of year, 9—5 daily. Admission: $9 adults; $4 ages 6—14; $6 age 62 and up.

IN A NUTSHELL: A shrine to the gridiron that's sure to put rabid football fans in hog (or pigskin) heaven. Six large exhibit areas chronicle the early days of

COURTESY OF INVENTURE PLACE
Paying homage to the great inventors in our nation's history, in Akron.

continued on next page

---

from Burke Lakefront Airport on the east side of North Coast Harbor.

OHIO CITY

A few blocks' walk south from the west bank of the Flats is the Ohio City Restoration Area, an eclectic mix of interesting homes, many of them in various stages of restoration. The neighborhood hosts an annual home tour on the third Sunday of May. Nearby, St. John's Episcopal Church was a station

GO to Cleveland, Ohio

the game when the gone-but-not-forgotten Canton Bulldogs and the first big-name pro, Jim Thorpe, played here in Canton. From Jack Kemp's No. 15 blue and white Buffalo Bills jersey to the shoe Garo Yepremian wore when he kicked a 37-yard field goal ending football's longest game (Miami over Kansas City on Christmas Day in 1971), to the origins of the Terrible Towel, little is left out. Plus there's Game-Day Stadium (a theater where the noise level reaches the pitch of a packed stadium), and interactive "Call the Play" and "Hall of Fame TeleTrivia" exhibits.

THE VENUE: A cluster of five buildings make up the museum complex. The entrance to the first hall is up a winding stadium-style ramp. Kind of like Three Rivers, but smaller and without the rivers.

COURTESY OF PRO FOOTBALL HALL OF FAME
The Pro Football Hall of Fame is located in Canton, Ohio, site of one of pro football's first teams.

FUN FACT: Despite the nickname, footballs are made out of cowhide, not pigskin.

QUOTABLE: *"My three children...each had a toy called a Super Ball...In the AFL-NFL Joint Committee meetings we had been referring to the "Final Game." Subconsciously, I may have been thinking about the Super Ball and one day, I just happened to come out and call the game the 'Super Bowl.' Somehow or other the name just stuck."*

Lamar Hunt, president
Kansas City Chiefs

of hope for slaves seeking freedom via the Underground Railroad.

JACOBS FIELD

Sports fans will want to head back into the heart of Cleveland's downtown, a few blocks south of Public Square along Ontario Street, where they'll find Jacobs Field, a 42,800-seat, open-air field of dreams for the Cleveland Indians baseball team. Next door is Gund

GO to Cleveland, Ohio

In Little Italy, the cafe life spills out onto the sidewalk.
GERRY WINGENBACH

Arena, home of the NBA Cavaliers and the IHL hockey-playing Lumberjacks. Even if you're not there on game day, both facilities offer tours.

UNIVERSITY CIRCLE

A 10-minute drive east of downtown is University Circle (around Euclid Avenue and East Boulevard), site of the nation's largest concentration of cultural arts and educational institutions centered within a square mile. At its heart is the Cleveland Museum of Art. Rodin's "The Thinker" is perched outside the main entrance (purchased from the artist in 1916). Inside, the museum showcases a rich collection of Asian and medieval European art, as well as American Indian treasures. Facing the museum is a long, stately garden perfect for strolling. On weekends, you're likely to see formal wedding parties posing here for photographs.

The nearby Cleveland Museum of Natural History explores the wonders of the natural world and the mysteries of the cosmos. The Health Museum, the first of its kind in the country, features more than 200 participatory exhibits and displays, including Juno, a transparent, talking model of a woman.

Also in the University Circle area is the Western Reserve Historical Society, Cleveland's oldest cultural institution and the largest private historical society in the United States. Period rooms re-create life

GO to Cleveland, Ohio

from the pre-Revolutionary War era through the early 20th century.

Visitors to University Circle should also view Severance Hall, renowned for both its architecture and the Cleveland Orchestra, which calls it home. If possible, try to catch a performance by the hometown orchestra that Time magazine recently dubbed "the best band in the land."

LITTLE ITALY

Cleveland was settled by a mix of nationalities and today's neighborhoods reflect that diversity. One of the most recognizable is Little Italy on the city's east side, just a short drive from University Circle. The heart of this colorful community of family-run restaurants and markets is the intersection of Murray Hill and Mayfield, where the cafe life spills out onto the sidewalk. The neighborhood streets are also peppered with wonderful art galleries and shops that sell locally produced fine art.

On a hill overlooking Little Italy is Lake View Cemetery, rich in both history and architecture. Particularly worthy of a stop is Wade Chapel, built for Cleveland industrialist Jeptha Wade. It has a spectacular 24-karat gold and Italian marble mosaic floor. Stained-glass murals highlight scenes from the Old and New Testaments. Stunning Tiffany windows that depict the resurrection are particularly impressive in the surreal glow of afternoon sunlight. Cemetery tours tie in well to the art of Little Italy and University Circle.

ZOO AND RAIN FOREST

Five miles south of downtown is the Cleveland Metroparks Zoo and The RainForest, which is lavishly spread over 165 wooded acres. The zoo houses more than 3,300 animals and the tropical rain forest has another 600 attractions.

SEA WORLD AND GEAUGA LAKE

Two family theme parks are located just beyond Cleveland's boundaries in Aurora, 30 minutes southeast of downtown (115 miles west of Pittsburgh). Sea World of Ohio (one of four Sea Worlds in the United States) features performances by trained marine life, among them dolphins, seals and penguins. Championship athletes perform high diving, waterskiing and gymnastics. More than 20 attractions are spread over 90 acres of rolling hills. Wear your walking shoes.

Nearby is Geauga Lake Park, with more than 100 amusement-type attractions. The roller coasters do half loops and complete loops. There's also a white water rapids ride, a beach with simulated ocean swells, and musical revues.

GO to Cleveland, Ohio

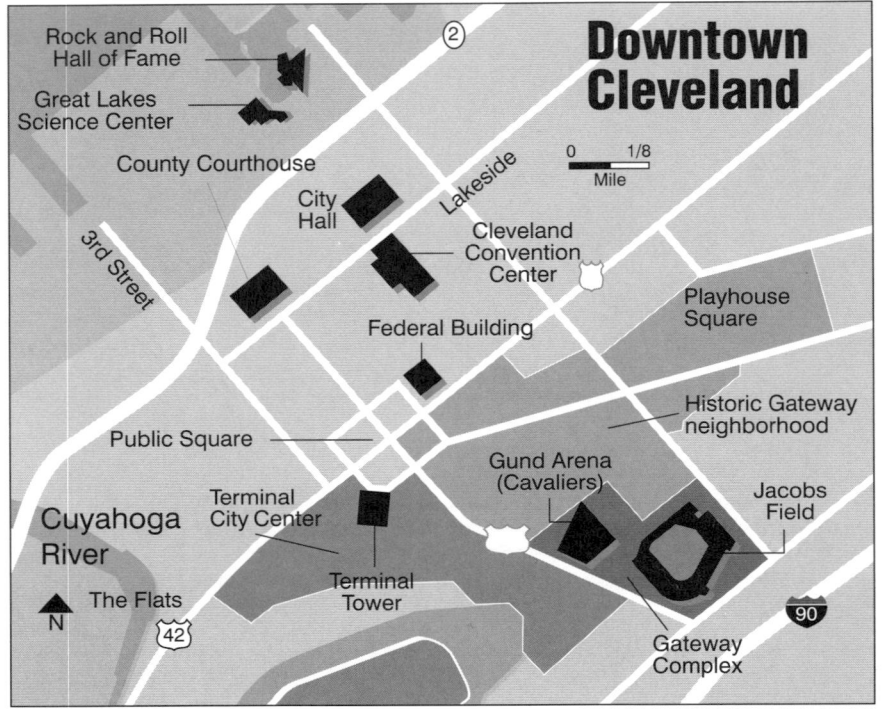

Downtown Cleveland

- Rock and Roll Hall of Fame
- Great Lakes Science Center
- County Courthouse
- City Hall
- Lakeside
- Cleveland Convention Center
- Federal Building
- Playhouse Square
- Public Square
- Historic Gateway neighborhood
- Terminal City Center
- Cuyahoga River
- The Flats
- Terminal Tower
- Gund Arena (Cavaliers)
- Jacobs Field
- Gateway Complex
- 3rd Street
- 42
- 90

0   1/8 Mile

DIANE JURAVICH/PITTSBURGH POST-GAZETTE

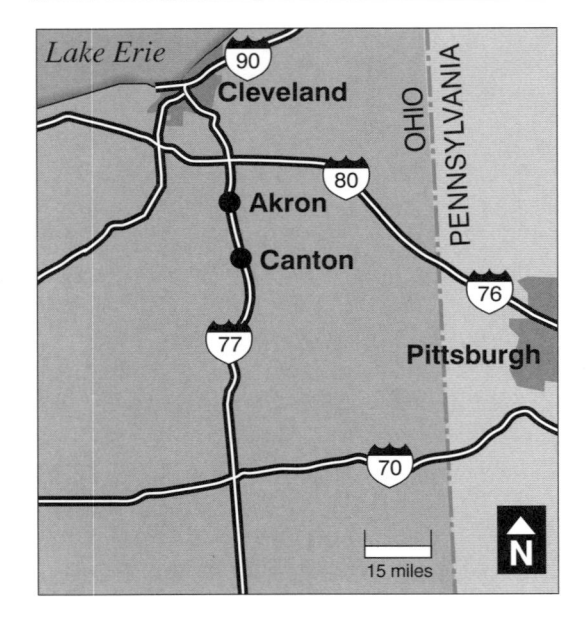

Lake Erie — Cleveland (90) — Akron (80) — Canton (77) — Pittsburgh (76) — (70)

OHIO | PENNSYLVANIA

15 miles

THE ROUTE

Take I-79 north to the Pennsylvania Turnpike west into Ohio, then I-80 west to I-77 north. **Round-trip mileage: 260**

40

GO to Cleveland, Ohio

MORE INFORMATION

➥ **Convention & Visitors Bureau of Greater Cleveland,** Suite 3100, Terminal Tower, 50 Public Square, Cleveland, OH 44113; (800) 321-1001 or (216) 621-4110

➥ **Advantix,** 31515 Euclid Ave., Fourth Floor; (800) 766-6048 or (216) 348-5323. Ticketing by phone for major entertainment and sporting events.

THINGS TO DO, PLACES TO SEE

➥ **Cleveland Museum of Art,** 11150 East Blvd. (at University Circle); (216) 421-7340. Hours: 10—5:45 Tues., Thurs., Fri.; 10—9:45 Wed.; 9—4:45 Sat.; 1—5:45 Sun. Admission: free. World-renowned gallery, particularly known for its Asian and medieval European collections.

➥ **Cleveland Metroparks Zoo and The RainForest,** 3900 Brookside Park Dr. (easy access from I-71 and I-480); (216) 661-6500. Hours: Labor Day—Memorial Day, 9—5 daily, except Christmas and New Year's; extended weekend and holiday hours in summer. Admission: $7 adults; $4 ages 2—11. More than 3,300 animals in one of the Midwest's largest zoological parks. Includes the 2-acre, glass-enclosed RainForest.

➥ **Rock and Roll Hall of Fame and Museum,** 1 Key Plaza; (800) 493-7655 or (216) 781-7625. Hours: Memorial Day—Labor Day, 10—5:30 Sun.—Tues.; 10—9 Wed.—Sat.; Labor Day—Memorial Day, 10—5:30 Thurs.—Tues., 10—9 Wed. Admission: $12.95 adults; $9.50 seniors and ages 4-11. Seven floors of memorabilia dedicated to rock and roll.

➥ **Great Lakes Science Center,** 601 Erieside Ave.; (216) 694-2000. Hours: 9:30—5:30 daily; Omnimax shows hourly. Admission: $6.75 adults; $6 seniors; $4.50 ages 3—17; combination tickets to galleries and Omnimax theater, $9.95 adults; $9 seniors; $7 children. More than 350 interactive exhibits explore the environment and technology.

➥ **Cleveland Museum of Natural History,** 1 Wade Oval; (216) 231-4600. Hours: 10—5 Mon.—Sat. (until 10 p.m. Wed.); 12—5 Sun. Admission: $6 adults; $4 ages 5—17 and seniors. Free admission 3—5 Tues. and Thurs. Planetarium admission: $1.50.

➥ **The African-American Heritage Trail;** (800) 322-7485 or (216) 921-2726. Guided tour to 16 Cleveland sites that figured in African-American history. Cost: $12 adults; $9 seniors; $8 ages 2-7.

➥ **Lake View Cemetery,** 12316 Euclid Ave.; (216) 421-2665. Hours: Apr.—Nov. 9—4. Cost: Free. Visitors can tour architecturally rich Wade Chapel and the cemetery.

➥ **Sea World of Ohio,** 1100 Sea World Dr., Aurora (30 miles southeast of Cleveland); (800) 637-4268. Hours: May—Sept., 10—7 daily, (until 11 p.m. June—Aug.). Admission: $27.95 adults, $19.95 ages 3—11. Marine-life attractions spread over 90 acres.

➥ **Geauga Lake Park,** 1060 N. Aurora Rd., Aurora (next to Sea World); (216) 562-7131. Hours: Memorial Day—Labor Day, 10—10 daily. Admission: $21.99; $7.99 children under 48 inches tall. Amusement park with more than 100 attractions including roller coasters and water slides.

ACCOMMODATIONS

➥ Chain lodgings, many of them clustered around I-90, include **Holiday Inn** (800-465-4329); **Comfort Inn** (800-228-5150) and **Days Inn** (800-325-2525).

➥ In the heart of Cleveland's downtown are: **Ritz-Carlton Cleveland,** 1515 W. 3rd St.; (800) 241-3333 or (216) 623-

GO to Cleveland, Ohio

1300. Rates: $149—$235. Deluxe downtown hotel connected to the Terminal City Center shopping complex.

➡ **Renaissance Cleveland Hotel,** 24 Public Square; (216) 696-5600. Rates: start at $125. Deluxe downtown hotel facing Public Square and listed on the national historic register.

➡ **Cleveland Marriott Downtown** at Key Center, 127 Public Square; (800) 228-9290 or (216) 696-9200. Rates: $129 and up. Deluxe downtown hotel close to North Coast Harbor.

➡ **Omni International Hotel,** 2065 E. 96th St.; (800) 843-6664 or (216) 791-1900. Rates: $129—$299. In University Circle area near museums.

RESTAURANTS

Cleveland's dining scene has become more diverse in recent years. From the lively eateries in the Flats to the upscale downtown restaurants to traditional ethnic favorites, the city offers something for all tastes. Here are some favorites among readers of Cleveland Magazine:

➡ **BEST FINE DINING: Classics,** Carnegie Ave. and E. 96th St. (in the Omni Hotel); (216) 791-1300. Dinner, $26.

➡ **BEST CASUAL DINING: Pastabilities,** 13915 Cedar Rd., South Euclid; (216) 321-8600. Dinner, $12. (It also got votes for Most Romantic and Best Pasta.)

➡ **BEST MICROBREW: Great Lakes Brewing Company,** 2516 Market St.; (216) 771-4404. Dinner, $16.

➡ **BEST SUNDAY BRUNCH: The Riverview Room at the Ritz-Carlton,** 1515 W. 3rd St.; (216) 623-1300. Brunch buffet, $32.

➡ **BEST PEOPLE WATCHING: Shooters on the Water,** 1148 Main Ave.; (216) 861-6900. Dinner, $12.

➡ **ADVENTUROUS DINING: Empress Taytu Ethiopian Restaurant,** 6125 St. Clair Ave.; (216) 391-9400. Dinner, $10—$15.

➡ **WILDEST HAPPY HOUR: Fagan's,** 996 Old River Rd.; (216) 241-6116. Drinks, 99 cents 4:30—9 daily; dinner, $15—$20.

➡ **OTHER CHOICES INCLUDE: Rock Bottom Brewery,** 200 Sycamore St. (west bank of the Flats); (216) 623-1555. Hours: 11:30 a.m.—12 a.m daily. Micro-brewed ales and lagers, interesting menu, especially the appetizers. Weekend entertainment. Dinner, $8—$18.

➡ **Watermark Restaurant,** 1250 Old River Rd. (east bank of the Flats); (216) 241-1600. Hours: 11:30—10 Mon.—Thurs.; 11:30—11 Fri.—Sat.; 11—2:30 and 5—10 Sun. Outdoor and indoor tables along the river, nice setting, popular Friday night seafood buffet. Dinner, $15.

➡ **Wilbert's Bar & Grill,** 1360 West 9th St.; (216) 771-2583. Hours: 11:30—8 Mon.; 11:30—2:30 a.m. Tues.—Fri.; 3—2:30 a.m. Sat.; 5 p.m.—1:30 a.m. Sun. Southwestern food with evening blues performances. Dinner, $5—$13.

BIG EVENTS

➡ **Grand Prix of Cleveland,** summer, Burke Lakefront Airport. (800) 321-1001 or (216) 621-4110.

➡ **Cleveland National Air Show,** Labor Day weekend, Burke Lakefront Airport. (800) 321-1001 or (216) 621-4110.

GO to Oil Country

Liberty Street is the main business thoroughfare in Franklin, a tidy town that boasts every architectural style popular in Western Pennsylvania from the 1830s to the 1930s.

TONY TYE/PITTSBURGH POST-GAZETTE

Oil Country

THINGS ARE GUSHING IN VENANGO COUNTY

Oil Creek, Oil City and Petroleum Centre aren't the sort of place names likely to provoke a stampede of nature lovers. But Venango County and its environs boast more pristine territory ideal for outdoor pursuits than its Oil Country moniker lets on.

This corner of Western Pennsylvania about an hour north of Pittsburgh got its first growth spurt in the 1860s after the world's first successful oil well was drilled in 1859 near Titusville. The discovery sparked a boom up and down the Oil Creek Valley and along the Allegheny River, as thousands of prospectors flooded in hoping to make their fortunes.

The oil industry still has a presence, but these days you're just as likely to meet people like Joey and Warren Simmons, former Arizonans who moved here to get away from it all and now run a cattle farm/bed and breakfast inn near Emlenton.

GO to Oil Country

This is a region of tidy farmland, solitary stretches of river and small towns. Though the oil industry isn't as pervasive as it once was, its role in shaping this area is apparent, from the aging refineries along the Allegheny River to the pleasant park that memorializes that first oil strike, to the mansions built by the beneficiaries of the black gold.

EMLENTON

A short hop off Interstate 80 brings you to Emlenton. The little town on the banks of the Allegheny River claims to have had the world's largest concentration of millionaires (seven in a town of 1,400) at one point in the past. (Trivia note: Emlenton is the hometown of socialite Martha "Sunny" von Bulow, the heiress whose husband, Claus von Bulow, was acquitted of causing her insulin-induced coma.)

Today, most residents live modestly on the slopes rising above the Allegheny. Two bed and breakfast inns face the river, and a greenbelt along the shore is a pleasant spot to watch the river drift by.

FOXBURG

To get out on the water, head three miles south on Route 268, dipping into Clarion County, where an old B&O Railroad bridge rusted to a deep cinnamon color leads over the river and into Foxburg.

Foxburg Livery and Outfitters faces the river, and here you can rent canoes and get recommendations on routes. The most popular float trip is the nine-mile stretch from Mill Creek south to Foxburg. (Figure on traveling two to three miles per hour.) If you fancy camping out along the river, the 38 miles from Franklin to Foxburg takes in some nice scenery.

This stretch of river is slow, sleepy and quiet. And residents seem to prefer it that way.

"We like canoes," said Dick Garrard, owner of Foxburg Livery. "We don't want the 150-horse-power guys sucking up booze and messing things up for other people."

Foxburg Livery also sells fish bait — minnows, maggots and mealworms are on the menu. Next door at Ye Olde Silver Fox Inne, the fare, ranging from prime rib to pizza, is more appetizing.

Foxburg was once the sole domain of a physician named Fox who, so the story goes, was owed a debt by William Penn. Penn said he'd pay him in land — "as much as could be walked from sun up to sun down." Fox, by all accounts a clever sort, hired an Indian scout and had him trek west on the longest day of the year. Fox ended up with title to 118,000 acres.

AMERICAN GOLF HALL OF FAME

One of Fox's heirs, Joseph Mickle Fox, settled in the area in the 1840s. In 1884, he traveled to Scotland,

GO to Oil Country

Liberty Street in Franklin, seen through the window of DeBence Antique Music World, which houses a collection of nickelodeons, music boxes, band organs and other antiques.
TONY TYE/PITTSBURGH POST-GAZETTE

where he took up golf. In 1887, he opened his own course in Foxburg, which claims distinction as the oldest continually operated golf course in the United States.

The clubhouse, a handsome, rambling, log structure originally built in 1924 as a vacation home, has a wraparound porch lined with comfortable old rockers and hanging baskets of flowers. On the second floor, the American Golf Hall of Fame Association houses a small museum where you can learn all sorts of historical trivia. Example: regulation golf balls circa 1400-1800 were stuffed with one silk top hat full of feathers per ball. The museum's oldest artifact is one of these 300-year-old "featheries."

FRANKLIN

Route 322 heading northwest is sprinkled with farm markets and hand-painted signs offering eggs and whole turkeys. The road eventually bumps into Franklin, a handsome town of well-maintained houses and businesses. The community is an architectural treasure-trove, boasting every popular architectural style in Western Pennsylvania from the 1830s to 1930s. A self-guided walking tour helps you sort out the late 17th-century Dutch colonials from the more elaborate Gothic Revival and Italian villa styles of the post-Civil War era when the oil

GO to Oil Country

A replica of Edwin Drake's derrick and well house sits on the site of the original well in Drake Well Park, near Titusville.
TONY TYE/PITTSBURGH POST-GAZETTE

boom brought new wealth to town.

DEBENCE ANTIQUE MUSIC WORLD

Two unusual museums in Franklin appeal to children, as well as adults. At DeBence Antique Music World, a cacophony of sound spills out of nickelodeons, calliopes, barrel organs and other obsolete tune-makers. The 125 "music machines" displayed in a 1906 dry goods store are from the collection of Jake and Elizabeth DeBence. Jake DeBence, a local dairy farmer who died in 1992, bought broken machines and tinkered with them until they sang again.

The single most valuable one is a $250,000 orchestrion. The 1912 one-machine band was built for silent movie houses and sounds like a 10-piece orchestra.

WILD WEST MUSEUM

Behind the Franklin fire department in a former Civil War armory, Dan Hardesty runs an auction house and Wild West Museum. Life-size bronzes of cowboys on rearing horses greet you at the entrance. Inside, is a repository of Civil War, American Indian and cowboy artifacts. Celebrity items include cowboy star Tom Mix's saddle, Gene Autry's holster and Apache Indian warrior Geronimo's burial shroud. There's a lot of interesting stuff in the auction rooms as well, like vintage jukeboxes and gasoline pumps, which are hot sellers in European markets.

OIL CREEK STATE PARK

Ten miles north of Franklin on the banks of Oil Creek, a former oil boomtown is now a haven for cyclists, fishers and hikers. Oil Creek State Park covers more than 7,000 acres from the village of Rynd Farm to Drake Well Park. It encompasses the remains of Petroleum Centre, a wild and woolly town that within three short weeks of its founding in the 1860s claimed 3,000 residents, thanks to oil fever. By the 1880s most had moved on in search of better prospects elsewhere.

Today, Mike Laskowski, owner of a bike rental and fly-fishing shop across from the park's visitors center, is the last holdout. A sign inside the 1860s house where he works and lives proclaims: Petroleum Centre: Pop. 1.

The parks department keeps the town's legacy alive, however, with a 45-minute, self-guided walking tour with photographs and explanatory notes posted at sites along the way. Several small graveyards also are relics of the boomtown days.

The park has a paved bike path that meanders along the creek and

TONY TYE/PITTSBURGH POST-GAZETTE
A house on 15th Street in Franklin, decked out for Independence Day festivities.

up to the Drake Well Museum. The 19-mile round-trip route takes about three hours, depending on how much you dawdle along the way.

PITHOLE

Nearby, the remains of Pithole, another oil boomtown that exploded to a town of 15,000 in a mere nine months, is now a state historic site, which also has a visitors center.

DRAKE WELL PARK

If you're driving through Oil Creek State Park, a loop road returns you to Route 8 south of Titusville and Drake Well Park, site of the first oil strike in 1859. Here, Edwin Drake, a former train conductor turned oil explorer, struck oil on the banks of Oil Creek. Vintage equipment, including a replica of the derrick and engine house are set up along the creek.

It's the largest concentration of

GO to Oil Country

oil-industry trappings you're likely to see these days in Oil Country, since much of the oil business ceased operation here in the 1980s.

OIL CREEK & TITUSVILLE RAILROAD

An ideal way to see the countryside is by taking a ride on the Oil Creek & Titusville Railroad. Trains run in the summer and fall from the Perry Street Station, a restored 1893 freight depot in Titusville. Inside is a concession stand selling train-related souvenirs and snacks. The first stop on the 2½-hour round-trip ride is just outside town at the Drake Well Museum. If you're traveling with a bicycle (they're allowed on the train) you can get off here and ride along 10 miles of paved trails through the Oil Creek Valley, then reboard the train at Rynd Farm Station, four miles north of Oil Creek. The train also has a flag stop at Petroleum Centre.

TONY TYE/PITTSBURGH POST-GAZETTE

Daryl Weaver, who helps run the pro shop, shows off the old-style comfort on the clubhouse porch at Foxburg Country Club.

GO to Oil Country

THE ROUTE

Oil country

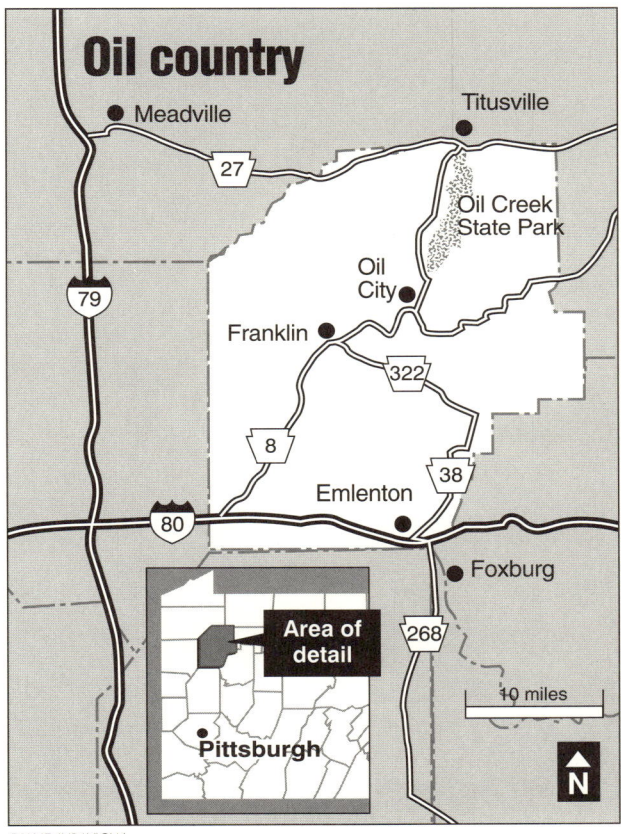

From Pittsburgh, take I-79 north to I-80 east. To go directly to Franklin and Oil City, head north on Rt. 8 (exit 3). For a back roads route, continue east on I-80 and exit on to Rt. 38 (exit 5) at Emlenton. A detour onto Rt. 268 south leads to the banks of the Allegheny River at Foxburg. From there, return to Venango County on Rt. 38 north, then take Rt. 322 west to Franklin. Rt. 8 leads north to Oil City and on to Titusville. Rt. 27 west to Meadville leads back to I-79. **Round-trip mileage: 250**

DIANE JURAVICH/
PITTSBURGH POST-GAZETTE

MORE INFORMATION

➡ **Oil Heritage Region Tourist Promotion Agency,** 248 Seneca St., National City Bank Building, Box 128, Oil City, PA 16301; (800) 483-6264

➡ **Emlenton Chamber of Commerce,** Box 212, Emlenton, PA 16373; (412) 867-1855

➡ **Franklin Chamber of Commerce,** 1259 Liberty St., Franklin, PA 16323; (814) 432-5823

➡ **Oil City Chamber of Commerce,** 102 Center St., Box 376, Oil City, PA 16301; (814) 676-8521

➡ **Titusville Chamber of Commerce,** 202 W. Central Ave., Titusville, PA 16354; (814) 827-2941

GO to Oil Country

THINGS TO DO, PLACES TO SEE

FOXBURG AREA

➡ **Foxburg Livery & Outfitters,** Main Street facing the Allegheny River; (800) 519-6877 or (412) 659-3752. Hours: Apr. 1 until after the leaves change, 8 a.m. daily (April—May, Sept.—Oct. weekends or by reservation only.) Rates: Weekend canoe rentals, $15 per canoe (2 people) for a 4-mile trip; $25 for a 9-mile trip; $60 for 2-day, 38-mile float. (Weekday rentals slightly less.) Kayaks also available. Transportation to put-in or take-out point included.

➡ **Foxburg Country Club and the American Golf Hall of Fame,** Harvey Road Foxburg; (412) 659-3196. Golf course open Apr.—Oct. Greens fees: $20 for 18 holes weekends; $15 weekdays. Cart rental $22. Museum admission: free. Public course claims to be oldest in continuous use in the United States. Rambling 1920s clubhouse houses American Golf Hall of Fame w/ historic golf memorabilia.

➡ **Nickleville Store,** off Rt. 38, 10 miles north of Emlenton; (814) 498-2873 or (800) 816-1679. Hours: Apr.—Dec., 11—5 daily; Jan.—Mar., 11— 5 Sat. or by appointment. Old general store sells antiques and collectibles.

FRANKLIN

➡ **"Walking Tours of Historic Franklin,"** available at Franklin Chamber of Commerce, 1259 Liberty St., outlines history and architectural styles of significant buildings. Cost: $1.

➡ **DeBence Antique Music World,** 1261 Liberty St.; (814) 432-5668. Spring/summer hours: 10—4 Tues.—Sat.; 12:30—4 Sun. Winter hours: 11—4 Thurs.—Sat. Admission: $6 adults; $5 seniors; $3 children.

➡ **Wild West Museum,** 1280 Franklin Ave.; (814) 432-8577. Hours: 10—5 Sat.; noon—5 Sun.; weekdays by chance. Call ahead. Admission: $4 adults; 12 and under free.

➡ **Samuel Justus Recreational Trail** covers 5.8 miles between Franklin and Oil City. Paved, level path is ideal for bicycling and in-line skating.

➡ **Allegheny River Trail,** runs 14 miles south from Franklin to Kennerdell, crosses wilderness areas, past Indian carvings and remnants of the railroad and oil industries.

➡ **Country Pedalers,** Rt. 322 (just east of Franklin by the 8th St. Bridge); (814) 432-8055 or (800) 707-6520. Hours: 9—7 daily. Bicycle rentals, $3 an hour; in-line skates, $5 an hour; canoes, $20—$40 per trip.

TITUSVILLE — OIL CITY

➡ **Oil Creek State Park,** 4 miles north of Oil City (turn right off Rt. 8 past the Rynd Farm Bridge); (814) 676-5915. Hours: 8 a.m.—sunset. Park has 36-mile loop of hiking trails w/ 2 overnight trail shelter areas (reserve through park office). Oil Creek is popular among fishers for its stocked and native trout; 9½-mile paved bike trail runs along an old railroad grade through Oil Creek Gorge.

➡ **Oil Creek Outfitters,** across from the Oil Creek State Park office; (814) 677-4684. Hours: 10—6 daily; closed Tue.—Thurs. Labor Day—Mar. 1. Bike rentals and fly fishing equipment.

➡ **Drake Well Museum,** RD 3, Titusville (turn right at the first stoplight as you enter Titusville and follow the signs); (814) 827-2797. Hours: 9—5 Tues.—Sat.; noon—5 Sun. Closed Mon. except

GO to Oil Country

Memorial Day, July 4 and Labor Day. Admission: $4 adults; $3.50 seniors; $2 ages 6—12; $10 families.

➡ **Pithole Historic Site,** off Rt. 227 between Pleasantville and Plumer; (814) 827-2797. Hours: site is open year round; visitors center open June — Labor Day, noon — 5 Wed.; 10 — 5 Thurs. — Sun. Admission: $2.50 adults; $2 seniors; 50 cents children; $5.50 families. 19th-century oil boomtown is now part of Drake Well Museum.

➡ **Tyred Wheels Museum,** Russell Corner Rd.(2¼ miles west off Rt. 227 between Plumer and Pleasantville). Hours: Memorial Day — Sept. 1, 1 — 5 daily; and to groups by appointment May — Oct. Admission: $3.50 adults, $2 ages 8—16. Small museum houses 25 vintage autos and thousands of miniature vehicles.

➡ **Oil Creek & Titusville Railroad,** Oil City; (814) 676-1733. 2½-hour narrated trips through Oil Creek State Park. Round-trip runs depart from Perry Street Station, a restored 1893 freight depot in Titusville from mid-June—Oct. at 2 p.m. Wed.—Sun. Extra runs are added on weekends in Oct. Other boarding points are at Drake Well Museum, Petroleum Centre Station and Rynd Farm. Fare: $9 adults; $8 seniors; $5 ages 3—17; and $1 for bikes. Tickets can be purchased in advance or at boarding points. The railroad also stages special holiday rides at Easter, Halloween and during the Christmas season, along with murder-mystery rides and special fall foliage excursions. Call for dates and ticket prices.

ACCOMMODATIONS

➡ **Apple Alley B&B,** 214 River Ave., Emlenton; (800) 547-8499. Rates: $40—$60. 6 guest rooms, 3 w/ private bath in 1884 house w/ broad front porch facing river.

➡ **Barnard House,** 109 River Ave., Emlenton; (412) 867-2261. Rates: $40. 1870s Queen Anne Victorian has 4 guest rooms, w/ shared bath.

➡ **Whippletree Inn & Farm,** Big Bend Road, Emlenton; (412) 867-9543. Rates: $50—$60. 100-acre farm accommodates horses as well as human guests. Farm also has cattle, sheep, ducks and other animals; 5 guest rooms (2 w/ private bath) furnished w/antiques.

➡ **Inn at Franklin,** 1411 Liberty St., Franklin; (800) 535-4052 or (814) 437-3031. Rates: $65—$125. Motel-style lodging in the center of town.

➡ **The Lamberton House B&B,** 1331 Otter St., Franklin; (800) 481-0776 or (814) 432-7908. Rates: $45—$75. Queen Anne-style house has 6 guest rooms, some w/ private bath and 4 w/ fireplaces.

➡ **Quo Vadis B&B,** 1501 Liberty St., Franklin; (800) 360-6598 or (814) 432-4208. Rates: $60—$80. Handsome 1867 Queen Anne in the town's historic district has 6 guest rooms furnished w/ heirloom antiques; private baths.

➡ **Holiday Inn,** 1 Seneca St., Oil City; (800) HOLIDAY or (814) 677-1221. Rates: $62.

➡ **Cross Creek Resort,** Rt. 8, Titusville (4 miles south of Titusville); (814) 827-9611. Rates: start at $95. Lodging has 94 guest rooms, 27-hole golf course, tennis courts and outdoor heated pool. Ask about golf packages and other specials.

➡ **Casey's Caboose Stop,** 221 S. Monroe St., Titusville; (814) 827-6597. Rates: $65—$75. Lodging in converted cabooses.

RESTAURANTS

➡ **Ye Olde Silver Fox Inne,** Main Street, Foxburg; (412) 659-5701. Bar

GO to Oil Country

hours: 11—11 Mon.—Thurs.; 11—1 a.m. Fri.—Sun. Dining room hours: 11—9 Sun.—Thurs.; 11—11 Fri.—Sat. Indoor and outdoor dining in a casual atmosphere. Eclectic menu, $6—$17.

→ **Leonardo's,** 1267 Liberty St., Franklin; (814) 432-8421. Summer hours: 11—10 Mon.—Thurs.; 11 a.m.—midnight Fri.—Sat. Winter hours: 11—10 Mon.—Sat. Extensive Italian menu, $6—$10.

→ **Yellow Dog Lantern,** 218 Elm St., Oil City; (814) 676-1000. Hours: lunch, 11—2 Mon.—Fri.; dinner, 5—10 Mon.—Sat. Steak and seafood. Dinners, $10—$20.

→ **Papa Carone's,** 317 S. Franklin St., Titusville; (814) 827-7555. Hours: 11—11 Mon.—Thurs.; 11—midnight Fri.—Sat.; noon—11 Sun. Italian food. Dinners, $6—$12.

BIG EVENTS

→ **Oil Heritage Week,** full week, ends last Sun. in July, Oil City. Sporting events, entertainment, arts and crafts. (814) 676-8521.

→ **Oil Festival,** full week in mid-Aug., Titusville. Barge race, oil baron's picnic and other events commemorate the discovery of oil. (814) 827-2941.

→ **Applefest,** 1st weekend in Oct., Franklin. Craft show, children's activities and other activities celebrate the harvest. (814) 432-5823.

GO to Cook Forest

An Amish farmer drives his team down a country road near Smicksburg.

GERRY WINGENBACH

Cook Forest

THE SPLENDOR OF A MAGIC REGION

On a summer day in 1910, Anthony W. Cook sat on a log in the midst of the towering woods near his home in the Clarion River Valley and vowed to preserve the forest. He was the grandson of John Cook, who had arrived in the valley in 1826 and made his fortune from logging that forest.

It took 15 years for Anthony Cook's declaration of preservation to become reality, but in 1925 — a century after his grandfather's sawmills took shape — the state of Pennsylvania purchased the land that would become Cook Forest State Park. Today the 6,600-acre tract is part of a four-county region that dubs itself the Magic Forests.

This driving trip east and north of Pittsburgh takes in parts of those "magic forests," plus a town that is

53

GO to Cook Forest

GERRY WINGENBACH

Clarion's 19th-century Queen Anne Victorian courthouse sports a 214-foot tower.

54

GO to Cook Forest

home to one of Pennsylvania's largest Amish communities; the hometown of the world's most famous groundhog; and a couple of towns whose historic main streets are so lovingly restored they could be a Disney stage set.

SMICKSBURG

Traveling north out of Pittsburgh on Route 28 to Kittanning, then east on Route 85, you eventually leave the suburban sprawl behind and enter an area of rural homes and scattered small farms. Turning north on Route 954, the first Amish buggies appear on the thin ribbon of asphalt near Smicksburg. More than 200 Amish families have lived and farmed in the area since the 1960s. The borough proper, however, has only about 60 residents. It was founded in 1827 by Lutheran minister John George Smick, who sold plots along Little Mahoning Creek for $10 each. By the 1930s, Smicksburg was a relatively lively town with four churches, a school, a hotel and shops. Unfortunately, much of it lay in a flood plain, and when the Mahoning Creek Dam was built in the 1940s to control flooding, the lower half of town was obliterated.

Today, a small, but growing arts community has begun to take root. And there's a surprising amount of commerce conducted here, considering the town's tiny size. The old Smicksburg bank building in the heart of town has been attractively restored and converted to a large, airy display space for Smicksburg Pottery. Visitors can view some of the creative process at the wood-fired kiln out back. Across the street, Thee Village Sampler sells kitchen gadgets, chocolates, apple butter and dried pasta. An adjoining bakery sells fresh-baked pies, cakes, sandwiches and quiche if you want to pick up the makings of a picnic.

Just south of Smicksburg's center on Route 954 are several older businesses, including a country store and deli, an old-fashioned mercantile selling Amish goods and bulk foods, and a chocolate shop. Also south of town is Yoder's Quilt and Gift Shop located in a two-story white frame farmhouse formerly occupied by an Amish family. Vestiges of their lives there, such as the kerosene lamps mounted to the walls, remain. Quilts made by local Amish women and sold on consignment are in a building next door. Though many of the quilts are designed in the subdued shades of blue, black and green traditionally favored by the Amish, the quilters use other colors, as well. They also accept special orders, but it's best to make your preferences known before winter, when the women do most of their quilting.

Among antiques shops in the area is the Coleman House, a historic farmhouse in the middle of a 1,600-acre cattle farm a few miles northwest of town. It sells an interesting collection of bonafide antiques, along with some craft items in a range of prices.

A number of Amish operate woodworking shops announced only by small, hand-painted signs posted on trees along Route 954. One of them just north of Smicksburg is owned by Dan Byler who gave up farming for furniture making. In a large workshop/display room surrounded by farm buildings, he crafts porch swings, Adirondack-style chairs and picnic tables from cedar; rockers from hickory; benches with those little heart-shaped cutouts that are ubiquitous in Amish country; and some less traditional designs.

DAYTON

A three-mile detour west leads to Dayton, just over the Armstrong County line, where several other sites might provoke a stop. They include the Marshall House, home of the area's first white settlers and a nicely restored example of a traditional 19th-century farmhouse. The Country Corner Flea Market on Main Street is full of new and used goods sold on consignment. North of town, Mahoning Creek Lake's forested shoreline has picnic tables, grills and hiking trails.

Back on Route 954 three miles north of Smicksburg is Windgate Vineyards, which produces 7,000 gallons of wine annually. Inside there's a tasting room and view of the fermentation room. Visitors can also learn about the history of the Pennsylvania wine industry, which dates back to William Penn, who encouraged the planting of vineyards. Picnic tables and a children's play area are set up outside next to 15 acres of wine grapes.

PUNXSUTAWNEY

A turn onto Route 210 north leads to Punxsutawney, 14 miles from Smicksburg. The town is best known as the home of Punxsutawney Phil, the weather-forecasting groundhog who makes an annual appearance at Gobbler's Knob. As thousands of spectators look on, Phil emerges from his burrow just after daybreak. If he sees his shadow, prepare for six more weeks of winter; if he doesn't, expect an early spring.

The origins of Groundhog Day actually lie in the European Candlemas Day, when, according to legend, "for as the sun shines on Candlemas Day, so far will the snow swirl till May." German immigrants brought the legend with them to the area; the groundhog burrowed its way into the tradition later. But it stuck. Now, every Feb. 2 the members of the Inner Circle of the Groundhog Club (local businessmen dressed up in top hats and tails) meet at Gobbler's Knob with thousands of revelers to await Phil's annual forecast.

Little did those early members of the Punxsutawney Groundhog Club realize back in 1902 when it was organized, what a lucrative industry

GO to Cook Forest

A number of Smicksburg shops sell Amish-made goods.

GERRY WINGENBACH

Groundhog Day would spawn. Today, groundhog business is big business in Punxsutawney. The chamber of commerce sells groundhog T-shirts, cookie cutters, coloring books and posters. Phil has his own Web site. His likeness is on phone calling cards. He has visited the White House, appeared on the Oprah Winfrey Show and was featured in the 1993 movie "Groundhog Day."

You can visit Gobbler's Knob anytime (it's a hilly 2½ acre spot a mile from downtown). Phil usually sees visitors, as well, from his roomy, glassed-in enclosure in the children's library at the Mahoning East Civic Center downtown.

Long before Punxsutawney became known for its groundhog, the area was prized for its abundant natural resources. Those who grew prosperous from coal, oil and lumber lived along West Mahoning Street, known as Millionaire's Row. One of the most notable structures, the McKibben House at 401 W. Mahoning, is now the site of the local historical society museum. The brick and frame house was built in 1903 by Stanford White, the preeminent architect of his day, for Edwin McKibben, manager of the Punxsutawney Iron Works. Seven museum rooms are open to the public and contain furniture, photographs and other artifacts of Punxsutawney's early history.

Eight miles south of town off

GO to Cook Forest

The Coleman House is one of the top antique shops in the Smicksburg area.
GERRY WINGENBACH

Route 119 is Silverbrook Farms, where exotic animals such as guanaco (a member of the llama family) are raised for their fiber. A petting area allows kids to see angora goats and rabbits up close. Farm tours not only explain the spinning process but also get into the colonial history of the area. Historic buildings on the site include a one-room schoolhouse, colonial cabin and 1805 barn. There's also a spinning wheel museum.

BROOKVILLE

Brookville, 20 miles north of Punxsutawney via Route 36, is the Jefferson County seat and an exceedingly attractive little town. The downtown historic district runs three blocks along Main and Jefferson streets between White and Franklin.

Victorian buildings, expertly restored and well-maintained, include shops, restaurants and private homes. It's a fitting spot for Brookville's popular Victorian Christmas Celebration in early December. Stop by the Meeting Place restaurant at 209 Main St., for a self-guided walking tour brochure that gives the details on 21 buildings in the district.

The tiny community of Coolspring lies mid-way between Punxsutawney and Brookville. The Coolspring General Store has been a local gathering spot since 1904. In winter, you can warm up in front of the ancient pot-bellied stove; in summer, order a deli sandwich and take it out. Nearby, the Coolspring Power Museum displays 250 internal combustion engines spanning more than a century.

CLEAR CREEK STATE PARK

Continuing north, Clear Creek State Park, just off Route 36 on Route 949 near Sigel, is a good spot for families. It has plenty of picnic tables, plus a beach with a lifeguard from Memorial Day to Labor Day. In winter, there's a lighted skating pond. Camping is allowed year round and 22 small, rustic cabins rent from mid-April to mid-December. About 15 miles of trails cut through the woods and along streams, ranging from ½-mile to under 2-miles long. The park's Ox Shoe interpretive trail follows an old logging route. Signs posted along the way explain how logging worked in the last century, when oxen dragged logs to Clear Creek where they were floated to the Clarion River and on to Pittsburgh.

COOK FOREST

The largest stand of virgin timber in the Eastern United States lies just ahead in the Cook Forest. Naturalists believe the forest's oldest trees date back to 1644 and grew after a drought and forest fire burned the existing area. Some of the oldest measure 3 to 4 feet around and stand 200 feet tall; just four trees of this size would be enough to build a six-room house.

This is a lush, fairy tale forest thick with conifers and hardwoods. In summer, the sunlight barely filters through the thick cover of foliage. In fall, it is a riot of color. In winter, 27 miles of trails provide a quiet place for cross-country skiing; snowmobilers get their own 20 miles of trails to race on and skaters gather at the ice rink on River Road well into the evening.

The old-growth forests are concentrated in the eastern side of the park in the Swamp, Seneca and Cathedral areas. The Cathedral, a National Natural Landmark located just behind the Log Cabin Inn Visitor Center on the Longfellow Trail, is the most accessible of the three. "The Unconquered," a 1946 movie starring Gary Cooper, was filmed in parts of the forest, including the rocky outcrop known as Seneca Point. This is a good spot for visitors who want to get into the thick of the woods without exerting too much energy. Park roads lead to a parking lot near the Seneca Point lookout (watch for signs on Route 36 near Ridge Camp). Nearby is an 80-foot fire tower that dates from 1929. Climb the 108 steps to the top and you'll be rewarded with a spectacular view of the Clarion River meandering through the valley.

The first white settler to arrive here was John Cook. He bought 765 acres, built a cabin near where Cooksburg is today and raised a family of 10. The logging business he built was expanded by his son, Andrew, who constructed three sawmills and other

GO to Cook Forest

buildings. The Cook legacy continued well into this century and besides the park itself, a number of places bear the Cook name. The family homestead, a white farmhouse at the intersection of Route 36 and River Road, is now a privately owned bed and breakfast. The family cemetery lies just outside the park. And the Cook Mansion, built by Anthony W. Cook, who led preservation efforts, sits on River Road. It is privately owned and not open to the public.

The old Cook sawmill remains, as well, and it has been put to good use as an arts center. The Sawmill Center for the Arts has since 1975 offered classes and other arts-related programs from May through October, along with festivals and children's programs. The Verna Leith Sawmill Theatre next door features stage performances from May through September. There's also an outdoor swimming pool here. The Sawmill Center for the Arts Site II on Breezemont Drive off Route 36, is located in an old strip mine garage and is open year-round. It hosts workshops, Elderhostel programs, summer theater and festivals. The shop also sells regionally made crafts as disparate as hand-woven baskets, wooden vases, blackberry jam and concrete stepping stones.

A number of state-operated visitors facilities are located within park boundaries, including Ridge Camp, a 226-site family campground open

GERRY WINGENBACH
Smicksburg Pottery occupies an old bank building.

GO to Cook Forest

year-round. It has both tent sites and trailer hookups, but shower and toilet facilities at the campground are closed from late October to late May.

The state also operates two groups of log cabins built in the 1930s by the Civilian Conservation Corps that are open from mid-April to late December. The River Cabins, on a hill overlooking the Clarion River, have four rooms and a fireplace and sleep six to eight people. They have cold running water from May to October, but no toilets. At a nearby site are the smaller one-room Indian Cabins that sleep up to four. They're arranged in a semi-circle around a large bathhouse behind the Log Cabin Inn, another CCC project that now serves as the park visitors center. A small stocked pond nearby is open to pint-sized fishers ages 12 and under.

Several private outfitters rent canoes for paddling on the Clarion River and mountain bikes for riding on forest trails. There also are several stables offering guided horseback rides in the forest.

Outside the boundaries of the Cook Forest, a multitude of commercial enterprises rev into full gear in warmer months. They include go-cart tracks, water slides and miniature golf courses. Whether they strike you as tacky clutter or fun amusements is a matter of perspective. They detract from the natural beauty of the area, but they're bound to perk up kids who are bored by a walk in the woods.

The Cook Forest area also has numerous private cabin rentals. These complexes are eclectic; individual cabins may differ vastly in layout, quality of furnishings and amenities, and some of these aging hostelries could use an overhaul. It's advisable to have a close look before you check in.

CLARION

The principle community in the Cook Forest vicinity is Clarion, whose quaint town center has a wealth of historic buildings, including a stately 1883 Queen Anne Victorian courthouse with a 214-foot tower. A gazebo-crowned park and a wide Main Street lined with shops and restaurants in restored buildings round out the old-fashioned downtown. The town was born in 1839 after Clarion County was created from parts of Venango and Armstrong counties. Within two years it had more than 700 residents, although the early structures were haphazard. "The town looked to me more like a camp meeting than the metropolis of a flourishing county," wrote a visitor in 1840.

More substantial and beautiful buildings went up in the last half of the 19th and early 20th centuries. You won't find The Gap or Border's bookstore here; you will find independently owned clothing stores, bookstores and restaurants. A free walking-tour map available at the library on Main Street between Sixth and Seventh avenues outlines the history of 40 downtown buildings.

GO to Cook Forest

THE ROUTE

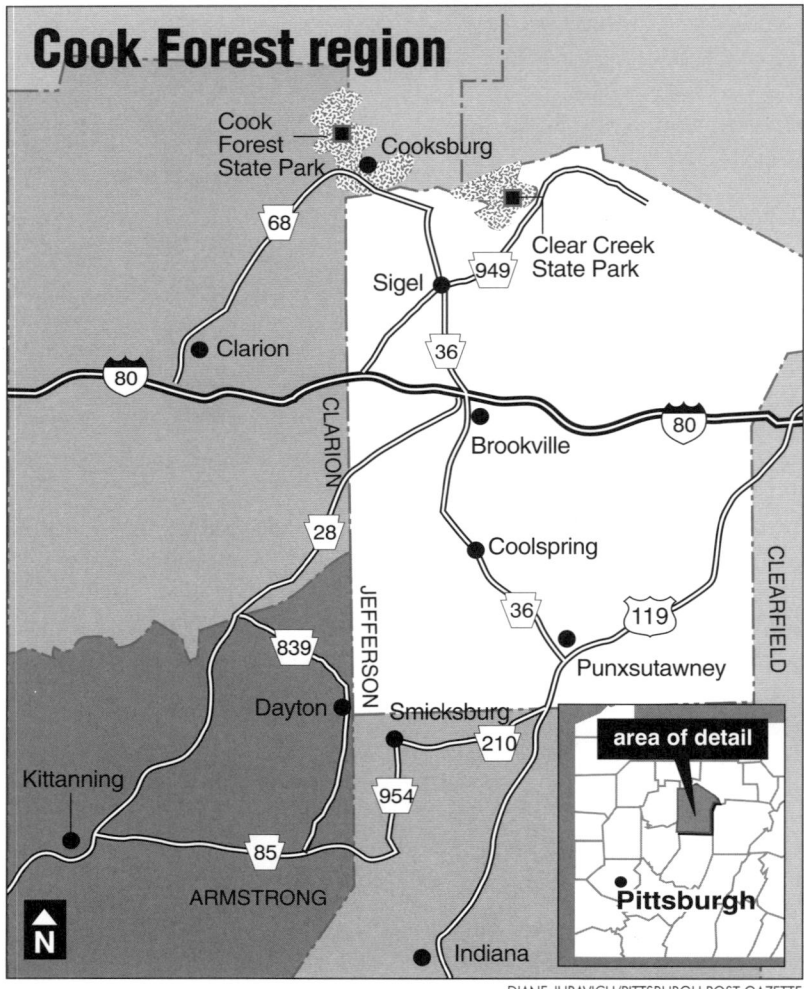

Cook Forest region

DIANE JURAVICH/PITTSBURGH POST-GAZETTE

From Pittsburgh, take Rt. 28 north to Kittanning then go east on Rt. 85 to north on Rt. 954 into Smicksburg. Rt. 954 joins Rt. 210 east of Smicksburg, then joins Rt. 119, 3 miles from Punxsutawney. Leave Punxsutawney via Rt. 36 north 20 miles to Brookville. Continue north on Rt. 36, about 27 miles to Cooksburg, where the road jogs west along Cook Forest State Park. Rt. 68 south leads into Clarion. From there, pick up I-80 west to I-79 south back to Pittsburgh. **Round-trip mileage: 220**

GO to Cook Forest

MORE INFORMATION

➡ **Brookville Area Chamber of Commerce,** 70 Pickering St., Brookville, PA 15825; (814) 849-8448

➡ **Cook Forest State Park,** Box 120, Cooksburg, PA 16217; (814) 744-8407

➡ **Magic Forests Visitors Bureau,** 175 Main St., Brookville, PA 15825; (800) 348-9393 or (814) 849-5197

➡ **Punxsutawney Chamber of Commerce,** 124 W. Mahoning St., Punxsutawney, PA 15767; (800) 752-PHIL (7445) or (814) 938-7700

THINGS TO DO, PLACES TO SEE

SMICKSBURG AREA

➡ **Armstrong County Historical Society Museum,** 300 N. McKean St., Kittanning; (412) 548-5707. Hours: Apr.—Nov., 2—4 Wed. and by appointment. Admission: donation. 1842 Federal-style home has two floors decorated w/ period furniture. Also, genealogical library open Apr.—Nov., noon—4 Tues.—Thurs. Admission: $2.

➡ **John G. Smick Memorial Museum,** Rt. 954, Smicksburg; (814) 257-8653. Hours: noon—4 Fri., Sun.; 11—4 Sat.; 8—4 Mon. Admission: free. Photos and artifacts chronicle the history of the community.

➡ **Yoder's Quilt and Gift Shop,** Rt. 954, Smicksburg; (412) 397-9645. Hours: 9—5 Mon.—Sat. (till 7 p.m. June—Aug.) Gift shop in former Amish home. Also, Amish quilts sold on consignment in separate building.

➡ **Smicksburg Pottery,** Rt. 954, Smicksburg; (814) 257-9879. Hours: 10—6 Mon.—Sat.; noon—5 Sun. Winter, weekends only (call for hours). Pottery made and sold in restored bank building.

➡ **Thee Village Sampler,** Rt. 954, Smicksburg; (814) 257-8035. Hours: 10—6 Mon.—Sat.; noon —5 Sun. Gift shop and bakery.

➡ **Windows Road Furniture,** 3 Windows Rd., Smicksburg (off Rt. 954). Hours: 8—6 Mon.—Sat. Amish-made furniture.

➡ **Coleman House Antiques,** North Point Trail (off Rt. 954), Smicksburg; (814) 257-8975. Antiques, crafts, Amish items. Hours: 10—5 Mon.—Sat.; noon—5 Sun. (Weekends only Jan.—Feb.)

➡ **Windgate Vineyards,** 3 miles north of Smicksburg off Rt. 954; (814) 257-8797. Hours: noon—5 daily. Wine-tasting and picnicking by the vineyards.

DAYTON

➡ **The Marshall House,** N. State St., Dayton; (814) 257-8260. Hours: Memorial Day—Labor Day, 2—4 Sat. and by arrangement for groups. Admission: free. Traditional country farmhouse on National Register of Historic Places.

➡ **Mahoning Creek Lake,** off Rt. 839 north of Dayton; (814) 257-8811. Picnic areas, camping and hiking trails on forested lakeshore. Boats limited to 10 horsepower; no swimming.

➡ **Country Corner Indoor Flea Market,** 1 W. Main St., Dayton; (814) 257-8491. Year-round garage sale features new and used goods, crafts, some antiques, Amish furniture. Hours: 9—5 Tues.—Sat.; 1—5 Sun.

GO to Cook Forest

PUNXSUTAWNEY AREA

➡ **Punxsutawney Groundhog Zoo,** Mahoning East Civic Center, E. Mahoning and Hampton; (800) 752-PHIL (7445). Permanent home of Punxsutawney Phil when he isn't forecasting the weather at Gobbler's Knob. Glassed-in den visible from outside the building.

➡ **Punxsutawney Area Historical & Genealogical Museum,** 401 W. Mahoning St.; (814) 938-2555. Hours: May—Nov., 10—4 Sat., Sun., and Thurs. during summer months. Admission: free. Historical exhibits in Stanford White-designed house.

➡ **Silverbrook Farms,** Marchand, 8 miles south of Punxsutawney; (412) 286-3317. Hours: shop, 10—6 Mon.—Sat.; 1—5 Sun. Farm tours, May—Oct., 10—4 Mon.—Sat.; 1—4 Sun. or by arrangement for groups. Tour admission: $3. Also group and children's rates. Natural fiber farm raises angora goats, angora rabbits, guanaco and other fiber-producing animals. Also, colonial buildings, petting area and spinning museum.

BROOKVILLE AREA

➡ **Jefferson County Historical & Genealogical Society Museum,** 232 Jefferson St., Brookville; (814) 849-0077. Hours: 2—5 Tues.—Sun. Admission: free.

➡ **My Mother's Treasures Antique Mall,** 113 Main St., Brookville; (814) 849-2461. Hours: 11—4 Tues.—Sat. (till 7 Fri); 11—3 Sun. Primitives, glassware, tools, linens and more.

➡ **Coolspring General Store,** off Rt. 36, Coolspring (10 miles north of Punxsutawney); (814) 849-2521. Hours: 9—5:30 Mon.—Fri.; 9—4 Sat. Old-fashioned country store in business since 1904 sells everything from deli sandwiches to antiques.

➡ **Coolspring Power Museum,** Rt. 36, Coolspring; (814) 849-6883. Hours: Apr.—Oct., third Sun. of month, noon—5 p.m. More than 250 internal combustion engines demonstrating 110 years of development.

CLEAR CREEK STATE PARK

➡ **Clear Creek State Park,** Rt. 949, Sigel (off Rt. 36); (814) 752-2368. River, beach and visitors center on 1,200 acres. Lighted ice rink in winter. Seasonal camping on 53 modern campsites, plus 22 rustic cabins (sleep up to 4) available mid-Apr.—mid.-Dec.

➡ **Belltown Canoe Rental,** Rt. 949, Sigel (at Belltown Bridge); (814) 752-2561. Hours: Apr.— Sept., 8—5 Wed.—Sat.; 8—6 Sun. Canoe rentals range from $16—$29 for day trips; $50 for overnight trips. Primitive camping, $6 a night.

➡ **The Farmer's Inn,** 2 miles north of Sigel on Rt. 949 (near Clear Creek State Park); (814) 752-2942. Hours: Mothers Day—Labor Day, 9—9 daily; spring/fall, 9—9 weekends. Wagon and pony rides, petting zoo, driving range, gift shop and restaurant.

COOK FOREST AREA

➡ **Sawmill Center for the Arts,** off the Cooksburg-Vowinckel Rd., Cooksburg; (814) 927-6655. Hours: May—Sept., 10—5 daily. Locally produced handcrafted items from more than 250 artisans; housed in the old Cook sawmill.

➡ **Sawmill Center for the Arts Site II,** Rt. 36, Breezemont Drive; (814) 744-9670. Hours: 10—5 daily, year round. Sales of locally produced crafts; craft classes, play area.

➡ **Double Diamond Deer Ranch,** Rt. 36, 3 miles south of Cook Forest State Park; (814) 752-6334. Hours: mid-Apr.—early Dec., 10 a.m.—dusk daily. Admission: $3.50; 4 and under free. Whitetail deer in their natural habitat; covered

GO to Cook Forest

walkways, trails and gift shop.

➞ **Knox & Kane Railroad,** Rt. 66, Marienville; (814) 927-6621. Hours: June—Oct. (call for times). Fare on 96-mile Marienville-Kinzua Bridge run, $20 adults; $13 ages 3—12. Cost for 32-mile trip from Kane to the bridge, $14 adults; $8 children. Tickets and box lunches can be ordered in advance by writing Knox & Kane Railroad, Box 422, Marienville, PA 16239. Scenic steam-powered train ride through the Allegheny Forest.

➞ **Silver Stallion Stables,** Vowinckel Rd. (3 miles north of Cooksburg Bridge), Cooksburg; (814) 927-6636. Horseback riding year round, weather permitting. 1-hour guided rides, $13.

➞ **Lance's Landing Canoe Rentals,** River Rd., Cook Forest (¼ mile off Rt. 36 next to Clarion River Lodge); (814) 927-8496. Hours: mid-May—mid-Oct., 10—5 daily. Canoe and kayak trips on the Clarion River; $15 for 4-mile trip; $20 for 9-mile trip. Mountain bicycles, $5 per hour.

CLARION

➞ **Anchor Village,** River Hill, just west of Clarion off Rt. 322; (814) 226-7142 or (814) 226-6545. Privately owned small, early 20th-century workers' town has vintage buildings, gas pumps, artifacts. Picnic area open to public free.

➞ **Clarion Antique Mall,** jct. Rts. 322 and 66 (4 miles north of I-80); (814) 226-4420. Hours: 10 a.m.—5 p.m. daily. More than 20 dealers sell books, furniture and more.

➞ **Sutton-Ditz House Museum and Library,** 18 Grant St., Clarion; (814) 226-4450. Hours: 10—4 Tues.—Sat. Admission: $1. Renovated 1850 house is decorated w/ late Victorian furnishings; also history exhibits.

➞ **Historical and architectural walking tour of Clarion,** available at Clarion Free Library, Main Street between 6th & 7th Aves. A walking tour of the county seat, 40 buildings of interest.

ACCOMMODATIONS

➞ Chain motels are concentrated along I-80 around Clarion and Brookville. Other options include:

➞ **Pantall Hotel,** 135 E. Mahoning St., Punxsutawney; (814) 938-6600. Rates: $58—$77. Restored Victorian 1888 downtown hotel has 75 rooms, restaurant, bar.

➞ **Clarion House Bed & Breakfast,** 77 S. 7th Ave., Clarion; (800) 416-3297 or (814) 226-4996. Rates: $65. 4 guest rooms w/ private bath and second-floor study in beautifully restored 1895 home.

➞ **Clarion River Lodge,** River Rd. (off Rt. 36), Cooksburg; (800) 648-6743 or (814) 744-8171. Rates: $94—$129 (includes continental breakfast). Motel-style rooms in building added onto former private retreat. Original lodge is pleasant w/ cherry paneling, oak beams and high ceilings. Nice river views. Packages available.

➞ **Cook Forest State Park** operates two sets of cabins within the park; (814) 744-8407. Rates: $168—$248 a week for Pa. residents. (Slightly higher for nonresidents.) Cabins sleep 4—8 people; some have access to bathhouses and fireplaces; some have running water, but no toilets. Rentals in summer are Friday to Friday only; can be rented nightly w/ 2-night minimum other times. Early reservations recommended for summer rentals.

➞ **Cook Forest Top Hill Cabins,** Vowinckel-Cooksburg Rd., Cooksburg; (814) 927-8512. Rates: $120—$150 weekend; $250—$300 Sun.—Fri.; $275—$390 week. 1-and 2-bedroom cabins, w/ kitchens, stone or brick fireplaces, TV.

➞ **Cook Homestead Bed & Breakfast,** Rt. 36 and River Rd., Cooksburg; (814) 744-8869. Rates: $70—$80. 8 guest rooms, 3 w/ private bath in 1870 house occupied by 5 generations of the Cook

GO to Cook Forest

family. Some family furniture remains.

➡ **Cook Riverside Cabins,** River Rd., Cooksburg; (800) 680-0160 or (814) 744-8300. Rates: $90—$150 a night; $350—$575 a week. 18 cabins on 13 partially wooded acres. Cabins vary in size, decor and location.

➡ **Gateway Lodge,** Rt. 36, Cooksburg; (800) 843-6862 or (814) 744-8017. Rates: $103—$115 for inn rooms (some w/ shared bath); $125—$175, 1—8 person cottages; $200—$212, suites w/ private bath, fireplace. Dining plans also available. 15 percent service charge added to room rate. Indoor pool and sauna.

➡ **MacBeth's Cabins,** Rt. 36, Cooksburg; (800) 331-6319 or (814) 744-8400. Closed early-Dec.—early-Jan. Rates: $40—$200 a night; $250—$800 week. 28 log cabins on Clarion River sleep up to 12; all have kitchens; some have indoor fireplaces. Nice setting facing river; cabins vary in layout, decor.

➡ **Mitchell Ponds Inne,** off Rt. 338, Knox (exit 7 off I-80, 20 minutes west of Clarion); (814) 797-1690. Rates: $100. Lovely farmhouse B&B w/ private guest house in back. Large outdoor pool, spa, sauna, steam, exercise room, fishing pond in beautiful rural setting. Dinner served by arrangement.

RESTAURANTS

➡ **Stockdale's Restaurant,** Main St., Dayton; (814) 257-8651. Hours: 6:30 a.m.—9 p.m. Mon.—Sat.; 8 a.m.—9 p.m. Sun. Soups, pies, Amish cooking. Lunch, about $3; dinners, $6. Amish wedding feast at noon and 5 p.m. Sat.; $12. (Reservations required for Amish feast.)

➡ **Country Villa,** Rt. 119, 1 mile south of Punxsutawney; (814) 938-8330. Hours: 6 a.m.—9 p.m. Mon.—Sat.; 8:30—7:30 Sun. Casual restaurant in rural setting w/ extensive menu. Lunch, $2—$5; dinner, $5—$11.

➡ **The Meeting Place,** 209 Main St., Brookville; (814) 849-2557. Hours: 8 a.m.—9 p.m. Mon.—Fri; 9—9 Sat.; 10—7:30 Sun. Hearty dishes like beef burgundy, baked chicken and rice and Italian entrees. Lunch, $5—$6; dinners, $7—$12.

➡ **Americo's Italian Restaurant,** Vowinckel-Cooksburg Rd. (3 miles from the Clarion River Bridge); (814) 927-8516. Hours: Apr.—Oct., 4—9 Mon.—Fri.; noon—9 weekends and holidays. Veal, prime rib, chicken, seafood; pasta specials on large deck, patio. Complete meals, $6—$15.

➡ **The Blue Heron,** River Rd., Cooksburg (in Clarion River Lodge); (800) 648-6743. Handsome stone and wood dining room in lodge across from Clarion River. Good salads and sandwiches; dinner menu has seafood, pasta, beef. Lunch, about $6; dinners, $12—$16.

➡ **The Captain Loomis Inn,** 540 Main St., Clarion; (814) 226-8400. Hours: 7 a.m.—9:30 p.m. Mon.—Thurs.; 7 a.m.—10 p.m. Fri.—Sat.; 7 a.m.—8 p.m. Sun. Extensive menu has chicken, seafood, beef and pasta served in century-old building. Lunch, $5—$7; dinners, $8—$12.

➡ **County Seat Restaurant,** 531 Main St., Clarion; (814) 226-6332. Hours: 6 a.m.—3 p.m. Mon.—Sat.; 8—2 Sun. Diner food served at booths or old-fashioned lunch counter. Sandwiches, about $4; dinners, $5—$6.

➡ **Kiva Han,** 611 Main St., Clarion; (814) 227-2688. Hours: 7 a.m.—6 p.m. Mon.—Wed.; 7 a.m.—12 a.m. Thurs.—Sat. Classic coffeehouse serves bagel sandwiches, desserts; latte, espresso and just plain coffee. Sandwiches, about $3.

➡ **Wolf's Den Restaurant,** exit 7 off I-80, Knox; (814) 797-1105. Hours:

GO to Cook Forest

11:30—9 Sun.—Thurs.; 11:30—10 Fri.—Sat. Restored 1831 barn has cooked up a good regional reputation for American cuisine. Specialties include prime rib. Lunch, $7; dinner, $9—$16.

BIG EVENTS

➡ **Groundhog Day,** Feb. 2, Punxsutawney. Nationally known weather forecaster Punxsutawney Phil emerges from his burrow to predict when winter will end. (800) 752-PHIL (7445) or (814) 938-7700.

➡ **Summer Fun Fest,** June, downtown Clarion. 4-day festival kicks off the season. (814) 226-9161.

➡ **Western Pennsylvania Laurel Festival,** 3rd full week in June, Brookville. Craft show, parade, music. (814) 849-2024.

➡ **Groundhog Festival,** 1st week in July, Punxsutawney. Games, music, special events. (814) 938-7700.

➡ **Woodcarving Competition & All-Wood Crafts Festival,** mid-July, Sawmill Center for the Arts, Cook Forest State Park. Competition and sales of wood crafts; also, soap-carving contests for children. Admission: $2 per car. (814) 927-6655.

➡ **Summerfest and Quilt Show,** mid-Aug., Sawmill Center for the Arts, Cook Forest State Park. 3-day art show and sales, music, drama, quilt competition and auction. Admission: $2 per car. (814) 927-6655.

➡ **Autumn Leaf Festival,** Sept. or Oct., Clarion. 9-day festival features craft and antique car shows; parade, carnival, concessions. (814) 226-9161.

➡ **Victorian Christmas Festival,** 1st weekend in Dec., Brookville. Street carolers, buggy rides, house tours, living-history walks in town's restored Victorian historic district. (814) 849-8448.

GO to Historic Small Towns

LIU XIN/PITTSBURGH POST-GAZETTE
Two young girls play in Diamond Square in the heart of Harmony.

Historic Small Towns

WHERE THE OLD AND NEW MEET AND THRIVE

You don't have to venture far from Pittsburgh to discover a wholly different environment offering an assortment of experiences. Along the not-too-distant back roads of Lawrence, Mercer, Butler and Beaver counties lie picture-perfect small towns, a large Amish settlement, two very different kinds of shoppers' havens, and several lovely state parks.

This itinerary takes a circular route that could be covered in a day if you keep stops to a minimum. To fully experience all there is to do, however, consider making a weekend of it, or break the trip into shorter outings.

NEW WILMINGTON

Traveling northwest out of Pittsburgh via the Pennsylvania Turnpike, exit onto Route 60 and go north to Route 208, then east toward New Wilmington. The narrow road is a pastoral portrait of grazing cows

GO to Historic Small Towns

and barbed-wire fences, rocket-straight silos and slightly askew newspaper boxes. Hand-painted signs advertise night crawlers, Saturday auctions and handmade rugs. In warmer months, roadside stands sell fresh produce and baked goods. Local businesses like the Cheese House west of town cater to practicality and impulse with an eclectic inventory that ranges from Shaker-style wooden boxes, to hickory rockers, to "Bless This House" shot glasses.

New Wilmington is a quaint town that retains the original 1824 design laid out by its founders. The town's crowning centerpiece is Westminster College, an idyllic ivy-covered stone-walled campus that dates to 1852. Five bed and breakfast inns operate nearby. They cater both to college traffic and to guests seeking a quiet weekend in the country.

Several shops in and around New Wilmington specialize in Amish furniture. A number of independent craftspeople sell out of their homes, as well; watch for signs along the back roads. In a small house off Route 18 south of town, for example, several Amish sisters make rag rugs and home-baked pies. Generous throw rugs are priced at around $30. Elsewhere along these country roads are homegrown harness shops and workshops turning out lawn furniture.

VOLANT

Four miles east of New Wilmington on Route 208 lies Volant, a 19th-century farming town on the banks of pretty Neshannock Creek. By the 1870s, the town had become a hub of commerce for surrounding farms, thanks to the grist mill at its heart. But during the Depression, businesses went into a decline. By the time the mill closed in the 1960s and the railroad stopped coming through in the 1970s, few outsiders would have hit the brakes as they cruised through town. Then in 1984, the old grist mill reopened as a store selling gifts, antiques and used goods. Other merchants gradually set up shop in nearby buildings and in a collection of railroad cars on Volant's narrow Main Street. Today, about 50 stores and restaurants attract shoppers by the busload, particularly during summer and fall. For nonshoppers, the broad, grassy banks of Neshannock Creek are a fine spot to enjoy an afternoon, and maybe even do a little fishing.

GROVE CITY

Route 208 continues east through rural suburbia. American flags and lawn jockeys and little cut-out wooden gewgaws adorn front lawns as the narrow road winds its way toward Grove City. At the intersection of Interstate 79 lies an exhaustive collection of outlet stores that is no less than nirvana for the diehard shopper. At last count the Grove City Factory Shops had topped 130 stores. As outlet malls go, this is

GO to Historic Small Towns

LIU XIN/PITTSBURGH POST-GAZETTE
Weeding the fields is a constant summer chore for the area's Amish women.

among the best, with all the retailers you usually find at these off-price havens, plus ones you normally won't, like Ann Taylor, Oshkosh, Sony and Saks Fifth Avenue.

Grove City's most heavily promoted attraction is the Wendell August Forge, which bills itself as the nation's oldest and largest forge. Indeed, it's been cranking out metalware since 1923. The forge moved to Grove City in 1932 and began producing gift ware later in the 1930s after Pittsburgh department store owner Edgar Kaufmann received an aluminum tray as a gift and decided to sell the line in his stores. Visitors can watch the craftsmen engraving, hammering and ornamenting the mostly aluminum items during weekday working hours. The gift shop is open daily.

OLD STONE HOUSE (SLIPPERY ROCK)

An eight-mile jaunt south from Grove City on Route 173 leads to Slippery Rock. A few miles south of town at the intersection of routes 173 and 8 is the Old Stone House. The handsome 1822 wayside inn for early travelers on the Butler and Mercer pikes was rebuilt from rubble in 1963. Tours led by Slippery Rock University interns are interesting and thorough. They take in the parlor room (where women and children ate and slept), the tavern (for men only) and upstairs sleeping rooms, where a small museum is housed. And yes, the inn has a ghost story.

JENNINGS ENVIRONMENTAL EDUCATION CENTER

A piece of true Midwestern prairie lies south of here on Route 528 and is part of the state-operated Jennings Environmental Education Center. This bit of prairie land is the easternmost part of what scientists believe was once a "prairie peninsula" stretching into Pennsylvania from the Midwest. The relict prairie was formed through four glacial periods thousands of years ago. As glaciers melted they deposited soil and plant seeds, which were transported miles away. Dr. Otto Emery Jennings, for whom the center is named, discovered the blazing star, a flower that is indigenous to the prairie, growing here and worked for the preservation of the land. Another endangered species, the Massasauga rattlesnake, also calls this prairie home.

The environmental center is on 300 acres with about six miles of trails, though only a small section is prairie. Rangers offer a variety of interpretive walks and programs, mostly during the school year. They include maple sugaring demonstrations in early spring, instruction in winter tracking, and wildflower walks.

MORAINE STATE PARK

Continuing south, Route 528 is a

GO to Historic Small Towns

A group of Amish women shop in Grove City.

LIU XIN/PITTSBURGH POST-GAZETTE

back-country road at its finest. It crosses Lake Arthur in Moraine State Park before running into Route 422 at the park's southern boundary. The sprawling 15,000-acre park (Lake Arthur alone has 42 miles of lakeshore) was reclaimed from strip-mined land pockmarked by 400 abandoned gas and oil wells. You'd be hard-pressed to detect its sorry past by the park's present appearance. It sports 16 miles of maintained hiking trails, seven miles of paved bike paths along the lakeshore and has 1,200 picnic tables, along with campgrounds and 11 modern cabins for rent. And if you're inclined to join the Bass Trackers out on the water, you can rent a canoe at the Bear Run Campground at the southwest edge of the park.

MCCONNELL'S MILL STATE PARK

Continue west on Route 422, crossing over I-79, then drop south on Route 19 to one of the prettiest natural spots in the region. McConnell's Mill State Park isn't large, but its setting in the Slippery Rock Creek Gorge is spectacular at any time of year. An 1800s grist mill spans the rapids of the creek. The mill ceased operation in 1928, but was restored in the 1960s. Park employees give free tours in the summer. Nearby is an 1874 covered bridge, one of two in Lawrence County.

GO to Historic Small Towns

White-water boating is possible through the gorge if you have an approved craft (no inner tubes or air mattresses allowed). Hiking trails cover 11 miles of beautiful, but rugged, terrain. The two-mile Kildoo Nature Trail is a good choice for those who don't want to go far. Park rangers also lead guided nature walks built around a variety of themes on summer weekends. And above the gorge in the upper portion of the park is a large, grassy picnic area and playground.

LIU XIN/PITTSBURGH POST-GAZETTE
Aluminum ware collected at Wendell August Forge in Grove City.

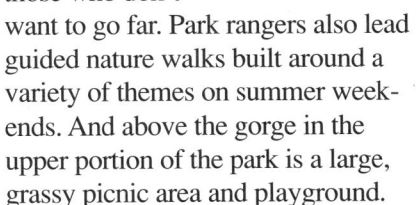

ANTIQUING ON ROUTE 19

Route 19 going both north and south from here is studded with a wealth of antique/junk shops selling everything from good china to old tractors. Keep your eyes open and pull over when something strikes your fancy. Or to better plot your route, write the Western Pennsylvania Antiques Dealers' Association for a brochure listing member shops. (See the Things to Do list for the address.)

HISTORIC HARMONY

Driving into Harmony you'll find vestiges of the original 800-member "Harmonie Society," a group of German separatists that formed in 1805 and came to this country seeking religious freedom. The community took root after leader Johann George Rapp bought 4,000 acres here, and with his communal group, established a thriving village. They built a church, grist mill, school, brewery and tavern. Many of those buildings coexist today with an Elks Lodge, Dodge dealership and new housing on the edge of town. But the central historic district, a National Historic Landmark, remains true to its 19th-century origins. Among the Harmonist places open to the public are a log house, a Mennonite meeting house and cemetery.

ZELIENOPLE

Next door in the town of Zelienople, a German aristocrat, Baron Dettmar Basse, had bought 10,000 acres two years before the Har-

GO to Historic Small Towns

A mix of old and young: Children play outside the 19th-century Harmony Museum.
LIU XIN/PITTSBURGH POST-GAZETTE

monists formed. (Part of that land later was sold to Rapp and would become Harmony.) Basse named the town for his daughter, Zellie, who arrived five years later with her new husband, Phillip Passavant. Their house, and the home of another early player in Zelienople's early years, Christian Buhl, can be toured during the summer. The 10-room 1805 Buhl house is the town's oldest building and contains family artifacts. The Passavant house, built between 1808 and 1810, holds genealogical records, family relics and photographs.

Elsewhere in Zelienople, Main Street is lined with interesting shops in historic buildings and makes for a pleasant place to stroll or browse. From there, it's a short hop back to Pittsburgh via I-79.

GO to Historic Small Towns

Historic small towns

THE ROUTE

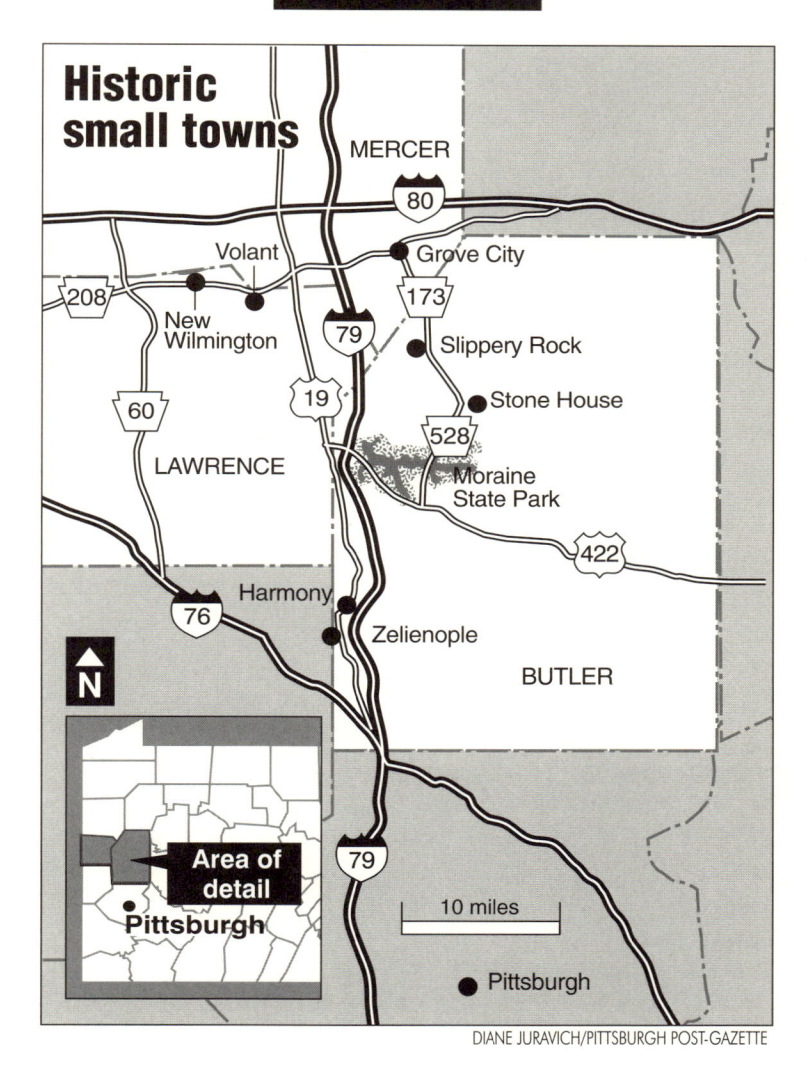

From downtown Pittsburgh take I-279 north to I-79 north to I-76 west. Take exit 1A onto Rt. 60 north 22 miles to Rt. 208 east to New Wilmington. Continue on Rt. 208 to Volant and Grove City. Leave Grove City on Rt. 173 south to Slippery Rock. South of Slippery Rock at Stone House, take Rt. 528 south through Moraine State Park. Pick up Rt. 422 west to Rt. 19 south, which leads to Harmony and Zelienople, and head south on I-79 back to Pittsburgh. **Round-trip mileage: 111**

GO to Historic Small Towns

MORE INFORMATION

➥ **Beaver County Tourist Promotion Agency,** 215B 9th St., Monaca, PA 15061; (800) 564-5009 or (412) 728-0212

➥ **Butler County Chamber of Commerce,** 201 S. Main St., Box 1082, Butler, PA 16003; (412) 283-2222

➥ **Lawrence County Tourist Promotion Agency,** 138 W. Washington St., New Castle, PA 16101; (412) 654-5593

➥ **Mercer County Convention & Visitors Bureau,** 835 Perry Hwy., Mercer, PA 16137; (800) 637-2370 or (412) 748-5315

➥ **Zelienople-Harmony Chamber of Commerce,** 111 W. New Castle St., Zelienople, PA 16263; (412) 452-5232

THINGS TO DO, PLACES TO SEE

➥ **Living Treasures Animal Park,** Rt. 422 (4 miles west of I-79, exit 29); (412) 924-9571. Hours: Memorial Day—Labor Day, 10—8 daily; May, Sept., Oct., 10—6 weekends. Admission: $5.50 adults; $5 seniors; $4.50 ages 3—11. Alligators, cougars, bears, reptiles and more.

➥ **Lawrence County Historical Society,** 408 N. Jefferson St., New Castle; (412) 658-4022. Hours: 9—5 Mon.—Fri.; 1—4 Sun. Admission: $2. Housed in turn-of-the-century mansion with period rooms. Permanent fireworks exhibit; large collection of Shenango china.

➥ **Patrick Henry Antiques,** 222 S. Market St., New Wilmington; (412) 946-8382. Hours: 10—5 Mon.—Sat.; noon—5 Sun. Several rooms of antiques, tapestries, gifts.

➥ **The Cheese House,** Rts. 18 and 208, New Wilmington; (412) 946-8558. Hours: 9—5:30 Mon.—Sat.; 10—5:30 Sun. Cheese, kitsch and Amish crafts.

➥ **Apple Castle,** Rt. 18, New Castle-Sharon Rd., New Wilmington; (412) 652-3221. Hours: Jan.—mid-July, 9—5:30 Mon.—Sat.; mid-July—Jan, 9—8 Mon.—Sat. Sales of produce from fifth-generation family farm.

➥ **The Amish Peddler,** 405 E. Neshannock Ave., New Wilmington; (412) 946-8034. Hours: 10—5 Mon.—Sat. Large selection of Amish-made furniture and crafts.

➥ **Volant shopping district,** Rt. 208, Volant. Hours: Most shops open 10—5 Mon.—Sat.; noon—5 Sun. Winter hours may vary. 50 shops and restaurants, some in historic buildings and old rail cars.

➥ **Harlansburg Station Transportation Museum,** Rts. 19 and 108, Harlansburg (17 miles north of Zelienople); (412) 652-9002. Hours: May—Sept., 10—5 Tues.—Sat., 12—5 Sun.; Mar.—Apr., weekends only; closed Jan.—Feb. Admission: $2 adults; $1 children. Railroad cars and equipment, plus vintage gas pumps, ticket booths and other artifacts related to transportation.

➥ **Grove City Factory Shops,** exit 31 off I-79, Grove City; (412) 748-4770. Hours: 10—9 Mon.—Sat.; 11—6 Sun. Major outlet mall has more than 130 shops.

➥ **Wendell August Forge,** 620 Madison Ave., Grove City; (800) 923-4438. Hours: 9—6 Mon.—Thurs. and Sat; 9—8 Fri.; 11—5 Sun. Nation's oldest and largest metal-working forge. Free tours of production facility 9—4 Mon.—Fri.

➥ **Old Stone House,** intersection Rts. 173 and 8, south of Slippery Rock; (412)

GO to Historic Small Towns

794-4296. Hours: 10—5 Fri.—Sun. Rebuilt 1822 wayside inn; tours and museum.

➡ **Jennings Environmental Education Center,** Rt. 528 (next to Moraine State Park), Slippery Rock; (412) 794-6011. Hours: interpretive center, 8—4 Mon.— Fri.; park trails, 8—sunset, daily. Prehistoric prairie ecosystem; trails and variety of interpretive programs. Call for scheduled events.

➡ **Moraine State Park,** exit 29 off I-79, Portersville; (412) 368-8811. Large lake set in 15,848-acre park; boat rentals, beach, horseback riding, 11 modern cabins.

➡ **McConnell's Mill State Park,** off Rt. 19 north of Portersville; (412) 368-8091. Historic mill, hiking on 2,534 acres. Free grist mill tours Memorial Day—Labor Day, 10:15—5:45. Guided nature walks on summer weekends. White-water rafting in approved craft. No camping.

➡ **Guide to antiques shops in Western Pennsylvania** is available by writing: Western Pennsylvania Antiques Dealers' Association, RD 3, Box 137, Buttermilk Hill Rd., Franklin, PA 16323.

➡ **Historic Harmony Museum,** 218 Mercer St., Harmony; (412) 452-7341. Hours: 1—4 Tues.—Fri. and Sun. Admission: $3.50 adults; $3 seniors; $1.50 under age 12; free under 5. 1805—1815 home of the Harmonists, a communal society of German immigrants. Includes 4 buildings and memorabilia.

➡ **Passavant and Buhl houses,** 243 and 221 S. Main St., Zelienople; (412) 452-9457. Hours: May—Oct., hour-long tours begin on the hour from 1—3 Wed. and Sat. Admission: $3.50 adults; $2.50 children. Furnished house museums of Zelienople's founding families contain historical artifacts from the area.

ACCOMMODATIONS

➡ Chain lodgings on the route include a **Super 8 Motel** (412-658-8849), **Days Inn** (412-652-9991) and **Comfort Inn** (412-658-7700), all in New Castle. Other options are:

➡ **The Jacqueline House B&B,** Rt. 956, 1 mile south of New Wilmington; (412) 946-8382. Rates: $60—$100. 5 rooms, 3 w/ private bath and 1 large suite w/ living room and kitchenette in new home. Swimming pool w/ lounge area.

➡ **Gabriel's Bed & Breakfast,** 174 Waugh Ave., New Wilmington; (412) 946-3136. Rates: $65—$95. 1880 Victorian has 1 suite w/ private bath; plus 2 rooms w/ shared bath.

➡ **Applebutter Inn,** 666 Centreville Pike, Slippery Rock; (412) 794-1844. Rates: $79—$99 weekdays; $95—$125 weekends. 1844 farmhouse has been extensively restored and converted to 11-room inn, all w/ private bath; some w/ gas fireplaces. Attractive public rooms w/ country decor.

➡ **The Teacher's Pet B&B,** 204 Bloomfield School Rd. (off Rt. 19), Portersville; (412) 368-8920. Rates: $75. Country farmhouse on quiet lane has 2 rooms both w/ private bath. Also on grounds is antiques shop and barn.

➡ **The Inn on Grandview,** 310 E. Grandview Ave., Zelienople; (412) 452-0469. Rates: $75—$95. 4 spacious rooms all w/ private bath (1 w/ fireplace and whirlpool tub); large common areas. Includes breakfast.

RESTAURANTS

➡ **B&B Charcoal Grill,** Rt. 422 east, New Castle; (412) 924-2612. Hours: 6 a.m.—9 p.m. Mon.—Thurs.; 6—10 Fri.; 7—9 Sat.; 2—9 Sun. Family-style cooking. Lunch, $4; dinner, $7.

➡ **The Tavern on the Square,** 108 N. Market St., New Wilmington; (412) 946-2020. Hours: 11:30—2; 5—8 Mon.—Thurs., 5—9 Fri.—Sat.; noon—6:30 Sun.; closed Tues. Fine-dining restaurant, American fare served in the home of the original town doctor. Lunch, $10; dinners, $15.

➥ **The Shortstop Inn,** 124 W. Neshannock Ave., New Wilmington; (412) 946-2424. Hours: 11—9 Mon.—Sat.; noon—8 Sun. Family restaurant known for their ribs. Entrees, $5—$8.

➥ **Isaly's Restaurant,** 147 S. Market St., New Wilmington; (412) 946-8630. Hours: 6 a.m.—8 p.m. Home-style cooking; daily specials. Lunch, $4; dinner, $5.

➥ **The Greenhouse,** 304 N. Broad St., Grove City; (412) 458-7730. Hours: 9:30—5 Mon.—Sat. Varied menu; 5 soups daily. Entrees, about $5.

➥ **Wolf Creek School Cafe,** 664 Centreville Pike, Rt. 173, Slippery Rock; (412) 794-1899. Hours: 11—8 Tues.—Sat. (till 9 Fri.—Sat.); 11—7 Sun. One-room schoolhouse-turned-restaurant. Lunch, $4—$6; dinner, $12.

➥ **Log Cabin Inn,** 430 Rt. 19, Harmony (2 miles north of Zelienople); (412) 452-4155. Hours: 11—10 Mon.—Thurs.; 11—11 Fri.—Sat.; 12—9 Sun. Original 1835 log cabin w/ newer additions in nice rural setting serves chops, steaks, seafood. Lunch, $5—$7; dinner, $10—$17.

➥ **Harmony Inn Food and Spirits,** 230 Mercer St., Harmony; (412) 452-5124. Hours: 11:30—9 Mon.—Thurs.; 11:30—10 Fri.—Sat.; 11:30—8 Sun. Varied menu roams the map from Mexican chimichangas to German sauerbraten. Lunch, $5 ; dinner, $8.

➥ **Kaufman House,** 105 Main St., Zelienople; (412) 452-8900. Hours: 7 a.m.—9 p.m. Sun.—Thurs.; 7 a.m.—10 p.m. Fri.—Sat. Seafood, steaks, specials in former downtown hotel. Lunch, about $7; dinner, $10—$19.

BIG EVENTS

➥ **Historic Harmony House Tour,** 1st Sat. in June, Harmony. Tour of historic buildings includes properties owned by the Harmony Museum. Admission: $10. (412) 452-7341.

➥ **Grove City Street Fair,** 1st full weekend in Aug., Grove City. Carnival rides, entertainment, food and retail sidewalk sales. (412) 458-6410.

➥ **Strawberry Days,** 2nd weekend in June, Grove City. Music and arts festival. (412) 458-6410.

➥ **Summer Steam Show,** 1st full weekend Aug., Rt. 19, Portersville Show Grounds (just north of town). Antique steam engines displayed in old-time village atmosphere; parades, tractor-pulling, flea market. (412) 452-9545.

➥ **Dankfest,** weekend before Labor Day, Harmony. Pioneer crafts, museum tours, ethnic food, entertainment. (412) 452-7341.

➥ **Slippery Rock Heritage Festival,** mid-Sept., university campus, Slippery Rock. Antique, classic and custom car show; entertainment and crafts show. (412) 794-3140 or (412) 738-2723.

➥ **Autumn Pumpkin Festival,** usually 1st Sat. in Oct., Volant. Harvest market, pumpkin-painting contest, outdoor barbecue and colonial-crafts demonstrations. (412) 533-2591.

➥ **Fall Fling,** 1st full weekend in Oct., Rt. 19, Portersville Show Grounds. Watch sorghum molasses and apple butter made, plus crafts sales, flea market, antique engine display. (412) 452-9545.

GO to Fall's foliage

Seeing red (and yellow, and orange...)

When will the fall colors peak? Trying to pinpoint an exact time may be more art than science. But certain seasonal conditions help determine the timing and brilliance of autumn.

"The two major triggers to a colorful fall are the decrease in the length of daylight, and frost," said Roger Fickes, a Pennsylvania state parks official. "The frost accelerates the color change in the leaves and causes more trees in a given area to change color at the same time. If the trees were to take their natural course, they may change at different times and appear as a scattering of color."

In Pennsylvania, experts predict approximate leaf-changing times by slicing the state into three horizontal zones. In the northern tier (roughly from Bradford to Scranton) it's the first two weeks of October. In the central and southwest areas of Pennsylvania (Williamsport to Somerset) the peak comes in mid-October. And in the southern zone (Allentown on down) fall comes a bit later in the month.

For foliage updates, the state tourism office operates a 24-hour hotline from mid-September until the leaves are gone — usually in mid-November. The hotline number is: (800) FALL-IN-PA (800-325-5467). The recording also dispenses information on attractions, state parks and local flora.

Following fall's celebrations

Dozens of communities in southwestern Pennsylvania and beyond make the most of the gorgeous, but fleeting, fall foliage season by throwing a party. Following is information on some of those festivals, listed in chronological order and by state. Call ahead to make sure dates and

continued on next page

GO to Fall's foliage

locales haven't changed.

A word of advice: As fickle as fall's timing can be, you should reserve ahead if you're planning anything more elaborate than a day's drive in the country. During festival weekends and even on weekdays in October, lodgings at some of the more popular fall destinations may be booked. Make reservations well in advance to avoid discovering too late there's no room at the inn.

PENNSYLVANIA

➡ **WINE COUNTRY HARVEST FESTIVAL,** last weekend in Sept., North East, Erie County. Art shows and winery tours celebrate the grape harvest. (814) 725-4262.

➡ **SPRINGS FESTIVAL,** 1st Fri. and Sat. in Oct., Springs, Somerset County. Farm crafts, Pennsylvania Dutch foods, live music and handmade items for sale. (814) 662-4158.

➡ **FESTIFALL,** last Sun. in Sept., Friendship Hill National Historic Site near Point Marion, Fayette County. Showcases bygone skills such as blacksmithing, soap making, weaving, spinning and candle making. (412) 725-9190.

➡ **APPLEFEST,** 1st weekend in Oct., Franklin, Venango County. Music, car and antiques shows, arts and crafts exhibits and an apple orchard tour. (814) 432-5823.

➡ **FALL FOLIAGE FESTIVAL,** 1st two full weekends in Oct., Bedford, Bedford County. Hundreds of crafts exhibitors; also parades featuring old farm equipment and antique cars; apple butter and cider making, square dancing and other entertainment. (800) 765-3331.

➡ **AUTUMN LEAF FESTIVAL,** early Oct., Clarion, Clarion County. Weeklong event includes crafts sales, a carnival and parade. (814) 226-9161.

➡ **HISTORICAL FORT LIGONIER DAYS,** 2nd weekend in Oct., Ligonier, Westmoreland County. Recalls the Oct.12, 1758, attack on British troops at Fort Ligonier by French and Indian forces; battle re-enactments, sidewalk sales and entertainment. (412) 238-9701.

➡ **GREENE COUNTY HARVEST FESTIVAL,** 3rd weekend in Oct., Waynesburg. Demonstrations and sales of crafts, blacksmithing, pottery making, corn grinding and spinning. (412) 627-3204.

MARYLAND

➡ **AUTUMN GLORY FESTIVAL,** 2nd weekend in Oct., Oakland. Parades, concerts and more. (301) 334-1948.

OHIO

➡ **OHIO PUMPKIN FESTIVAL,** last weekend in Sept., Barnesville (between Wheeling, W.Va., and Cambridge, Ohio). Quilt and antiques shows and music. (614) 695-4359.

➡ **COVERED BRIDGE FESTIVAL,** 2nd weekend in Oct., Jefferson,

GO to Fall's foliage

Ashtabula County. Parade and tour of 14 antique bridges. (216) 576-9090.

WEST VIRGINIA

➡ **WELLSBURG APPLEFEST,** 1st full weekend in Oct., downtown Wellsburg. Apple fritters, pies, cider and entertainment. (304) 737-0801.

➡ **OGLEBAYFEST,** 2nd weekend in Oct., Oglebay Park near Wheeling. Fireworks, parades and contests. (304) 243-4000.

➡ **MOUNTAINEER BALLOON FESTIVAL,** 3rd weekend in Oct., Morgantown. Mass ascensions by dozens of hot air balloons, and entertainment. (304) 296-8356.

Tourism experts' favorite sites for viewing fall foliage

Who better to recommend fabulous fall foliage spots than people who work in the tourism business? Here are some favorite places and plans of Western Pennsylvania travel experts.

A lovely fall drive is to Bedford along Route 30 (the old Lincoln Highway), returning on Route 31 to Mount Pleasant, and Route 119 to the New Stanton interchange of the Pennsylvania Turnpike. "It's a neat circle trip. And if you find it's taking you longer than you had thought, you can hop on the turnpike."

— **GEORGE DEBOLT, DEBOLT UNLIMITED TRAVEL SERVICE**

The territory around Indiana in Indiana County is hilly and wooded and the fall colors are usually good. If you need a break from driving, drop by the Jimmy Stewart Museum, the town's salute to its most famous son. Cruises down the Ohio River between Pittsburgh and Wheeling, W.Va., also are a prime way to see the leaves. "I don't think there's anything prettier than leaves on the water."

— **KATHLEEN NYE, LENZER COACH LINES**

Tioga County in north-central Pennsylvania has several ideal foliage spots. One is the Grand Canyon of Pennsylvania, just south of Wellsboro. Formed by the Pine River, the canyon is about 50 miles long and up to 1,000 feet deep and has spectacular panoramas. Two state parks on either side of the canyon, Leonard Harrison and Colton Point, also are great for foliage viewing.

— **HARRIET SLEAR OF AMERICAN TOURS**

continued on next page

GO to Fall's foliage

The drive along the Allegheny River in Armstrong County via Route 128 from Freeport north to Ford City, then Route 268 north from Kittanning through East Brady to Parker in Clarion County, is particularly scenic in autumn. "You'll see about 50 miles of the river. There are some places where you won't be right on the river, but it's all beautiful farmland and wooded hillsides."
— SUSAN TORRANCE OF THE ARMSTRONG COUNTY TOURIST BUREAU

The covered bridges of Bedford County, especially those in Bedford and Breezewood, are lovely in fall. "They were called kissing bridges. You'd pull your horse and buggy in where no one could see you and you could kiss your honey there."
— DENNIS TICE OF THE BEDFORD COUNTY CONFERENCE AND VISITORS' BUREAU

Take a journey along routes 711 and 381 through parts of Fayette, Westmoreland and Somerset counties in southwestern Pennsylvania. The route starts at the Conemaugh Gap in Westmoreland County, goes through Ligonier, Donegal and to the Frank Lloyd Wright-designed home, Fallingwater, and ends at Ohiopyle State Park in Fayette County.
— LYNN BARGER OF THE LAUREL HIGHLANDS VISITORS BUREAU

Following the back roads of Beaver County can be an adventurous way to see autumn colors. There are a few roads where you can still ford streams with your car. Prime back roads are near Route 60, including roadways off Green Garden Road toward Service Creek Reservoir and dirt roads near the Ambridge Reservoir. "It's not developed, and it's really gorgeous. If you have a case of wanderlust and have the time, just take a turn right and left onto the roads and let them take you."
— APRIL KOEHLER OF THE BEAVER COUNTY TOURIST PROMOTION AGENCY

Brady's Bend in Clarion County is an especially good place to view foliage. At a spot on Route 68, two miles east of East Brady, is a 1,500-foot panoramic view of the Allegheny River.
— DEBBIE HENRY OF THE MAGIC FORESTS VISITORS BUREAU

GO

SOUTH

GO to Northern West Virginia

MARTHA RIAL/PITTSBURGH POST-GAZETTE

Central West Virginia lives up to the state's boast of being wild and wonderful.

Northern W.Va.

LAND OF EARTHLY AND OTHER PLEASURES

For those who revel in the wild and wonderful outdoors, north-central West Virginia is paradise. A sprint down I-79 from Pittsburgh is a jumping-off point that leads to old-growth forests, mountain biking and hiking trails, white water rafting, fishing holes and other natural assets.

The territory also harbors restored forts and historic homesteads, antiques shops and farmers markets, and a few unusual attractions, as well.

If you tried to cram all the activities in this 400-mile circuit into a

GO to Northern West Virginia

GERRY WINGENBACH

A park at the childhood home of Confederate Civil War hero and West Virginia native Stonewall Jackson.

single weekend, you'd experience little more than the drive. So pick the attractions that appeal to you; skip the ones that don't. Or slice off a piece of the route and save the rest for a later trip.

PRICKETT'S FORT

Traveling south on I-79 into West Virginia, exit 139 two miles north of Fairmont leads to historic Prickett's Fort, situated in a peaceful meadow on the banks of Prickett's Creek. Inside the log walls of the reconstructed 1774 fort, costumed interpreters re-enact life as it was when early settlers took refuge here from Indian attacks. The 16 spartan cabins, meeting hall and storehouse tucked inside the fort's walls offered security, but few comforts. The words of settler Keziah Batten Shearer posted on a wall in the park's small museum also offer a glimpse into 18th-century life here.

"The living in old times was hard. Women and children cried a great deal and the men and boys cussed a lot... But mostly we all just laughed, about nothing much to eat ... and the Indians sneaking around."

The little graveyard near the fort, its older tombstones worn down to pointy shards like broken teeth, tells its own tales of hard lives and early deaths. One headstone relates how Isaiah Prickett was captured and killed by Indians in 1774 while "forting" near the mouth of Prick-

GO to Northern West Virginia

Part of West Virginia's character is its music. Bluegrass is a local favorite.

ett's Creek. Others, like Charity Prickett, defied the odds. A new stone on her grave records that Prickett, believed to be the first white woman to cross the Alleghenies, died in 1833 at the age of 95.

CLARKSBURG

Fifteen miles south of the fort, Clarksburg blossomed after the Civil War as a manufacturing center for glass and tin. Today, it's a pleasant, if somewhat weathered town. But a number of stately buildings remain, among them Waldomore, a Federal-style house set back off Pike Street. It was built in 1839 by a wealthy local merchant and served as the public library from the 1930s until 1975, when it became a repository of local history and genealogy.

On the second floor tucked among more serious historical records, is the Gray Barker UFO Collection amassed by one of Clarksburg's more colorful residents. The UFO buff and author of works such as, "They Knew Too Much About Flying Saucers," Barker collected hundreds of documents relating to the paranormal from the 1950s until his death in 1984. Copies of Barker's "Saucer News" are stuffed in file cabinets. Theatrical photographs — more comic than macabre — of a blood-smeared Barker playing dead are on display, along with publications from his company, Saucerian Press.

Clarksburg is also the birthplace of Confederate Civil War hero, Stonewall Jackson, though he was raised 20 miles south of here near Weston. Costumed interpreters show visitors around the 18th- and 19th-century cabins in the compound at Jackson's Mill Historic Area. The family's reconstructed 1794 grist mill, where Jackson worked as a boy, is still operating, and you can buy fresh-ground cornmeal with a recipe for Civil War cornbread.

A 200-year-old grave near Prickett's Fort.

BUCKHANNON

Turning east onto Route 33 brings you to the tiny college town of Buckhannon. Several antiques shops are ripe for browsing and a number of grand old dwellings line the side streets. One of them, the Post Mansion Inn, was built in 1891 by state Sen. William Post. The 25-room, neo-classical house was in disrepair when Buckhannon native Juanita Reger bought it in 1991. She'd lived out West for decades and told family members the only way she'd move back was if she could fulfill her childhood dream of owning this house. As fate would have it, the house went up for sale, Reger bought it and opened the bed and breakfast inn a year later. The interior features intricate inlaid floors and stained-glass windows. Tours are offered by appointment.

Four miles east of Buckhannon in the midst of rolling farmland is Deer Park, a truly wonderful inn hidden from view down a tree-shaded lane. Patrick and Liz Haynes bought 100 acres here with an 1870 farmhouse that incorporates a 1770 cabin as its central room. They've added a modern kitchen and a two-story

GO to Northern West Virginia

The area is a natural for active getaways, but there are lots of quiet spots as well.
MARTHA RIAL/PITTSBURGH POST-GAZETTE

lodge built of old logs, with a wide wraparound porch, creating an ideal spot to comfortably drop out of the mainstream.

ELKINS

Elkins, an attractive college town that nudges up against the vast Monongahela National Forest, lies 30 miles east of Buckhannon. The commercial heart of downtown runs along Davis Avenue. Here you can sip an espresso, browse through new and used bookstores and antiques and art shops. A walking tour map (available at the tourist office) steers you past more than a dozen early structures built around the turn of the century in this former railroad boomtown. The Davis & Elkins College campus is perched on a hill overlooking town. Graceland, a grand Victorian mansion built as a summer home by town co-founder and U.S. Sen. Henry Davis Elkins has been renovated and opened as a public lodging in 1996.

Hiking and mountain biking on trails that lace through the nearby national forest are popular warm-weather activities. Rafting and inner-tubing on the Shavers Fork of the Cheat River just outside of town also draw vacationers.

CANAAN VALLEY

East of Elkins, Route 33 joins Route 32 at Harman and climbs north into the Canaan Valley, a rugged mountain valley with several all-sea-

GO to Northern West Virginia

West Virginia's streams provide a place where those of all ages can commune with nature.

sons resorts. From here on, the highlights of this trip are mostly natural, with a few creature comforts located at convenient intervals. Canaan Valley State Park, one of West Virginia's full-service "resort parks" consists of a sprawling 250-room lodge, 23 cabins and 34 campsites. Add to that amenities like a golf course, health club, tennis courts, conference center, ski area, skating rink and indoor and outdoor swimming pools, and you could forget you're in a National Wildlife Refuge. But there are miles of back country here for hiking, along with secret fishing holes that local outfitters can steer you to.

BLACKWATER FALLS

Blackwater Falls State Park, 10 miles north of the Canaan Valley Resort, has a smaller lodge (55 rooms), fewer facilities and, as a consequence, a more backwoods atmosphere. A boardwalk path gives easy access to an overlook where Blackwater Falls tumbles five stories into an eight-mile-long gorge. Trails thread deep into the park for hikers seeking more challenging terrain.

CATHEDRAL STATE PARK

Cathedral State Park, about 20 miles north of Blackwater Falls, rounds out this trio of natural beauties. With just 133 acres, it's small compared to the other two parks, but this old-growth hemlock forest is well worth a stop. Located just off Route 50 in Preston County, Cathe-

GO to Northern West Virginia

A sign welcomes visitors to a wildlife wonderland. — GERRY WINGENBACH

dral State Park was preserved due to the efforts of Branson Haas, a worker at a hotel that once stood on the property. He bought the acreage in 1922 and sold it to the state 20 years later with the stipulation that no trees could be cut.

OUR LADY OF THE PINES

Before you reach Cathedral State Park, there's a notable roadside attraction on Route 219 in Silver Lake, 10 miles north of Thomas. Our Lady of the Pines claims to be the smallest church in the lower 48 states. It's small all right — about the size of a one-car garage. The church was built in 1958 by local auto dealer Peter Milkint and his wife, Elizabeth, in memory of their parents. The couple have passed on, but the tiny shrine remains popular, drawing up to 125 visitors daily in the summer and fall. Next door is a closet-sized postal office with infrequent delivery — every Friday the 13th, according to the sign. Actually, a caretaker picks up the postcards left by visitors and drops them in a mailbox.

ROUTE 50

Beyond Cathedral State Park, Route 50 slithers around 20 mph curves, either side shrouded by thick foliage. Eventually, it hugs the Cheat River and continues through communities too small to rate mention on the state map.

Another roadside relic lies farther along Route 50. Cool Springs Park, a fixture since 1929, looms large with a giant cow on its roof and an EAT sign whose neon sparked out long ago. Inside the merchandise-crammed general store, there's a central U-shaped lunch counter and a diverse inventory of lawn jockeys, rubber snakes, camouflage hunting clothes and Indian moccasins.

RIVER RAFTING

A short detour off Route 50 north onto Route 72 leads to Rowlesburg, where two outfitters, USA Raft and Appalachian Wildwaters, run half-day trips down the Cheat River on guided trips, or you can rent smaller, individual craft.

TYGART LAKE

Continuing west on Route 50 brings you to Grafton. Tygart Lake

GO to Northern West Virginia

GERRY WINGENBACH

Reconstructed homes keep alive the legacy of early settlers.

State Park lies just south of the town off Route 119. The 13-mile lake, created in the 1930s by the Army Corps of Engineers, winds through wooded valleys. Besides boat rental and launch areas, the park has a 20-room lodge and restaurant overlooking the lake, 10 cabins and a 40-site campground.

ARTHURDALE

If you return north by taking tiny Route 92 off Route 50, you'll reach Arthurdale (16 miles southeast of Morgantown), a town with a fascinating history and a place on the National Register of Historic Places. At the peak of the Depression, Arthurdale became the first of about 200 homesteads and farmsteads created by the U.S. government. This New Deal project was a favorite of Eleanor Roosevelt, who insisted that all of Arthurdale's homes have electricity and running water at a time when many in these rural areas did not. The homesteading experiment put unemployed West Virginians, many of them from impoverished coal mining towns, into self-sustaining communities.

In Arthurdale, the project consisted of 165 homes, each with enough acreage for gardens. Blacksmiths, carpenters, weavers and other skilled workers, were sought out as residents. A community forge produced pewter work that was regarded for its high quality. A central administration oversaw a number of

GO to Northern West Virginia

Prickett's Fort, near Fairmont, W.Va., is a reconstructed fortress from 1774.

other cooperatives, including pottery and furniture making and textile enterprises, and established a progressive vocational school.

The U.S. government released its hold on the land in 1947. Some buildings were bought by individuals; others fell into disrepair. But some of the original homesteaders remain. So does the administration building, now a museum chronicling through words and pictures how Arthurdale came to be. Organizers have plans to convert the former community building into a catering hall and public canning kitchen, and hope to once again attract craftspeople to the forge and other vacant facilities.

"Some people say Arthurdale was not a success," said resident Jennifer Bonnette, whose grandparents were among the first residents. "But it is. The original spirit is still here."

GO to
Northern West Virginia

DIANE JURAVICH/PITTSBURGH POST-GAZETTE

THE ROUTE

Take Interstate 79 south to Fairmont. To get to Jackson's Mill, take Rt. 19 at Jane Lew and follow the signs. Rt. 19 leads to Weston, where you can pick up Rt. 33 east to Buckhannon and Elkins. Rt. 33 turns north outside of Elkins, joins Rt. 32 at Harman and continues to Canaan Valley State Park and Blackwater Falls State Park. At Thomas, turn onto Rt. 219 to Silver Lake, then pick up Rt. 24 north, which connects with Rt. 50 and Cathedral State Park. Continue on to Clarksburg and meet up with I-79, or take a slightly shorter, back roads route by turning north off Rt. 50 onto Rt. 92, just west of Fellowsville. Rt. 92 meets Rt. 7 north of Arthurdale, jogs west and meets Route 68 in Morgantown. **Approximate round-trip mileage: 400**

GO to Northern West Virginia

MORE INFORMATION

➡ **West Virginia Division of Tourism,** 2101 Washington St. E., Charleston, WV 25305; (800) CALL WVA (800-225-5982)

➡ **Bridgeport/Clarksburg Convention and Visitors Bureau,** 158 Thompson Dr., Bridgeport, WV 26330; (800) 368-4324 or (304) 842-7272

➡ **Harrison County Chamber of Commerce,** 348 W. Main St., Clarksburg, WV 26301; (304) 624-6331

➡ **Convention & Visitors Bureau of Marion County,** 110 Adams St., Fairmont, WV 26555; (800) 834-7365 or (304) 368-1123

➡ **Monongahela National Forest,** 200 Sycamore St., Elkins, WV 26241; (304) 636-1800

➡ **Randolph County Convention & Visitors Bureau,** 200 Executive Plaza, Elkins, WV 26241; (800) 422-3304 or (304) 636-2717

➡ **Tucker County Convention & Visitors Bureau,** Box 565, Davis, WV 26260; (800) 782-2775 or (304) 259-5315

THINGS TO DO, PLACES TO SEE

CLARKSBURG TO ELKINS

➡ **Prickett's Fort State Park,** Rt. 3, Fairmont (exit 139 off I-79 and follow signs 2 miles to park); (304) 363-3030 or (800) CALL WVA. Hours: mid-Apr.—late-Oct., 10—5 Mon.—Sat.; noon—5 Sun. Also open for annual Christmas market the first 3 weekends after Thanksgiving. Admission: $5 adults; $4.50 seniors; $2.50 ages 6—12.

➡ **Waldomore,** 400 W. Pike St., Clarksburg; (304) 624-6512. Hours: 9—8 Mon.—Thurs.; 9—5 Fri., Sat. The 19th-century mansion's downstairs rooms have period furniture (tours by request). Upstairs is a genealogical library and the UFO collection of Gray Barker.

➡ **Valley Falls State Park,** off Rt. 310 south of Fairmont. Falls up to 18-feet-high tumble into the Tygart Valley River. Day-use park has picnicking, fishing, a playground and hiking trails.

➡ **Tygart Lake State Park,** Grafton (Rt. 119 south to Rt. 50 to Grafton); (304) 265-3383 or (800) CALL WVA. Open mid-Apr.—Oct. A 13-mile man-made lake winds through a forested valley; rooms in 20-room lodge are $64—$70; 10 cabins range from $455—$589 weekly (including tax). Campsites also available.

➡ **Masterpiece Crystal Outlet,** Trolley St., Jane Lew (exit 105 off I-79 to Jane Lew and follow the signs); (800) 624-3114. Hours: 9—5 daily. Free glass factory tours 9—3 Mon.—Fri. every half hour except 11 a.m. Small outlet store sells hand-blown goblets, paperweights and other glass objects.

➡ **Jackson's Mill Historic Area,** Weston (2 miles off U.S. 19 between Jane Lew and Weston); (304) 269-5100. Hours: Memorial Day—Labor Day, 10—5 Tues.—Sun. Weekends only in early May and early Oct. Guided tours of Stonewall Jackson's boyhood home. Admission: $3 adults; $2 under 12;

GO to Northern West Virginia

under 6, free. Also, conference center and lodgings on extensive grounds available for group rentals, and occasionally, to individuals.

➡ **Buckhannon Antique Mall,** 3 miles north of Buckhannon on Rt. 20; (304) 472-9605. Hours: 10—5 Mon.—Sat.; noon—5 Sun. 20-plus dealers sell everything from postcards to furniture. No crafts.

➡ **Antiques & Collectibles,** corner Main and Kanawha streets, Buckhannon; (304) 472-1120. Hours: 9—5:30 Mon.—Fri.; until 5 Sat.

➡ Walking tour maps of historic downtown Elkins are available at the **Randolph County Visitors Bureau,** 200 Executive Plaza. Also available are guides to bicycle routes and a complete list of antiques stores in the area.

CANAAN VALLEY

➡ **Canaan Valley Ski Resort,** Davis; (800) 622-4121. Ski season runs Dec.—Apr., weather dependent. 3 lifts service 34 slopes; adult lift tickets, $18—$36; children, $14—$28, depending on time. Also cross-country skiing. After ski season, the lifts continue running, offering scenic rides up and down the mountain from 10—5 daily; $4 adults; $2 children 6—12.

➡ **Timberline Four-Seasons Resort,** off Rt. 32, 10 miles south of Davis; (304) 866-4801 (ski lodge); or (800) 633-6682 (lodging). Downhill and cross-country skiing from mid-Dec.—mid-Apr.; adult lift tickets, $25—$36; ages 6—12, $19—$25. Also, mountain biking and scenic ski lift rides other times.

➡ **White Grass Cross Country Ski Area,** Freeland Rd. (off Rt. 32, 10 miles south of Davis); (304) 866-4114. Cross-country skiing Dec.—Mar. on 35 miles; 25 miles are machine set. Adult trail pass, $8; children, $3.

➡ **The Art Company of Davis,** Main St., Davis.; (304) 259-4218. Fine arts and crafts made by West Virginia artists and crafters. Hours: 10—5 Mon.—Fri.; 10—6 Sat; 11—6 Sun; closed Wed. in winter.

➡ **Cathedral State Park,** off Rt. 50, west of Rt. 219; (304) 735-3771. Picnic areas and trails; no camping, hunting or fishing.

➡ **USA Raft,** Rowlesburg; (800) USA RAFT. Half-day and longer trips on the Cheat River depart from Cheat River Outdoor Center in Rowlesburg (Rt. 72 off Rt. 50). Rates: Guided trips start at $42 per person weekends; $35 weekdays.

➡ **Appalachian Wildwaters,** Rowlesburg; (800) 624-8060. Full-day guided raft trips on the Cheat River. Rates: $77—$97, depending on day.

➡ **Arthurdale Historic District,** Rt. 92, Arthurdale; (304) 864-3959. Hours: Memorial Day—Labor Day, 10—1 Mon.—Fri.; noon—5 Sat.; 2—5 Sun. Other times, 10—1 weekdays. Buildings and displays from the nation's first Depression-era federally run homestead project. Museum and self-guided driving tour. Admission: $2 adults; $1 seniors, students and children.

ACCOMMODATIONS

➡ Elkins has plenty of chain motels including a **Best Western** (800-528-1234), an **Econo Lodge** (800-553-2666) and a **Days Inn** (800-325-2525).
Among the other choices:

➡ **Deer Park Bed & Breakfast, Lodge & Inn,** Buckhannon; (800) 296-8430 or (304) 472-8400. Rates: $90—$150 weekends; 20 percent less Sun.—Thurs. Beautiful lodge several miles outside of Buckhannon has 6 rooms or suites (3 in main house; 3 in lodge), all w/ private bath.

➡ **Post Mansion Inn,** 8 Island Ave.,

GO to Northern West Virginia

Buckhannon; (800) 301-9309 or (304) 472-8959. Rates: $80—$100. 5 guest rooms, 3 w/ private bath in historic mansion.

➡ **Baxa Motel,** 21 N. Kanawha St., Buckhannon; (304) 472-2500. Rates: $36—$45. Newly refurbished, reasonably priced motel.

➡ **Graceland Inn & Conference Center,** 100 Campus Dr., Elkins; (304) 637-1600. Rates: May—Oct. $90—$115 standard, $175 suites; Nov.—Apr. $75—$95 standard, $135 suites. 13 guest rooms in former 1893 private mansion on campus of Davis & Elkins College. Also, rooms in adjoining conference center (a former dormitory). Rates: May—Oct. $55—$70; Nov.—Apr. $45—$60.

➡ **Warfield House B&B,** 318 Buffalo St., Elkins; (888) 636-4555. Rates: $65—$75 weekends; $55 weekdays. Next to Davis & Elkins College. 5 guest rooms, 3 w/ private bath.

➡ **Cheat River Lodge,** Rt. 1; (304) 636-2301. Rates: $48 weekdays; $53 weekends for lodge rooms. Cabin rates: $151 for 2 guests weekends; $131 weekdays; $10 for each additional person. Weekly rates also available. Lodge and cabins have hot tubs and view of the Cheat River.

➡ **Canaan Valley Resort,** Davis; (800) 622-4121. Rates: start at $74 and up during peak season for standard lodge rooms, lower other times. Weekly rate for cabins: $621 for 2 bedrooms to $966 for 4 bedrooms. Nightly rates, $137—$213. State-run full-service resort park has golf, skiing, swimming, hiking, restaurants and more. Ask about special packages.

➡ **Deerfield Village,** Canaan Valley; (800) 342-3217. Rates: mid-Mar.—mid-Dec. $125 for 1-bedroom condo; $230 for 4 bedrooms. Late-Dec.—mid-Mar., $135—$250. Resort complex has restaurant, bike and ski rentals and other facilities.

➡ **Blackwater Falls State Park Lodge,** Davis; (304) 259-5216 or (800) CALL WVA. Rates: $48—$63 in lodge, depending on season. Cabin rates: $80—$88 for 2 people; $100—$116 for 8 guests. Weekly rates are lower; rates vary according to season. Another West Virginia parks facility in a gorgeous setting.

➡ **Best Western Alpine Lodge,** Rt. 32, Davis; (800) 528-1234 or (304) 259-5245. Rates: about $50.

RESTAURANTS

➡ **Starr Cafe,** 224 Davis Ave., Elkins (at the rear of Augusta Books); (304) 636-7273. Hours: 9—9 Mon.—Sat.; 10—2 Sun. Creative menu includes a good selection of nightly specials. Lunch, $2—$5; dinner, $8—$14.

➡ **C.J. Maggie's American Grill,** 309 Davis Ave., Elkins; (304) 636-1730; also, 5 E. Main St., Buckhannon; (304) 472-2490. Hours: 11—9 Sun.—Thurs.; 11—10 Fri.—Sat. Pizzas baked in wood-fired oven, plus large selection of pasta dishes. Lunch, about $6; dinner, $12—$15.

➡ **Sirianni's Cafe,** Main St., Davis; (304) 259-5454; also at Deerfield Village in Canaan Valley; (304) 866-3388. Hours: 11—10 Mon.—Thurs.; 11—11 Fri.—Sat. (Deerfield Village open to midnight Fri., Sat.); noon—10 Sun. Pizzas, hoagies, pasta. Lunch, $4—$6; dinner, $10—$15.

BIG EVENTS

➡ **West Virginia Strawberry Festival,** 3rd weekend in May, Buckhannon. Parades, art shows and other events.

➡ **Augusta Festival,** 2nd weekend in Aug., Augusta Heritage Center on the

GO to Northern West Virginia

Davis & Elkins College campus, Elkins. 3-day music festival. (304) 637-1209.

➻ **Stonewall Jackson Jubilee,** Labor Day weekend, Jackson's Mill State Park near Weston. Festival of traditional arts.

➻ **Leaf Peeper's Festival,** last weekend in Sept., Davis. Music, games, antiques and car show.

➻ **Mountain State Forest Festival,** late Sept.—early Oct., Elkins. (800) 422-3304. State's largest festival is a week-long celebration of mountain music and arts.

ALSO IN THE AREA

➻ **For Civil War buffs:** The U.S. Forest Service has outlined a Civil War auto tour of the Monongahela National Forest that takes in 16 sites that lie roughly between Parsons and Marlington. For a copy, contact Monongahela National Forest, 200 Sycamore St., Elkins, WV 26241; (304) 636-1800.

➻ **Potomac Eagle Scenic Railroad,** Romney; (800) 22 EAGLE (800-223-2453). Scenic rides along the south branch of the Potomac River. Operates daily during the summer and Oct.; weekends only in May and Sept.

➻ **Dolly Sods Scenic Area,** Seneca Rocks Visitor Center, Box 13, Seneca Rocks, WV 26884; (304) 257-4488 or (304) 567-2827. 10,000-acre back-country area on the Allegheny plateau studded with unusual plants, bogs and wind-stunted trees.

➻ **Seneca Rocks,** near the town of Seneca Rocks on Rt. 55. 1,000-foot quartzite rock face popular among hikers.

➻ **Smoke Hole Caverns,** Rt. 28/55, west of Petersburg; (800) 828-8478. Guided tours of caves used by the Seneca Indians for smoking game, and during the Civil War for ammunition storage. Open year-round. Winter 9—3:30 daily; summer 9—8 daily.

➻ **Seneca Caverns,** off Rt. 33/28, 3 miles southeast of Riverton; (304) 567-2691. Open year-round, weather permitting; call for hours. Guided tours of caves up to 165 feet underground.

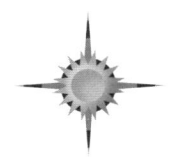

GO to Western Maryland

GERRY WINGENBACH
Kicking back outside Bill's Place in Little Orleans, Md. The combination bait shop, saloon, restaurant and mayor's office is the tiny town's major enterprise.

Western Maryland

A LAND OF BACK ROADS BEAUTY

The history of Western Maryland can be summed up in a single word: movement.

Nineteenth-century pioneers eager to expand the nation's boundaries of commerce and culture pushed westward through the slender finger of Western Maryland, first along the muddy wagon ruts that would become the National Road, and later via an ingenious canal system, and finally by railroad.

It's still possible to make tracks via all these modes of transport on a road-canal-rail trip through Western Maryland. Route 40 follows the path of the old National Road, the nation's first highway. The C&O Canal towpath, once the domain of mules pulling canal boats upriver, ends its 184-mile journey from Washington, D.C., at Cumberland. And a steam railroad carries pleasure-trippers through the mountainous terrain between Cumberland

GO to Western Maryland

and Frostburg.

If the essence of a road trip is movement, then this route is a classic.

En route from Pittsburgh just over the West Virginia border Interstate 68, the late-20th-century incarnation of the National Road, heads east. A couple of worthwhile stops lie just off the freeway before the Maryland state line.

CHEAT LAKE, W.VA.

One of them, Cheat Lake, is 1,730 acres of placid water ringed by forested shoreline. The lake, 10 miles east of Morgantown, W.Va., was created in the late 1920s by a power dam. Old-timers like marina owner John Blosser will tell you the area has changed little since then.

"One of the beauties of the lake is that it's like it was 60 years ago," said Blosser, whose family has done business here since 1929. "It never got built up like so many other places."

Limited road access is one reason for the relative serenity. Private homes and a few small marinas dot the lakefront. The major development is the Lakeview Resort & Conference Center, a full-service resort with a lodge, condos, golf courses and health club. But it's barely visible from most of Cheat Lake.

COOPERS ROCK

Continuing a few miles east on the interstate, Coopers Rock State Forest (exit 15 off I-68) is worth a detour, if only to take in the spectacular view from the Coopers Rock overlook. A paved trail leads onto the rocks, which jut out over the Cheat River flowing through a thickly forested valley 1,200 feet below. Stone and wood pavilions with tables and huge fireplaces near the overlook make a nice spot for a picnic.

DEEP CREEK LAKE

After crossing into Maryland, a 25-mile detour south down Route 219 leads to Deep Creek Lake, the state's largest freshwater lake and a year-round recreation area. In summer, most of the activity is centered close to Deep Creek Lake and its 65 miles of shoreline. Boating, fishing, hiking, bicycling, horseback riding and golf are all popular warm-weather pastimes. Several marinas rent boats and other water-sports equipment. Two championship golf courses — the Oakland Golf Club in Oakland and the Golf Club at Wisp Resort in McHenry — are open to the public. And as an added bonus, summer temperatures average 10 degrees cooler than in Pittsburgh.

Fall is festival season. Garrett County's biggest event, the Autumn Glory Festival in mid-October, draws up to 40,000 people. The festival features the Maryland state banjo and fiddle championships,

GO to Western Maryland

CREATING LIFE IN WOOD

For 20-odd years Gary Yoder has occupied a 1775 settler's cabin in the Spruce Forest Artisan Village, carving birds so lifelike they appear as if they might fly off his worktable. His prize-winning carvings are highly collectible, and most of Yoder's work is done strictly by commission. It's also costly. A small songbird sells for about $1,000; major works reach five figures.

But Yoder isn't here to sell. Instead, he chats with curious visitors, who marvel at his creations. His comments reveal that even he sometimes wonders how such intricate creatures manage to spring from blocks of ordinary wood. "To me carving is as natural as breathing. I pick up a piece of wood and I just know where to go," he said.

Like other artisans in the village, Yoder comes and goes, but you'll usually find him in his cabin from spring through October.

"I stay open until I can't stand to talk to people anymore and then I shut the door until I can't stand to be alone anymore."

➡ **Spruce Forest Artisan Village,** 177 Casselman Rd. (next to Penn Alps); (301) 895-3332. Hours: 10—5 Mon.—Sat. Admission: free. Artisans demonstrate their skills from May—Oct. in historic buildings. Several are in residence year-round.

GERRY WINGENBACH
Gary Yoder carves one of his lifelike birds.

along with parades and arts and crafts sales in a brilliant fall setting.

WISP RESORT

In winter, Wisp Ski Resort, Maryland's only downhill ski area, delivers skiers to an elevation of 3,080 feet with stunning views of Deep Creek Lake. Cross-country skiing is popular on the hiking trails that weave around the lake. When the snow melts, mountain biking and in-line skating rule at Wisp.

Though the Deep Creek area is peppered with a growing number of exclusive vacation home developments, a range of accommodations is available, from attractive lakeside inns, to the sprawling resort at Wisp, to mom-and-pop motels. There's also plenty of camping space. Garrett County boasts more than 70,000 acres of public land, most of it in the state parks of Deep Creek Lake, Swallow Falls, Herrington Manor, Big Run and New Germany. All have camping areas. In addition, Herrington Manor has 20 modern cabins for rent; New Germany has 11 cabins.

Deep Creek Lake was created in the 1920s by a hydroelectric dam 1½ miles above the lake at the confluence of Deep Creek and the Youghiogheny River. The 3,900-acre lake flooded farmland with an average of 26 feet of water. Submerged relics, including old farm vehicles, are popular haunts for scuba divers.

DEEP CREEK LAKE STATE PARK

On the eastern side of the lake 10 miles northeast of Oakland (the Garrett County seat), Deep Creek Lake State Park sports a bathhouse and picnic sites spread along a mile of beach. The swimming area has been cleared of tree stumps that protrude from the bottom of much of the lake. A limited number of docks are available for private boats; there's also a public boat launch. Rowboats are for rent at the park office.

Anglers can try their luck fishing for more than 22 types of fish that thrive in the lake, including small mouth bass, bluegill and yellow perch. Johnny's Bait House on Route 219, just south of McHenry, is the oldest and largest supplier of bait. It also sells and rents gear and has updates on the best fishing spots.

You'll also find excellent fishing in the nearby Savage River and at the Savage Reservoir, where power boats are prohibited. The river and reservoir areas are undeveloped and the drive there along wooded, winding Dry Creek Road is beautiful.

GRANTSVILLE

From Deep Creek Lake, return north on Route 219 or take the more scenic Route 495 near New Germany State Park to old Route 40 at Grantsville. The Casselman Inn, an old National Road stagecoach stop at the eastern end of town (now operated by Mennonites who provide spotless, but spartan rooms, good food and, in the basement, a tempting bakery), sells maps outlining a 16-mile route that weaves through nearby Amish farmland, just north of the Pennsylvania border in southern Somerset County. This pleasant drive along hidden back roads pass-

The view from inside the Carmel Cove Bed & Breakfast on Deep Creek Lake, Md.
JOHN BEALE/PITTSBURGH POST-GAZETTE

es an Amish school and meeting house, a buggy shop and historic mill, among other sites. The map also points the way to several area sugar camps, which are in a frenzy of activity in early spring when the maples are tapped for their sweet sap.

PENN ALPS

Back on old Route 40 just east of the Casselman Inn, lies tiny Casselman River Bridge State Park, site of the nation's largest single-span stone arch bridge when it was built on the National Road in 1813. Visitors can still walk across the bridge and picnic in its shadow on the banks of the river. Penn Alps, a restaurant and nonprofit crafts center housed in a remodeled 19th-century log stagecoach stop, is nearby.

Next to Penn Alps in a wooded grove, the Spruce Forest Artisan Village showcases practitioners of bygone arts who demonstrate their talents in historic buildings that have been restored and moved to the site. It's an informal atmosphere in which visitors can wander into the workshops and watch the artists at work. A blacksmith, basket weaver, carver and quilter, among others, also sell their creations.

FROSTBURG

Alternate Route 40 continues to parallel Interstate 68 as it weaves east through the mountains from Grantsville to Cumberland. Midway

GO to Western Maryland

LIFE AT BILL'S PLACE

On late summer afternoons, the atmosphere around Bill's Place can get so sleepy it hardly registers a pulse. But then, this venerable establishment has been around for so long, you can hardly blame it for seeming a bit worn out.

Proprietor Bill Schoenadel is lively enough, though he only permanently came on the scene in 1968. The Place, on the other hand, has been around since 1832. So long that this weathered, clapboard building predates both the Chesapeake and Ohio Canal and B&O Railroad that originally drew people to the area.

Bill's Place sits at the end of Orleans Road, which in turn is just yards from Fifteen Mile Campground, one of three drive-in camping spots on the C&O Canal. Today it is the hub of Little Orleans, Md., which is very little, indeed. A sign outside advises that Bill's Place is not only the mayor's office (unofficially, anyway — the town isn't incorporated), but it's also the spot to rent canoes, stock up on basic camping supplies and quaff something cold after a day of boating on the river or hiking along the towpath.

Or listen to Schoenadel, a longtime habitue of the canal, tell stories of how it used to be along this quiet stretch of river 30 miles southeast of Cumberland.

"The canal up here didn't get a lot of recreational use until around 1975. In the early '60s we'd come here to camp and fish. It wasn't much. There were no bridges and you'd just drive out onto the towpath. But it was our favorite place to camp. And if someone else came along, why, we'd just get our axes out and clear them out a place."

➡ Bill's Place, Orleans Road, Little Orleans (exit 68 off I-68, 5 miles south to the end of the road); (301) 478-2701. Canoes rent for $20 a day. Sites at the Park Service campground are available on a first-come basis.

---

between the two is Frostburg. It's a quiet college town, but certain oddities point to a wilder past.

Failingers Hotel Gunter on Main Street is one of them. It may be that this restored Victorian-era relic is the world's only hotel with a jail and cock-fighting arena. The jail housed in-transit prisoners while their guards slept upstairs. These days,

GO to Western Maryland

Mennonite girls greet the Western Maryland Scenic Railroad at the Cumberland station. GERRY WINGENBACH

the cell is strictly a curiosity. But the cock-fighting arena has found new life as a sports bar. (Watch for Redskins football players here during their summer training camp at Frostburg State University.)

Also on Main Street are several restaurants, including Greek, French and new American, whose menus go beyond the beef-chicken-fish repertoire of many small-town eateries.

WESTERN MARYLAND SCENIC RAILROAD

Frostburg is the western terminus of the Western Maryland Scenic Railroad, which begins its route in Cumberland and pulls into the historic Frostburg depot 45 minutes later. In between, it chugs through a mile-long gorge called "The Narrows," through the 914-foot Brush Mountain Tunnel, and climbs 1,300 feet into the Allegheny Mountains, burning three tons of coal in the process. Passengers (about 50,000 a year) usually begin the round trip in Cumberland, then have lunch and wander through the souvenir shops at Frostburg's Old Depot before climbing back on board for the return trip.

CUMBERLAND

Cumberland's long history includes some notoriety as the place where George Washington launched and ended his military career. A downtown walking trail covers the area where the French and Indian War-era Fort Cumberland stood in the 1750s. In the basement of the Emmanuel Episcopal Church is a 23-foot replica of the fort. Self-guided walking tours are also outlined for the Washington Street Historic District, a preserved six-block area of homes and buildings from the mid-1800s.

C&O CANAL VISITORS CENTER

But perhaps the best place to begin a visit to Cumberland is at the Western Maryland Station Center, a restored 1913 train depot that is the home of the Western Maryland Scenic Railroad. It also houses the C&O Canal Visitors Center, the Allegany County Visitors Bureau, and the Transportation and Industrial Museum.

The C&O Canal Visitors Center offers a rundown on the history of the canal in words and pictures. Or you can walk a few yards outside and see where it ended 22 years after the first shovel of earth was turned 184 miles away in Washington, D.C. The canal was originally conceived as a natural highway into the nation's interior. Ironically, in 1828, the year digging started, construction also began on the Baltimore and Ohio Railroad. By the time the C&O canal reached Cumberland in 1850, it was already outpaced by the faster, more weather-resistant railroad. A flood in 1889 dealt a major financial blow, forcing the canal into receivership. By 1924, another flood put it out of business for good.

For decades, the C&O deteriorated. Then in the mid-1950s, Supreme Court Justice William O. Douglas led a movement to preserve it as a hiking and biking trail. Finally, in 1971 the canal was officially named a national historical park. It's the narrowest national park in the country and the mostly level towpath where mules once pulled canal boats now seems custom-made for hikers and bicyclists.

PAW PAW TUNNEL

Twenty-eight miles beyond Cumberland along Route 51 is the canal's 3,118-foot-long Paw Paw Tunnel. Billed as one of the Wonders of the World when it was completed in 1850, crews dug and blasted through a mountain to avoid having to dig the canal alongside a curvy six-mile stretch of the Potomac. It shortened the canal by five miles, but took 14 years to complete.

The drive back to Cumberland along Route 51 follows the Potomac River and is lovely at any time of the year. It's an excellent back roads way to complete the excursion.

GO to Western Maryland

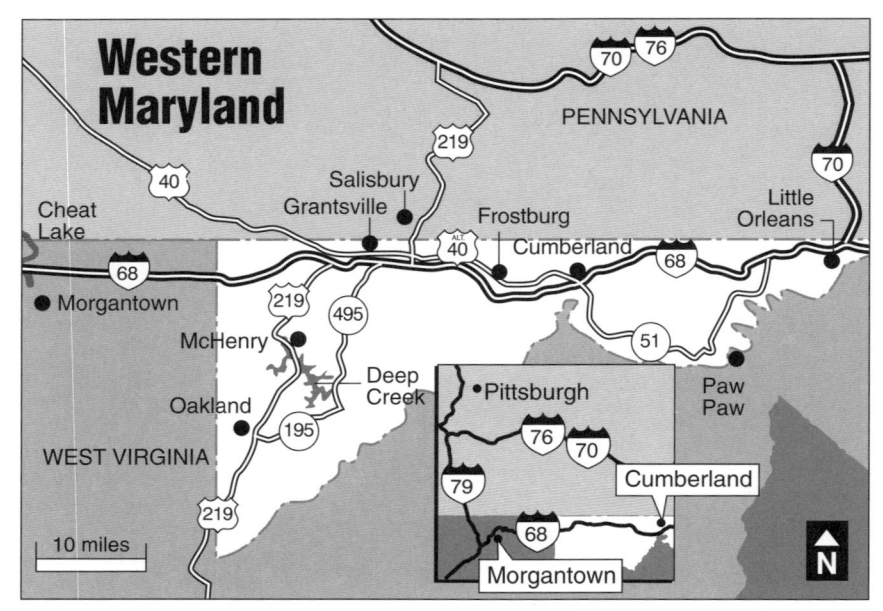

THE ROUTE

Take I-79 south to Morgantown, W.Va., then go east on I-68. (A 25-mile detour south on Rt. 219 leads to Deep Creek Lake.) To travel part of the old National Road, leave I-68 at exit 19 at Grantsville, Md., and join Alt. Rt. 40, which rejoins I-68 at Cumberland. To get to the C&O Canal towpath at Fifteen Mile Campground, continue east past Cumberland, exit I-68 at exit 68 and continue 5 miles to Little Orleans at the end of Orleans Rd. For a lengthier but more scenic return to the interstate, follow Rt. 51 along the Potomac River back west and north to Cumberland. **Approximate round-trip mileage: 375**

MORE INFORMATION

➞ **Allegany County (Md.) Visitors Bureau,** 13 Canal St., Cumberland, MD 21502; (800) 508-4748 or (301) 777-5905

➞ **Deep Creek Lake-Garrett County Promotion Council,** Garrett County Courthouse, 200 S. 3rd St., Oakland, MD 21550; (301) 334-1948

➞ **C&O Canal National Historical Park Headquarters,** 16500 Shepherdstown Pike, P.O. Box 4, Sharpsburg, MD 21782; (301) 739-4200

GO to Western Maryland

THINGS TO DO, PLACES TO SEE

CHEAT LAKE, W.VA.

➡ **Blosser's Lighthouse Marina,** Mont Chateau Rd. (exit 10 off I-68); (304) 594-2541. Open Apr.—Oct., weather dependent. Canoes rent for $5 an hour; $25 a day. Pontoon boats start at $25 per hour; $125—$175 day.

➡ **Edgewater Marina,** Mont Chateau Rd.; (304) 594-2630. Open May 1—Oct. 1. Pontoons rent for $50 an hour.

➡ **Coopers Rock State Forest,** exit 15 off I-68, 15 miles east of Morgantown; (304) 594-1561. Hiking trails crisscross lush forests. Highlights include the Coopers Rock overlook and the Henry Clay iron furnace. Picnic areas and 25 campsites with electricity available on a first-come basis from Apr. to early Dec.; 5 sites available by reservation.

DEEP CREEK LAKE, MD.

➡ **Deep Creek Lake State Park,** 3 miles south of McHenry on the lake; (301) 387-5563. Improved campsites, plus rowboat rentals, swimming beach and interpretive program featuring guided walks and campfire programs.

➡ **Herrington Manor State Park,** 5 miles northwest of Oakland on Herrington Manor Rd.; (301) 334-9180. Canoe and paddle boat rentals, campsites and cabins, food concession, plus interpretive programs.

➡ **New Germany State Park,** New Germany Rd. off Rts. 40 and 219 (6 miles south of Rt. 40); (301) 895-5453 or (301) 746-8359. Fishing, boating, camping and nature programs. Also 11 modern cabins, swimming and winter activities.

➡ **Swallow Falls State Park,** 9 miles northwest of Oakland on Swallow Falls Rd.; (301) 334-9180. Boasts the state's highest waterfall, the 52-foot Muddy Creek Falls. Several miles of hiking trails and winterized campsites.

➡ **Wisp Ski Resort,** next to Deep Creek Lake in McHenry; snow report, (301) 387-4911; reservations, (800) 462-9477. Maryland's only downhill ski area has a 610-foot vertical drop from a 3,080-foot elevation. 23 trails on 100 skiable acres. Summer activities include golf and mountain biking. Package deals offered.

➡ **Garrett County Historical Museum,** 107 S. 2nd St., Oakland; (301) 334-3226. Hours: June—Aug., 10—4 Mon.—Fri. Admission: free. Exhibits focus on the people and history of the area, including military and Indian artifacts.

GRANTSVILLE, MD.

➡ **Farmers' Market & Springs Museum,** off Rt. 669, 3 miles north of Grantsville. Hours: Memorial Day—Labor Day, 9—2:30 Sat. Admission: donation. Pastries, produce, quilts, antiques and flea market items for sale. The museum features local historic artifacts.

➡ **Penn Alps,** 125 Casselman Rd. (Rt. 40); (301) 895-5985. Hours: Memorial Day—Oct., 7 a.m.—8 p.m. Mon.—Sat.; Nov.— May, 7— 7 Mon.—Thurs.; 7—8 Fri., Sat.; 7—3 Sun. Restaurant and nonprofit crafts shop near the historic Casselman River Bridge.

FROSTBURG, MD.

➡ **Frostburg Depot,** 19 Depot St.; (301) 689-1221. Hours: 11—10 Mon.—Fri., 11—11 Sat., 11—9 Sun. Restaurant and train-themed gift shop are housed in an 1891 freight depot and restored 19th-century rail cars.

➡ **Thrasher Carriage Museum,** 19 Depot St.; (301) 689-3380. Hours: May—Sept., 11—3 Tues.—Sun.; Oct., 11—3 daily; Nov. and Dec., 11—3 weekends only. Admission: $2 adults; $1.75 seniors; $1 ages 5—12. Formal carriages, milk wagons and sleighs are among the 19th- and 20th-century vehicles on display.

➡ **Frostburg Museum,** corner of Hill

GO to Western Maryland

and Oak streets; (301) 689-1195. Hours: May—Oct., 1—4 Tues.—Fri.; 2—4 weekends. Admission: donation. Highlights include displays on the National Road and coal mining exhibits.

CUMBERLAND, MD., AREA

→ **Western Maryland Scenic Railroad,** 13 Canal St.; (800) 872-4650 or (301) 759-4400. Operates Tues.—Sun. and Mon. holidays from May—Sept.; daily in Oct. and weekends Nov.—Dec. Fares from Oct.—mid-Dec., $18 adults, $17.50 seniors, $10.75 ages 2—12; from May—Sept., $16 adults, $14.50 seniors, $9.75 children. A 1916 steam engine pulls vintage cars between Cumberland and Frostburg on a 3-hour, round-trip run, including a 1½-hour layover in Frostburg. Inquire about dinner and murder-mystery excursions.

→ **Chesapeake and Ohio Canal Visitors Center,** 13 Canal St. (in the Western Maryland Station Center); (301) 722-8226. Hours: May—Oct., 9—5 Tues.—Sun; Dec.—Apr., 9—5 Tues.—Sat. Admission: free. Exhibits and artifacts on the history of the C&O Canal. Call ahead for a schedule of seasonal interpretive programs and events.

→ **Transportation and Industrial Museum,** 13 Canal St. (in Station Center); (301) 777-5905. Hours: May—Oct., 10—noon and 2—4 Tues.—Sun; through mid-Dec. weekends only. Admission: free. Displays focus on 19th-century water and land transportation.

→ **Washington Street Historic District,** Baltimore St. to the 600 block of Washington St.; (301) 777-5905. Self-guided walking tours of an area of 19th-century buildings. Maps available at the Allegany County Visitors Center.

→ **C&O Canal Boat Replica,** Rt. 51 S.; (301) 729-3136. Hours: June—Sept., 9—noon Mon.—Fri.; 1—4 Sun. and by appointment. Admission: donation. A restored 93-foot canal boat (complete with stable for the mules that pulled it) is next to canal lock No. 75. There's also a restored lock house.

→ **Cumberland Theatre,** 101 Johnson St.; (301) 759-4990. Professional theatrical productions from June—Nov.

→ **History House,** 218 Washington St.; (301) 777-8678. Hourly tours: 11—4 Tues.—Sat.; also, 1:30—3:30 Sun., June—Oct. Admission: $3 adults; $1 children. 1867 Victorian home is headquarters of the Allegany County Historical Society.

→ **Allegany Expeditions,** 10310 Columbus Ave., NE (exit 45 off I-68); (800) 819-5170 or (301) 722-5170. Customized, guided adventure tours for small groups include rock climbing, backpacking, canoeing and caving. Also canoe rentals.

→ **Allegany Adventures,** 14419 National Highway, LaVale; (301) 729-9708. Tour packages include weekend and day hiking and bike trips.

→ **Artist Co-op Gallery,** Western Maryland Station Center; (301) 777-2787. Hours: 10—4 weekdays; 10—3 weekends. More than 30 area artists sell their wares in train station.

→ **Historic Cumberland Antique Mall,** 55 Baltimore St.; (301) 777-2979. Hours: 10—5 Mon.—Sat.; noon—5 Sun.; closed Tues. Jan.—Apr. 32 dealers sell goods on 5 floors in downtown Cumberland.

→ **C&O Canal Paw Paw Tunnel,** Rt. 51, 28 miles southeast of Cumberland, near Paw Paw, W.Va.; (301) 722-8226. Hours: dawn to dusk daily. Visitors can walk through this 3,000-foot brick-lined tunnel.

→ **Rocky Gap State Park,** exit 50 off I-68 east of Cumberland in Flintstone; (301) 777-2139; camping information, (301) 777-2138. Spectacular mountain scenery, good hiking trails and picnic areas along with boating, beaches and a modern bathhouse on Lake Habeeb. Winter sports include ice skating and sledding. Heated chalet sleeps 8.

GO to Western Maryland

ACCOMMODATIONS

Chain motels are clustered along I-68 around Morgantown, W.Va., and Frostburg and Cumberland, Md.

Other options include:

➡ **Lakeview Resort & Conference Center,** 1 Lakeview Dr., Morgantown; (800) 624-8300. Rates: early Apr.—mid-Nov., $145; mid-Nov.—early Apr., $105. Full-service resort on Cheat Lake has an attractive lodge with 2 restaurants, health club, golf and other amenities. Suites and condos available; also golf packages.

➡ **Failingers Hotel Gunter,** 11 W. Main St., Frostburg (exit 34 off I-68); (301) 689-6511. Rates: $60. Restored Victorian hotel with individually decorated rooms on Frostburg's main drag sports its own jail, a converted cock-fighting arena and offbeat historical displays.

➡ **The Inn at Walnut Bottom,** 120 Greene St., Cumberland (exit 43A off I-68); (800) 286-9718 or (301) 777-0003. Rates: $74—$95. Country inn a block from Cumberland's historic district has 12 guest rooms, some w/ shared baths. Rates include breakfast served in the Oxford House Restaurant below the inn.

➡ **Town Hill Hotel,** scenic Rt. 40, Little Orleans; (301) 478-2794. Maryland's first "tourist hotel," circa 1921, is now a 7-room B&B perched atop Town Hill Mountain, 23 miles east of Cumberland. Rates: $60—$70. Rooms are small, but views from the mountain are spectacular. Restaurant.

➡ **The Castle Bed & Breakfast,** 15925 Mt. Savage Road, Mt. Savage (9 miles west of Cumberland); (301) 264-4645. Rates: $72—$120. Rambling 1840 Gothic revival inspired by a Scottish castle went through several incarnations after its owner left in 1930. Among them: dance hall, brothel and casino. It's now a National Historic Landmark and a 6-room inn, 4 w/ private bath.

➡ Deep Creek Lake has numerous private homes, cottages and condos for rent. For information contact **Coldwell Banker Deep Creek Realty,** (800) 769-5300; **Railey Realty,** (800) 447-3034; **A&A Realty,** (800) 336-7303. A number of roadside motels are in Oakland, south of the lake. Other lodgings are in McHenry.

Among the inns and resorts on or around Deep Creek are:

➡ **Carmel Cove Bed & Breakfast,** Glendale Rd., Oakland; (301) 387-0067. Rates: $80—$100. Former monastery converted to 6-room country lodge. A path leads 200 yards through the woods to the lakefront and dock. Fishing equipment, canoe and bicycles provided for guests; also hot tub and tennis court.

➡ **Lake Pointe Inn,** 174 Lake Pointe Dr., McHenry; (800) 523-5253 or (301) 387-0111. Rates: mid-June—mid-Oct., $138—$178 weekends; $123—$163 weekdays. Off-season rates, $108—$148 weekends; $93—$133 weekdays; incl. breakfast. (Holiday weekend rates are higher in the off-season.) Arts and Crafts style house with wraparound porch and hot tub has been attractively renovated. Great views of lake and ski slopes. Kayaks, canoes and bikes provided.

➡ **Savage River Inn,** Dry Run Rd., McHenry; (301) 245-4440. Rates: $80—$120. Sits on 20 acres just off Rt. 495, 10 miles south of Grantsville, within easy driving distance of Deep Creek Lake. 3 guest rooms, all w/ private bath; 2-story great room w/ massive stone fireplace; hot tub.

➡ **Red Run Lodge,** 175 Red Run Rd., Oakland; (800) 898-7786 or (301) 387-2626. Rates: $75—$110 in season; $65—$95 Labor Day— Memorial Day; incl. breakfast. 6 guest rooms, sandy beach and boat dock just steps away on the lakefront; adjoining restaurant and lounge.

➡ **Wisp Resort Hotel and Conference Center,** Marsh Hill Rd., McHenry; (800) 462-9477 or (301) 387-5581. Rates: $79—$225. Year-round resort has skiing, golfing, biking and hiking in

GO to Western Maryland

scenic surroundings near the lake.

RESTAURANTS

➥ **Reflections on the Lake,** Lakeview Resort & Conference Center (at Cheat Lake), 1 Lakeview Dr., Morgantown; (800) 624-8300. Hours: 6—10. Elegant room with expansive views of the lake. Dinner, $8—$22. Also at the resort, The Grille Room, lunch, $5—$8.

➥ **Ruby and Ketchys,** exit 10 off I-68 near Cheat Lake; (304) 594-2004. Hours: 7 a.m.—8 p.m. daily. Home cooking since 1958. Lunch, $2—$4; dinner, $6—$13.

➥ **McClive's Restaurant & Lounge,** Deep Creek Dr., McHenry; (301) 387-6172. Hours: 5—10 p.m. daily. Lakefront dining overlooking Wisp Resort. Prime rib, grilled chops, seafood. Dinners, about $13.

➥ **Uno Restaurant & Bar,** Rt. 219 on Deep Creek Lake; (301) 387-4866. Hours: 11 a.m.— midnight Mon.—Thurs; 11—1 a.m. Fri., Sat.; 11—11 Sun. Casual family dining. Lunch from $4.50.

➥ **Tombstone Cafe,** 60 E. Main St., Frostburg; (301) 689-5254. Hours: 9 a.m—11 p.m. Mon.—Wed.; 9 a.m.—12 a.m. Thurs.—Sat.; 9—8 Sun. Coffeehouse/restaurant was once a gravestone carver's shop — hence the name. Sandwiches, snacks and dinner specials in the $7 range. Great desserts.

➥ **Petit Paris,** 86 E. Main St., Frostburg; (800) 207-0956 or (301) 689-8946. Hours: 6 p.m.—9:30 p.m. Tues.—Sat. Local institution serves classic French food. Dinner, $11—$44.

➥ **Acropolis,** 45 E. Main St.; (301) 689-8277. Hours: 4—9 Tues.—Thurs; 4—10 Fri., Sat. Greek food. Dinners, most under $13.

➥ **The Melting Pot,** 11601 Winchester Rd., LaVale; (301) 729-1960. Hours: 10—10 daily. Eclectic menu includes vegetarian specialties, seafood, egg rolls. Dinners, $7—$10.

➥ **Gehauf's,** 1268 National Highway, LaVale; (301) 729-1746. Hours: 7 a.m.—10 p.m. Fri.—Sat.; 7 a.m.—9 p.m. Mon.—Thurs.; 8 a.m.—8 p.m. Sun. Homemade soups and daily specials. Dinners, $7—$15.

BIG EVENTS

➥ **McHenry Highland Festival,** 1st Sat. in June, Garrett County Fairgrounds, McHenry. Features bagpipe bands, Scottish country and highland dancers. (301) 334-1948.

➥ **Allegany County Fair & AG Expo,** July, County Fairgrounds, Rt. 220 S., Cumberland. Agriculture exhibits, midway rides and nightly entertainment. (301) 777-0911.

➥ **Autumn Glory Festival,** mid-Oct., Oakland. Fall foliage festival features state banjo and fiddle championships, arts and crafts. (301) 334-1948.

➥ **Maryland Rail Fest,** usually early Oct., Western Maryland Station Center, Cumberland. Autumn event features steam train rides, kids' games and entertainment. (800) 872-4650 or (301) 759-4400.

➥ **Springs Folk Festival,** 1st Fri. & Sat. in Oct. Springs Museum and Crafts Building, Springs, Pa. (southern Somerset County on Rt. 669, 3 miles north of Grantsville, Md.). Fall celebration of arts, crafts and culture. (814) 662-4158.

GO to Bed & Breakfasts

B&Bs can make vacations special if chosen wisely

Staying at a bed and breakfast inn can make a trip more memorable — for better or worse.

B&Bs generally are operated in private homes, with two to five rooms available for overnight guests, along with the use of some public gathering areas. Some travelers wouldn't stay anywhere else; others would sooner stay just about anywhere else.

B&Bs are run by individuals and they reflect that. There are broad differences in ambience, amenities, the amount of privacy guests can expect, and other factors. But generally, B&Bs are a good bet for people who enjoy the camaraderie and comfort of staying in a home-like atmosphere. Travelers who enjoy meeting other guests, either in the evening while sitting around the living room, or over a shared table at breakfast, will probably enjoy a B&B experience. Moreover, the owners can be valuable sources of information on the local scene.

But because there can be big variations in B&Bs, and because innkeepers make their own policies, here are some things to consider (and ask) before you make a reservation.

Does the room have a private bath? If so, is it connected to the room or is it down the hall?

Does the rate include a full breakfast or just a continental breakfast? Is breakfast served at flexible or set hours? Is it served in the dining room, or can you have it delivered to your room?

Are children welcome?

Are credit cards accepted?

Is there television/telephone in the room or in a public area?

Is smoking permitted?

Are pets allowed? And, conversely, do they have any pets you might not want to be around?

Are there any restaurants in the area? (This is especially pertinent in rural areas, where dinner may be miles away.)

We've included a range of

continued on next page

GO to Bed & Breakfasts

The Savage River Inn B&B near Deep Creek Lake, Md.
JOHN BEALE/PITTSBURGH POST-GAZETTE

B&Bs with most of the itineraries in this guide. For a wider range of choices in various geographical areas, contact the following agencies.

PENNSYLVANIA TRAVEL COUNCIL, (800) VISIT-PA or (717) 232-8880. A free Pennsylvania B&B Directory lists B&Bs, country inns and farm stays throughout the state.

For a comprehensive list of **OHIO B&BS,** contact the state travel office at (800) BUCKEYE.

For a **WEST VIRGINIA B&B DIRECTORY,** call the state tourism office at (800) CALL-WVA.

GO

EAST

GO to National Road

JOHN BEALE/PITTSBURGH POST-GAZETTE

Fallingwater, the great creation of architect Frank Lloyd Wright for the Kaufmann family.

National Road

FOLLOW RT. 40 TO PENNSYLVANIA'S GLORY

Before there was a Lincoln Highway or a Route 66 or any of the other byways that loom large in the American consciousness, there was a National Road. The origins of the nation's first federal roadway lie in a rutted wagon trail forged around 1811. Today, the road most Pennsylvanians know as Route 40 cuts at a diagonal from Addison on the Maryland border to Washington, Pa., then follows Interstate 70 into West Virginia.

Along the way are 19th-century taverns, a historic battlefield, a couple of excellent restaurants, some quirky roadside attractions, two houses designed by Frank Lloyd

GO to National Road

Wright, plus hiking, biking and rafting amid miles of gorgeous scenery.

The circular route outlined here starts on the Pennsylvania Turnpike heading east from Pittsburgh, then follows back-country roads through the Laurel Highlands, before joining Route 40 in the village of Farmington. From the turnpike, take exit 9 at Donegal (50 miles east of Pittsburgh) and leave the fast lane behind. Head south on Route 381 toward Ohiopyle State Park and what some regard as the most famous private house ever built.

BOB DONALDSON/PITTSBURGH POST-GAZETTE

A number of the original cement mile markers remain on the National Road.

FALLINGWATER

Fourteen miles and a world away from the turnpike is Fallingwater, Frank Lloyd Wright's residential masterpiece set on 5,000 acres now owned by the Western Pennsylvania Conservancy. A five-minute walk from the visitors center down a shady path leads to the sandstone dwelling. Jutting over the falls of Bear Run, the house appears as naturally formed as the rocks, trees and ferns that embrace it. Fallingwater's interior remains true to Wright's vision, as well, from the earth-toned built-in sofas, to the polished stone floors and Berber rugs, to the artwork and books that belonged to the family that commissioned it.

Besides architectural information, the 45-minute tours are laced with anecdotes about the interaction between the master architect and

GO to National Road

CELEBRATING NATURE'S SWEETNESS

From November to March the rolling farmland of southern Somerset County lies silent under a thick, white blanket of snow. Come spring, the sweet action begins. It is as imperceptible as a bud popping into full flower, but inside those maple trees lining the narrow country lanes the sap is beginning to flow.

Most visitors wouldn't detect a thing if it weren't for the tin buckets strung around the tree trunks like chunky silver beads on a slender neck. When the sap begins to flow, farmers tap the trees, attach the buckets and make daily rounds to collect the sugar water, which they boil down into syrup. The process continues for a scant six weeks, usually beginning in mid-February. By the time the signs of spring are inescapable — when the buds appear and the birds return to the groves — the farmers stop collecting sap.

Then they throw a big party.

In Meyersdale and Salisbury, both on Rt. 219 in southern Somerset County, the celebration lasts for two consecutive weekends in April. Four area sugar camps — Wagner's, Milroy Farms, Brennemans and Short Brothers — are major participants, opening their operations to public view. But drive along the winding back roads in the area and you're likely to spot other camps that welcome visitors.

This is Amish country, where farmers like Albert Hertzler supplement a dairy business with the seasonal rite. On a cool, late winter morning you might find him at Keim's Kamp, wearing thick

continued on next page

Fallingwater's owners, Pittsburgh department store magnate Edgar Kaufmann and his wife, Liliane. Even after the Kaufmanns took possession, Wright maintained an influence over the place. For example, he strongly objected to the three-legged Italian chairs Liliane Kaufmann bought for the dining room (though guides point out that they're more stable on the stone floors than four-legged chairs would be). When the architect visited, the Kaufmanns were careful to remove offending objects, such as the living room coffee tables made of chestnut trees.

"Mr. Wright did not like them. He said trees do not grow upside down," a guide recounted.

In 1963, the Kaufmanns' only

GO to National Road

work gloves and a wide-brimmed straw hat, stoking the fire of an ancient boiler inside a rickety sugar shack. The camp still bears the name of the former owner, even though Hertzler bought the 227 acres of maple-studded farmland a decade ago. Clouds of sweet steam billow up, warming the drafty barn and providing the power to boil five large pans of sugar water. The liquid circulates from one pan to the next, growing thicker and thicker until at the end of the line, the sap emerges as a caramel-colored syrup.

The whole family gets involved in the process, selling syrup from the farmhouse porch (except on Sundays). The Hertzlers also make a soft, chewy maple sugar candy that bears little resemblance to the hard, crystallized stuff usually found in stores. The treat doesn't last long, however. By June, the summer heat has reduced it to a sticky mess.

Up Tub Mill Run Road from Hertzler's place at Wagner's Sugar Camp, Dale Jeffrey and his mother, Dorothy, cultivate 115 acres of maples. Sap collecting may be a seasonal chore, but shipping the products of spring's labor is a year-round enterprise.

Dorothy Jeffrey, who grew up on the farm that has been in her family for 125 years, will tell you the maple syrup business is a lot more art than science. Ideal conditions include cold weather and plenty of moisture in January, then warmer days in February to get the sap flowing. Nights should remain cold, however, to retard bud growth. Once the trees bud, the sap gets bitter, signaling it's time to quit collecting it. As her father used to say: The worse the weather, the better the sugar season.

As with other kinds of agricultural pursuits, seasonal success is

continued on next page

---

child, Edgar Kaufmann Jr., donated to a trust what has been described as one of the best-known private homes in the world. Since then, thousands of visitors have toured the place. But this house-turned-museum retains a lived-in quality, as if the owners just stepped out. And that is part of its beauty.

You can purchase your own Wright-inspired masterpieces in Fallingwater's gift shop, which is stocked with reproductions ranging from $70 pillows to a $15,000 partner's desk.

OHIOPYLE

Continuing down Route 381 brings you to the tiny village of Ohiopyle, surrounded by almost

GO to National Road

based on some factors that lie beyond the control of the farmers.

There's no rule of thumb, Mrs. Jeffrey explained. "It's nature and nature is unpredictable. But you don't make much syrup after Easter. There's a full moon at Easter and that usually means a change of weather. It's pretty much the truth, not fiction."

🍁 🍁 🍁

The Pennsylvania Maple Festival is held the last two weekends in April at the Somerset County Fairgrounds, about a mile from Meyersdale, and at the Maple Festival Park in the heart of town on Meyers Avenue. The park consists of Maple Manor, a historic homestead, cobbler shop, country store and sugar camp. Festival activities include live entertainment, carnival rides, pancake and sausage dinners and lots of maple-flavored treats. More information: (814) 634-0213.

Eight miles south of Meyersdale on Route 219, Salisbury also celebrates the season with Maple Sugarin' Time pancake and sausage meals served by the local Lions Club in the Salisbury Community Building.

Area sugar camps are open for tours during the festival. But to see production in full swing, plan to visit between the second week and last week of March. For a map to the camps, drop by O'Donnell's Old Firehouse Restaurant, 110 Ord St., Salisbury.

19,000 acres of adventurous possibilities in Ohiopyle State Park. Rafting trips on the Youghiogheny River usually operate from March through October on the lower Yough, which runs through Ohiopyle. However, the seven-mile trip over class III and IV rapids is a bit too adventurous for some. (Children under 12 aren't allowed.) Calmer waters flow on the middle Yough along nine miles of class I and II rapids between the town of Confluence and Ohiopyle. If you prefer a dryer experience, rent bikes (or bring your own) to ride along a 28-mile abandoned railroad right-of-way that skirts the banks of the river.

In the winter, those same trails are ideal for cross-country skiing. The southern end of the 70-mile Laurel Highlands Hiking Trail leads into Ohiopyle State Park. More than 40 miles of hiking trails crisscross the area.

NEMACOLIN

Route 381 hits Route 40 at Farmington. Nemacolin Woodlands Resort, the main commercial attraction here, is hard to miss. What began as a 30-room inn built in 1970 has

GO to National Road

George Washington and his troops built Fort Necessity in 1754, then lost it to the French.

taken on theme-park proportions under the ownership of lumber tycoon Joe Hardy. In the past decade, it has expanded into a check-in-and-never-leave resort with two golf courses, an equestrian center, a full-service health spa, three swimming pools and five restaurants. An upscale 125-room wing modeled on the venerable Paris Ritz opened in 1997. Other recent additions to the resort are the Heritage Court Shoppes, an indoor shopping arcade whose facades mimic historic buildings along the National Road, and a ski hill. Even if you aren't checking in, it's worth a stop to check out Hardy's $20-million art collection displayed throughout the public spaces. It includes Tiffany glass, Alexander Calder watercolors, J. Seward Johnson sculptures and original Audubon books. For kids, there are virtual-reality games, an 8,500-gallon salt water aquarium and an ice cream parlor.

FORT NECESSITY

Ten miles beyond Farmington on Route 40 lies Fort Necessity National Battlefield, site of 22-year-old George Washington's first command and first (and only) defeat, in 1754. The young Lt. Col. Washington called it a "charming" field for an encounter, a description whose meaning in the parlance of the era was probably akin to "excellent." A stockade and cabin have been reconstructed from archeological finds uncovered in 1953. They aren't as spectacular as some other reconstructed forts in the region, but the visitors center offers an engaging account of the battle that sparked the French and Indian War, along with other displays.

MOUNT WASHINGTON TAVERN

Just west of Fort Necessity is the Mount Washington Tavern, a 19th-century watering hole and lodging for weary travelers. Almost 300 taverns once stood along a 300-mile stretch of the National Road from Baltimore to Wheeling, W.Va. A surprising number remain today, though you won't always recognize them as such. Some have been converted to gift shops or restaurants, or stand empty and dilapidated. The price of admission to the battlefield entitles you to tour the Mount Washington Tavern, built in the late 1820s. A small museum in the tavern contains artifacts and history of the National Pike, including an original white obelisk mile marker. (Watch for others as you travel along Route 40.)

Another less historic but still illustrious lodging is the Summit Inn in Farmington, which has been hosting guests since 1907. The guest register bears the names of notables such as Thomas Edison and Henry Ford. Guest rooms are a bit dated, but the large Mission-style lobby is pleasant and so is the setting.

A cannon stands guard at Fort Necessity.
BOB DONALDSON/PITTSBURGH POST-GAZETTE

CHALK HILL

Continuing west, Route 40 enters the village of Chalk Hill, where the Lodge at Chalk Hill sports basic, motel-style rooms at moderate prices on spacious grounds.

The village has a number of gift shops, some of them housed in historic buildings. Watch for a classic roadside attraction here: the Farm Implement Museum on the grounds of the Laurel Highlands Motel. A jumble of no-longer-functioning equipment has been transformed into what could be art or junk, depending on your perspective. A 1941 Chalk Hill fire engine sitting amid this riot of rusted sculptures forms the centerpiece.

KENTUCK KNOB

Also in the area is Kentuck Knob, another Frank Lloyd Wright-designed house, which opened for public tours in the spring of 1996. The sleek 1950s house built of red cypress and native fieldstone sits on a wooded knoll six miles down a country lane from Chalk Hill. On display is artwork collected by owner Lord Peter Palumbo, an English real estate mogul who collects architecturally important houses the way some people collect stamps.

The tomb of British Gen. John Braddock, killed in the French and Indian War in 1754, is located near Fort Necessity.

LAUREL CAVERNS

A different sort of shelter can be found inside Laurel Caverns, a maze cave with more than two miles of passages. (The turnoff to the cave is just east of the Summit Inn.) Independent explorers have been venturing inside since the 1700s; guided tours have been offered since 1964.

Bring a jacket, it's chilly inside.

HOPWOOD

A couple of worthwhile stops await travelers who skip the bypass and follow Route 40 into the little town of Hopwood, just east of Uniontown. One is The Art Warehouse, where 200 or so artists display original art in a variety of media. Prices range from $12 for

GO to National Road

Searight's Tollhouse is one of only two remaining National Road tollhouses.

earrings to $5,000 for an oil painting. Also in Hopwood is Chez Gerard, a restaurant serving classic French food in an 1816 stone house-turned-tavern that claims to have hosted seven early U.S. presidents.

SEARIGHT'S TOLLHOUSE

For a glimpse of one of two remaining National Road tollhouses (the other is in Addison), watch for Searight's Tollhouse west of Uniontown. It was one of six tollhouses constructed to collect revenue for maintenance along the Pennsylvania stretch of road. You can tour the inside during the summer months.

NEMACOLIN CASTLE

Farther west in Brownsville, the grand Nemacolin Castle on the banks of the Monongahela River, dates back to the era when this town served as the river gateway to the West. The core of the house is a stone trading post built in the late 1780s. In the 1790s, owner Jacob Bowman added Tudor trappings, a tower and battlements. Twenty-two furnished rooms are on the tour.

GO to National Road

Don't miss the view of the valley from the upstairs balcony.

SCENERY HILL

Crammed edge to edge in a short stretch of Route 40 in the town of Scenery Hill is a cluster of antiques and gift shops housed in historic buildings. (Most are closed on Mondays.) At the west end of town is the Century Inn, a hostelry that has been serving roadside travelers since 1794. It's a handsome pillared stone house full of antiques, faded Oriental rugs and polished wood. Guest rooms are furnished with period pieces; all have private baths and all but one have fireplaces. The restaurant downstairs is a good place for a leisurely meal in pleasant surroundings, whether or not you're spending the night. If you're only hungry for a snack, try a slice of homemade pie at the Huffman House Restaurant across the street.

From here, Route 40 continues another eight miles or so to Interstates 70 and 79, faster tracks that seem worlds away from the 19th-century wagon road that started it all.

BOB DONALDSON/PITTSBURGH POST-GAZETTE
A view of the National Road from a bedroom window of Mount Washington Tavern, near Fort Necessity. The rooms are decorated in 19th-century style.

GO to National Road

National Road

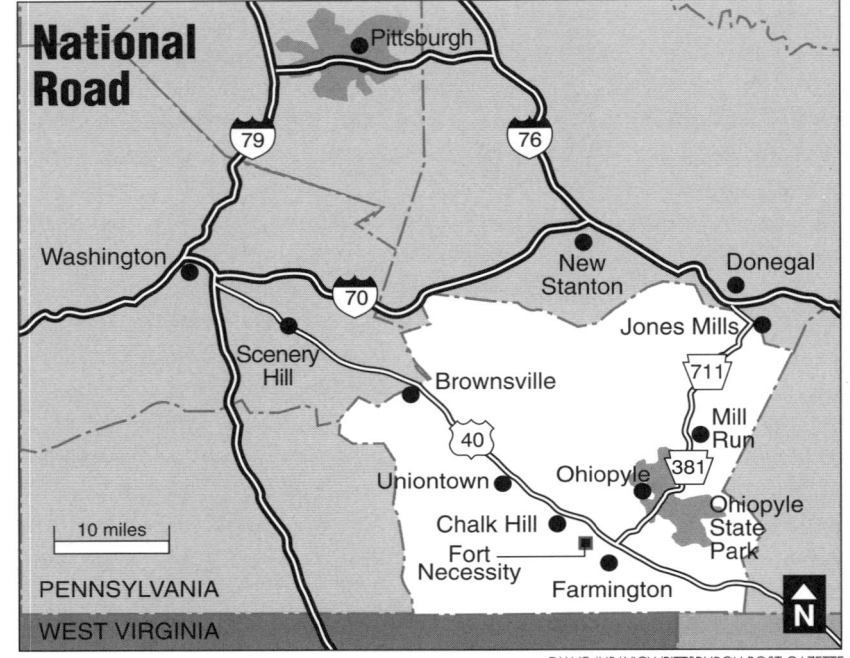

Map locations: Pittsburgh, 79, 76, Washington, 70, New Stanton, Donegal, Scenery Hill, Brownsville, Jones Mills, 711, Mill Run, 40, Uniontown, Ohiopyle, 381, Ohiopyle State Park, Chalk Hill, Fort Necessity, Farmington, PENNSYLVANIA, WEST VIRGINIA, 10 miles

DIANE JURAVICH/PITTSBURGH POST-GAZETTE

THE ROUTE

Take the Pennsylvania Turnpike east to exit 9 at Donegal, then Rt. 31 east to Jones Mills. Turn south on Rt. 381/711 to Fallingwater past the village of Mill Run. Ohiopyle State Park is several miles beyond. Rt. 381 meets Rt. 40 at Farmington. Head northwest about 45 miles to I-79 to return to Pittsburgh. **Round-trip mileage: 150**

MORE INFORMATION

➡ **Laurel Highlands Visitors Bureau,** 120 E. Main St., Ligonier, PA 15658; (800) 925-7669 or (412) 238-5661

➡ **Ohiopyle Information Center,** Trail Head, Ohiopyle, PA 15470; (412) 329-1127 (open May—Oct.)

➡ **National Road Heritage Park,** 3543 National Pike, Farmington, PA 15437; (412) 329-9380

GO to National Road

THINGS TO DO, PLACES TO SEE

➡ **Fallingwater,** Mill Run (between Mill Run and Ohiopyle on Rt. 381); (412) 329-8501. Hours: Apr.—mid-Nov., 10—4 Tues.—Sun.; mid-Nov.—Mar., 11—3 Sat., Sun. Tours of architect Frank Lloyd Wright's best-known creation last 45 minutes to an hour and are limited to 13 people; reservations required. Admission: $12 weekends and holidays; $8 weekdays. Also, in-depth tours at 8:30 a.m. in the summer and 10 a.m. in winter, run from 1 to 1½ hours; admission: $35 weekends; $30 weekdays. Children under 9 aren't permitted on tours, but there is a child-care center ($2 an hour). Also on the site are a cafe and interpretive nature trail.

➡ **Ohiopyle State Park,** Ohiopyle; (800) 637-2757. The Youghiogheny River Gorge cuts through the heart of this 19,000-acre gateway to the Laurel Mountains. A broad, grassy picnic area in the village of Ohiopyle by Ohiopyle Falls has day-use facilities. Also, biking on 28 miles of trails and rafting on the Yough River. Bike rentals and guided and unguided raft trips are available from several outfitters in town.

➡ **Fort Necessity National Battlefield,** Rt. 40, Farmington (11 miles east of Uniontown); (412) 329-5512. Hours: 8:30—5 daily, except Christmas. Admission: $2; under 16 free. Site where French and Indians surrounded George Washington's "fort of necessity" in 1754, leading to the French and Indian War. Admission includes entrance to rebuilt fort and nearby Mount Washington Tavern. Hiking, bike and ski trails are also in the park.

➡ **Kentuck Knob,** Kentuck Rd., Chalk Hill; (412) 329-1901. Hours: 10—4 Tues.—Sun. by reservation only. Admission: $15 weekends and holidays; $10 weekdays. It's recommended children be at least 12 years old. Frank Lloyd Wright home with grand view of the Youghiogheny River Gorge.

➡ **Laurel Caverns,** RD 1, Farmington; (412) 438-3003. Hours: One-hour tours depart every 20 minutes from 9—5 daily May—Oct.; weekends only Mar., Apr. and Nov. Admission: $8 adults; $6 ages 12—17 and $5 ages 6—11. Also a 3-hour adventure tour, $19. Guided and independent tours of Pennsylvania's largest cave.

➡ **Searight's Tollhouse,** Rt. 40, Uniontown; (412) 439-4422. Hours: Memorial Day—mid-Oct., 10—4 Tues.—Sat.; 2—6 Sun. Admission: $1 adults. One of two remaining tollhouses on the National Road.

➡ **Nemacolin Castle,** Front St., Brownsville; (412) 785-6882. Hours: Easter—mid-Oct., 11—5 weekends; June—Aug, 11—5 Tues.—Sun. Admission: $5 adults; $4 seniors; $2 children. Guided tours of 22-room mansion.

➡ **The Art Warehouse,** Bus. Rt. 40 at Bennington Road, Hopwood; (412) 439-1667. Hours: 11—5, Mon.—Sat.; noon—5 Sun.; closed Tues. Original work by more than 100 artists for sale.

ACCOMMODATIONS

➡ **Nemacolin Woodlands Resort,** Rt. 40, Farmington; (412) 329-8555 or (800) 422-2736. Rates: May—Oct., lodge rooms and suites $215—$495; condos, $245. Nov.—April, lodge rooms and suites, $180—$424; condos, $195.

➡ **Summit Inn Resort,** 2 Skyline Dr., Farmington; (800) 433-8594 or (412)

GO to National Road

438-8594. Open late Apr.—Oct. Rates: $75—$105. Call for discounts and special package deals. Historic hotel with swimming pool and tennis on 1,200 acres. Guest rooms vary in size and decor.

➦ **The Lodge at Chalk Hill,** Rt. 40, Chalk Hill; (800) 833-4283 or (412) 438-8880. Rates: $65—$75 weekends; $54—$64 weekdays. Lake-side lodging with small patios opening onto spacious grounds.

➦ **Stone House Hotel,** Rt.40, Chalk Hill; (412) 329-8876. Rates: $65—$125. 10-room historic inn, 4 w/ private bath, opened in fall 1996 in 1822 home. Guest rooms furnished w/ Victorian antiques.

➦ **The Century Inn,** Rt. 40, Scenery Hill; (412) 945-6600. Rates: $80—$140, including breakfast. Historic National Road tavern has 9 rooms furnished w/ antiques, all w/ private bath.

➦ **The B&B Inn of the Princess and European Bakery,** 181 W. Main St., Uniontown; (412) 425-0120. Rates: $85—$125. Restored home features Mission-style decor and antiques. 5 guest rooms, all w/ private bath.

➦ **Mountain View Bed and Breakfast,** Mountain View Road, Donegal (1 mile east of exit 9 off the Pennsylvania Turnpike); (800) 392-7773 or (412) 593-6349. Rates: $95—$150. Attractive 1850s farmhouse and converted barn in lovely rural setting, have 7 antiques-furnished guest rooms, all w/ private bath.

➦ **Yough Plaza Motel,** Ohiopyle; (800) 992-7238. Rates: $80 for up to 4 in room; $150 for 2-bedroom efficiencies. New motel close to Ohiopyle park office and outfitters.

➦ A number of commercial campgrounds are in the Ohiopyle State Park area. For information on camping within the park, call (800) 637-2757.

RESTAURANTS

➦ **Chez Gerard,** Bus. Rt. 40, Hopwood; (412) 437-9001. Hours: daily except Tues., lunch 11:30— 2; dinner 5:30—9. Fixed-price 3-course lunch, about $16.50; fixed-price 6-course dinner, about $35. Also a la carte menu. Classic French food served in a historic inn.

➦ **The Stone House Restaurant and Hotel,** Rt. 40, Chalk Hill; (412) 329-8876. Hours: noon—9 Tues.—Thurs.; noon—10 Fri.—Sat.; noon—9 Sun. Casual menu w/ emphasis on Italian-American cuisine served in 1822 house. Entrees, $7—$17.

➦ **The Lardin House Inn,** Rt. 21, Masontown (8 miles west of Uniontown); (412) 583-2380. Hours: 11—9:30 Tues.—Thurs.; 11—10 Fri., Sat.; 11—4 Sun. Continental menu w/ Mediterranean twist served in 230-year-old house. 5 small dining rooms and tavern room. Lunch, $5—$10; dinner, $12—$20.

➦ **The Century Inn,** Rt. 40, Scenery Hill; (412) 945-6600. Hours: lunch daily, noon—2:30; dinner, 4:30—7:30 Mon.—Thurs. and until 8:30 Fri.—Sat.; and 3:30—6:30 Sun. Closed Dec.30—mid-Mar. Lunch entrees, $7—$9; dinners, $12—$25.

➦ **River's Edge Cafe,** 203 Yough St., Confluence; (814) 395-5059. Hours: Memorial Day—Aug., 11—9 Tues.—Sun; mid-Apr.—May and Sept.—Oct., Fri.—Sun. only. Lunches, $5—$7; dinners $10—$14. Fish, grilled chicken and steak served indoors or out.

BIG EVENTS

➦ **National Pike Festival,** mid-May. Wagon train encampments and festivi-

GO to National Road

ties are staged in communities along Rt. 40; (412) 329-1560.

➤ **Laurel Highlands Wine and Food Festival,** mid-Aug., Seven Springs Mountain Resort, Champion. Pennsylvania wineries showcase their vintages; (800) 452-2223.

➤ **Pennsylvania Maple Festival,** last 2 weekends in Apr., Meyersdale; (814) 634-0213.

➤ **Pennsylvania Arts & Crafts Country Festival,** 4th weekend in May, Fayette County Fairgrounds, Rt. 19; (412) 863-4577.

ALSO IN THE AREA

➤ **Seven Springs Mountain Resort,** Champion; (800) 452-2223. Pennsylvania's largest ski area is open year round with a variety of seasonal festivals and events. Accommodations in the lodge, condominiums and cabins. Call for rates and special golf, ski and festival packages. From Pittsburgh, take exit 9 off I-76, then take Rt. 31 east for 2 miles to Rt. 711 south, 2 miles to County Line Road. The resort is 6 miles down the road.

➤ **Hidden Valley Resort,** 1 Craighead Dr., Hidden Valley; (814) 443-8000. Golf, tennis, a small ski area and other outdoor activities in a 2,000-acre resort community. Lodging in condos, townhouses and homes. Call for information and rates on special packages. From I-76, take exit 9 and go east on Rt. 31 for 8 miles to the entrance.

➤ **Horizon Outlet Center,** Somerset (exit 10 off I-76 to Rt. 601 north); (800) 866-5900 or (814) 445-3325. Hours: 10—8 Mon.—Sat.; 12—6 Sun.; winter 10—6 Mon.—Sat., 11—6 Sun. Outlet mall stores include Jones New York, Mikasa, Ralph Lauren and dozens more.

GO to Lincoln Highway

GERRY WINGENBACH
The Lincoln Highway is notable not only for what is along it, but also for its wonderful vistas.

Lincoln Highway

ROUTE 30 WINDS ITS WAY THROUGH HISTORY

Bedford County is a place to make tracks — or follow them, as the case may be. To 14 covered bridges tucked back out of sight along country roads. To orchards and farm markets heaving in fall with the fruits of summer's labors. To historic streets in the restored downtown of its county seat. To rolling back roads ideal for cycling, and off-road trails great for hiking.

The old Lincoln Highway, better known to Western Pennsylvanians as Route 30, is the track that leads to it all. The first transcontinental highway is layered with 250 years of transient history from its roots as part of the Forbes Road forged by colonists during 18th-century Indian wars, to its evolution as the Lincoln Highway in the early days of automobile travel. Along the way are

GO to Lincoln Highway

dozens of historic and natural attractions, along with classic roadside architecture that has survived the age of turnpike service plazas.

The directions are straightforward enough. From Pittsburgh, simply get on Route 30 and head east. The stretch from Pittsburgh to Greensburg can be a maddening snarl of traffic. So if you aren't planning stops until Ligonier, avoid the slow lane by taking the Pennsylvania Turnpike directly to exit 9 at Donegal, then take Route 711 north.

GREENSBURG

However, there are some things in and around Greensburg worth stopping for. One is the Westmoreland Museum of American Art in the heart of downtown. The permanent collection includes works by Mary Cassatt, Winslow Homer, Thomas Eakins and Andrew Wyeth, along with paintings by Pennsylvania artists.

Greensburg is the oldest county seat established west of the Alleghenies (it was incorporated in 1799). Take notice of the county courthouse, built in 1906. It's a French Renaissance beauty located south of the museum on Main Street.

HANNA'S TOWN

Three miles north of Greensburg between routes 119 and 819 is Hanna's Town, the original county seat, which was destroyed by fire in 1782. Some structures have been rebuilt, including the courthouse/tavern and a log fort. Costumed interpreters offer tours of the site from spring through fall.

SAINT VINCENT COLLEGE

East of Greensburg, a short detour off Route 30 north on Route 981 leads into Latrobe, where Saint Vincent College is an engaging place to visit — even when the Pittsburgh Steelers aren't in residence at their summer training camp here. The nation's oldest Benedictine college was established in 1846 and its campus is set amid lovely rolling hills. The centerpiece is a Romanesque basilica built in 1905. Nearby is a gristmill where Benedictine monks have been milling flour since 1854. Free tours are offered on Tuesday and Thursday afternoons.

LATROBE

Elsewhere in Latrobe is the Latrobe Brewing Co., makers of Rolling Rock Beer. Though there are no brewery tours, you can watch a 12-minute video on the beer-making process and a small museum displays Rolling Rock memorabilia, such as tap knobs, bottles and cans. There's also a company store selling everything from brand name buckets to gym shorts — but no beer.

East of here you leave the billboards, golden arches, car lots and the rest of Route 30's commercial jumble behind and glide into rural territory, where a Honda sign more

GO to Lincoln Highway

likely means they're selling off-road vehicles than Accords. The Loyalhanna Gorge Scenic Recreation Area opens up east of Latrobe. This 3½-mile stretch follows Loyalhanna Creek and is a great spot for a picnic or a short stroll. A mile-long nature trail is accessible from Route 30.

GERRY WINGENBACH
The sign beckons beer fans to one of Latrobe's landmarks — although no beverages are for sale.

IDLEWILD PARK

For more than a century, families have delighted in the manufactured sights at Idlewild Park, three miles west of Ligonier. Established in 1878 by Judge Thomas Mellon as a means of getting more passengers on his narrow gauge Ligonier Valley Railroad, the park, if not the railroad, has endured. Besides amusement rides, there's a water park and picnic areas. Also here is Story Book Forest, where Mother Goose's creations come to life in a wooded setting.

LIGONIER

Route 30 detours around Ligonier, but this pleasant little town is worth a visit, if only to wander through the shops or sit for a while in its central diamond-shaped park. If Hollywood were casting for a town that exudes quaintness, it could do no better than this. Attractive homes line swept streets, flower baskets hang from lamp posts and flags fly from storefronts. It even has a white gazebo in the park. The downtown area has dozens of shops selling gifts and antiques. Several B&Bs also are within walking distance.

FORT LIGONIER

Ligonier's main historical attraction is Fort Ligonier. It is a full-scale re-creation of the first British fort in the Alleghenies, which was built in 1758 during the French and Indian War. Dioramas, period rooms and the fort itself, depict life of the era. Special educational guides designed for families with children are available at the desk.

LINN RUN AND POWDERMILL

Just east of Ligonier, a nine-mile detour south on Route 381 leads to lovely Linn Run State Park, which

GO to Lincoln Highway

has hiking trails and 10 rustic cabins that sleep two to eight people.

Nearby is the Powdermill Nature Reserve, a biological field station operated by the Carnegie Museum of Natural History. A nature center on the grounds features a natural history exhibit with dioramas depicting plants and animals of the region. Also here are a three-quarter-mile hiking trail and butterfly and herb gardens. Special programs are conducted on Sunday afternoons from January through October.

A covered bridge near Shawnee State Park.
GERRY WINGENBACH

COMPASS INN MUSEUM

Back on Route 30, the Compass Inn Museum sits a mile east of Ligonier in Laughlintown. The core of the museum is the original stagecoach stop, a handsome log and stone building that dates back to 1799. It went through a number of incarnations including tavern, general store, post office, doctor's office and antiques shop before the Ligonier Valley Historical Society bought and restored it. Reconstructed outbuildings include a kitchen (with working beehive oven), blacksmith shop and barn.

In its day, this was considered a fine inn — no more than five to a bed, quipped an employee. Guides also work a bit of etymology into the tours. For instance, the word "toast" (in the drinking sense of the word) originated from the days when liquor, though popular, wasn't of the highest quality. So drinkers slipped a piece of toast in the bottom of their mugs to sop up the sediment and other gunk. When you drank to someone's health, you drank to the bottom, or the toast.

LAUREL SUMMIT

East of Laughlintown, the four-

GO to Lincoln Highway

Benedictine monks have been milling flour since 1854 at the St. Vincent College gristmill.

mile climb to the 2,684-foot Laurel Summit begins. Access to the 15,000-acre Laurel Ridge State Park is at the summit. The park, which follows the Laurel Ridge from Ohiopyle State Park north to Johnstown, has more than 70 miles of hiking and cross-country ski trails linking one end to the other.

JENNERSTOWN

Coming down off the summit you'll enter Jennerstown, founded in 1822 and reportedly named after Dr. Edward Jenner, who introduced vaccination. In the early days of the Lincoln Highway there was a tourist camp here (a pre-motel lodging where motorists parked and erected tents). Watch for stone gate posts at the western edge of town marked "Jenner Pines" and "Camping Park."

But a century before motorized vehicles buzzed through town, horse-drawn wagons ruled the road. Inns, like the building that now houses 1806 Antiques, were the one-stop watering, dining and resting spot. The 1806 building is the oldest hostelry in Somerset County and its owners tell many colorful stories about its past.

Also in Jennerstown is the Jennerstown Speedway (south of town on Route 985), where NASCAR races are run from April through October.

SOMERSET HISTORICAL CENTER

Seven miles south of Jennerstown

GO to Lincoln Highway

on Route 985 is the Somerset Historical Center, which re-creates 18th- and 19th-century Western Pennsylvania life. On the grounds are log cabins and barns, a maple sugar camp, covered bridge, smokehouse and general store. There's also a visitors center, genealogical library, and displays of early farm machines and buggies.

MOUNTAIN PLAYHOUSE

A half-mile north of Jennerstown on Route 985, the Mountain Playhouse has been presenting summer-stock theater in a converted 1805 gristmill since 1939. Performances are from mid-May to mid-October. Even if you aren't staying for the show, the Green Gables Restaurant, adjacent to the theater, serves good food in a beautiful lakeside setting.

BUCKSTOWN

Route 30 rises between Jennerstown and Buckstown, offering some of the most gorgeous views of the trip. If you need to stretch your legs, stop off at Duppstadt's Country Store in Buckstown, which has been catering to travelers since 1903, about the time the first auto rolled by. Among the eclectic offerings: maple syrup, trout bait, cowboy boots and hickory rockers.

GERRY WINGENBACH
The Romanesque basilica at St. Vincent College in Latrobe.

BEDFORD COUNTY

Just inside the Bedford County line the 1930s Ship Hotel, perched on the edge of the road near Reels

GO to Lincoln Highway

GERRY WINGENBACH
The Coffee Pot restaurant in Bedford has been closed for some time, but the building is vintage roadside architecture.

States and 7 Counties" beckons a chipped and faded sign. True to its claim, the views from this spot near the 2,464-foot summit of Allegheny Ridge are spectacular.

SCHELLSBURG

The next six miles from here to Schellsburg closely mimic the old Lincoln Highway and the Forbes Road before it. Two miles west of Schellsburg, watch for bison roaming in a field on the north side of Route 30. Cedarrow's Farm has been raising and selling bison since 1988. They sell the meat along with bison-themed souvenirs in the gift shop on the south side of Route 30.

Corners, was built to resemble an ocean liner, presumably because its owner was reminded of the sea when he looked into the valley beyond on foggy days. Today, more than a decade after it closed, the hotel looks more like a shipwreck adrift in the Alleghenies. (An old pickup has crashed right through the front door.) But this classic piece of roadside architecture meant to lure tourists still does just that. "See 3

At the western edge of Schellsburg in the heart of the Schellsburg Cemetery is an old one-room log and mortar church, beautiful in its simplicity. Inside, are a wine-glass pulpit, narrow wooden benches on rough pine floors, and on the walls, an honor roll of local residents who died in battle. Three of the names date back to the Revolutionary War. Wander among the headstones in the cemetery and you'll spot others from the era.

SHAWNEE STATE PARK

Schellsburg is a pretty little town whose main street (Route 30) can be strolled in a matter of minutes. Antiques shops outnumber any other type of commercial establishment. It is also home to Shawnee State Park, a year-round park that has a lake with a long sandy beach, boat rentals, good fishing, 12 miles of hiking trails, campsites and a lakefront cottage for rent.

COVERED BRIDGES

Several of Bedford County's 14 covered bridges are near Schellsburg. The tourist bureau publishes a map that will lead you to all of them, along with other maps outlining backroads cycling trips and routes to local orchards and small farm markets. Ten or so of those farm markets are in a scenic agricultural stretch along Route 96 north of Route 30 and along Route 4003, which runs parallel to Route 96. Most stands are open summer through fall.

Kayaking the calm waters of Shawnee State Park.
GERRY WINGENBACH

VINTAGE LODGINGS

A remnant of the Lincoln Highway's glory days sits off the road just east of Schellsburg. The Lincoln Motor Court is a horseshoe of one-room gray-shingled tourist cabins

GO to Lincoln Highway

GERRY WINGENBACH

Some graves in Schellsburg Cemetery date back to the Revolutionary War.

built between the '30s and the '50s for the auto trade. The current owners have added showers, televisions and phones, but in many respects the cabins, with their knotty pine paneling and lace curtains, belong to another era.

Directly across Route 30 is the former Hotel Lincoln whose scars from a notorious past include 40-some bullet holes above the bar in the back. The old dance hall/hotel/cathouse was converted into an antiques store around 1990. The Hotel Lincoln has lost its woolliness but it's still kind of wild. The proprietor specializes in finding the hard-to-find. Past procurements include a steam locomotive, a portable jail cell and an armored personnel carrier.

The more straight-laced Jean Bonnet Tavern, between Schellsburg and Bedford, is a fieldstone building on the National Register of Historic Places. A travelers' watering hole since the 1760s, it has large fireplaces and thick-beamed ceilings. The ground floor is a restaurant; upstairs are bed and breakfast rooms.

BEDFORD

Coming into Bedford, you're greeted by a couple of delightful examples of roadside architecture. One of them, the Coffee Pot, a two-story rendition of the object complete with handle and spout, is now empty and could use some polishing. Not so Dunkle's Gulf Station down the road. Its 1934 blue, yellow and green art deco tile is as dazzling as the day it opened. Gulf Oil built the station and Dick Dunkle, whose name is immortalized in that tile, ran the place for years, eventually purchasing it from the oil company. His son, Jack, now operates it.

In its long history, Bedford never experienced a major boom, but then, it didn't suffer a significant decline, either. The stability of this borough of 3,500 or so may account for the number of historic buildings that remain largely unmarred by the sort of well-intentioned renovation that later brings regret.

Many buildings serve different functions from the originals, of course. The 18th-century gray stone building at 203 Pitt St., for example, is now the Graystone Galleria, an antiques store. Similarly, Founders Crossing at the corner of Pitt and Juliana streets is a sprawling flea market and antiques shop that once housed a five-and-dime store.

FORT BEDFORD

There are no traces left of the original 1758 British stockade that spawned Bedford. But a replica has been constructed on the banks of the Raystown branch of the Juniata River. The original layout of the town, designed in 1766 around a central public square, remains. So do many of the historic buildings. Free walking-tour maps available at the fort or from the tourist bureau will lead you to them. Among the most historic is the 1766 Espy House on Pitt Street. It served as George Washington's headquarters in 1794 when he was in Bedford reviewing federal troops sent to quell a citizen protest against taxes on whiskey in what would become known as the Whiskey Rebellion. Another important historical figure, abolitionist John Brown, stayed in the Grand Central Hotel at the corner of Pitt and Juliana streets on his way to Harper's Ferry, W.Va. Unfortunately, the structure, now a bank, bears little resemblance to the original building.

OLD BEDFORD VILLAGE

Forty or so late-18th-century buildings have been reconstructed and moved to what is now Old Bedford Village, a 72-acre living-history museum north of Route 30 (exit 11 off I-76). The nonprofit enterprise includes log cabins, a schoolhouse, a church, a working colonial farm and a number of crafts shops. Costumed interpreters are on hand to explain life as it was in the late 1700s.

JOHNSTOWN

Forty miles northwest of Bedford, Johnstown remembers a horrific moment in history when a poorly maintained dam broke in 1889 killing 2,200 people. When the earthen dam collapsed in a torrential rainstorm that May, it sent a wall of water

GO to Lincoln Highway

GERRY WINGENBACH

Dunkle's Gulf Station in Bedford is noted for its colorful Art Deco exterior.

rushing at 40 mph down a channel of the Conemaugh River into town, leaving death and destruction in its wake. Two sites in Johnstown recall the disaster. The Johnstown Flood Museum in the former Carnegie Library has exhibits detailing how it happened. It also shows a 1989 Academy Award winning film about the flood. Northeast of the city, the National Park Service maintains the Johnstown Flood National Memorial, which overlooks the site of the original dam.

For a view of Johnstown, take a ride on the Inclined Plane. Rising 900 feet at a 71 percent grade, it's billed as one of the world's steepest. It was constructed in 1891, but a number of tourist-attracting improvements have been added over the years. Among them, a visitors center, restaurant and pub, observation deck and a 1¼-mile sculpture trail lined with steel works by local artist James Wolfe.

GO to Lincoln Highway

Lincoln Highway

DIANE JURAVICH/PITTSBURGH POST-GAZETTE

THE ROUTE

Take Route 30 east out of Pittsburgh and follow it all the way to Bedford. If you want to skip the congested areas from Pittsburgh to Greensburg, pick up I-76 to Route 711 (exit 9 at Donegal), and go north to Rt. 30 at Ligonier. Johnstown is 40 miles northwest of Bedford via Rt. 56. For a faster return to Pittsburgh from Johnstown, head southeast on Rt. 56 to south on Rt. 219, 33 miles to Somerset, where you can pick up I-76. An alternate scenic way back to Pittsburgh is via Rt. 56 northwest to Rt. 22 west.
Round-trip mileage: 210

MORE INFORMATION

➡ **Bedford County Conference & Visitors Bureau,** 141 S. Juliana St., Bedford, PA 15522; (800) 765-3331 or (814) 623-1771

➡ **Laurel Highlands Visitors Bureau** (Westmoreland, Somerset and Fayette counties), 120 E. Main St., Ligonier, PA 15658; (800) 925-7669 or (412) 238-5661

➡ **Cambria Country Tourist Council,** 111 Market St., Johnstown, PA 15901; (814) 536-7993

GO to Lincoln Highway

THINGS TO DO, PLACES TO SEE

GREENSBURG/LATROBE

➡ **Westmoreland Museum of American Art**, 221 N. Main St., Greensburg; (412) 837-1500. Hours: 11—5 Wed.—Sun. (till 9 p.m. Thurs.) Admission: $3 adults; 12 and under free. Permanent collection includes 19th-century art and southwestern Pennsylvania artists. Also changing exhibits of American art.

➡ **Hanna's Town**, 3 miles north of Greensburg off Rt. 119; (412) 836-1800. Hours: Memorial Day—Labor Day, 10—4 Tues.—Sat. and 1—4 Sun.; May, Sept., Oct., 10—4 Sat. and 1—4 Sun. Admission: $2 adults; $1 children. Recreation of 18th-century town with living-history demonstrations.

➡ **Saint Vincent College**, Latrobe; (412) 537-4560. Self-guided tours of the campus including summer theater, a 4-story wooden gristmill and a 1905 Romanesque basilica. Free tours of gristmill on Tues. and Thurs. afternoons. Pittsburgh Steelers summer training camp afternoon practices open to public during first 2 weeks of July; call (412) 323-1200 for details.

➡ **Latrobe Brewing Company Store**, 119 Jefferson St., Latrobe; (412) 539-3394. Hours: 9:30—5 Tues.—Wed., 9:30—6 Thurs.—Fri. and 9:30—3 Sat. Makers of Rolling Rock Beer sell brand merchandise. Also, small museum.

➡ **Laurel Highlands Railroad** departs from Rt. 819 off Rt. 119 S., Scottdale; (412) 887-4568. Hours: May—Oct., weekends, 3 trips daily. Fare: $8 adults; $6 ages 5—12 for 1-hour trip; $12 adults; $10 ages 5—12 for 2½-hour trip. Scenic steam train trips in Laurel Highlands.

LIGONIER AREA

➡ **Fort Ligonier**, intersection of Rts. 30 & 711, Ligonier; (412) 238-9701. Hours: Apr.—Oct., 10—4:30 Mon.—Sat.; 12—4:30 Sun. Admission: $5 adults; $2.25 ages 6-14. Full-scale, on-site reconstruction of 1758—1766 British fort w/ period rooms, exhibits and living-history activities.

➡ **Linn Run State Park**, off Rt. 381, Rector (9 miles south of Ligonier); (412) 238-6623. 10 rustic cabins sleep 2-8.

➡ **Powdermill Nature Reserve**, Rt. 381, Rector; (412) 593-6105. Hours: Apr.—Oct., 8—4 Wed.—Sat. and noon—5 Sun. Also, Sun. afternoon programs Jan.—Oct. Other times of year, hours determined by staff availability. Admission: free. Biological field station on 2,200 acres has butterfly and herb gardens. The Florence Lockhart Nimick Nature Center has dioramas of local flora and fauna.

➡ **Compass Inn Museum**, Rt. 30, Laughlintown (3 miles east of Ligonier); (412) 238-4983. Hours: May—Oct., 11—4 Tues.—Sat; 12—4 Sun. Admission: $4 adults; $2 ages 6-16. Restored stagecoach stop dating from 1799, and outbuildings furnished w/ period pieces.

➡ **Graham's Antique Mall**, Rt. 30, Ligonier; (412) 238-8611. Hours: 10—5 daily, closed Tues. More than 40 dealers.

➡ **Idlewild Park**, Rt. 30, Ligonier (3 miles west of town); (412) 238-3666. Hours: Memorial Day—Labor Day, 10 a.m.—closing (time announced daily); closed Mon., except holidays. Admission: $13.95 weekdays; $14.95 weekends; $7.50 seniors; ages 2 and under free. Amusement park w/ rides, water slide and entertainment.

SOMERSET COUNTY

➡ **Somerset Historical Center**,

GO to Lincoln Highway

10649 Somerset Pike, Somerset (exit 10 off I-76); (814) 445-6077. Hours: 9—5 Wed.—Sat.; noon—5 Sun. Closed holidays except Memorial Day, July 4 and Labor Day. Admission: $3.50 adults; $3 seniors; $1.50 ages 6-17. Museum of rural life traces 18th- and 19th-century development of Western Pennsylvania with re-created buildings and other exhibits.

➡ **Glades Pike Winery,** Rt. 31, Somerset; (814) 445-3753. Hours: 12—6 daily. Housed in 1868 barn; tastings and tours.

➡ **Mountain Playhouse,** Rt. 985, Jennerstown (½ mile north of Rt. 30); (814) 629-9201. Dramas and musicals performed from mid-May to mid-Oct. in historic gristmill-turned-theater.

BEDFORD COUNTY

➡ **Shawnee State Park,** Rt. 96, Schellsburg; (814) 733-4218. Nature programs, trails on 3,983 acres; also swimming, fishing, boating on large lake w/ beach; wheelchair accessible fishing area. 300 campsites have picnic tables and fire rings; showers and flush toilets are nearby. Also, renovated caretaker's house sleeps 8. Contact park office for rates and availability.

➡ **Cedarrow's Bison Farm,** Rt. 30 (2 miles west of Schellsburg); (814) 733-2323. Hours: Memorial Day—Labor Day, 10—5 daily; rest of year, 10—5 Thurs.—Sat.; noon—5 Sun. Admission: free. Bison-related gifts and bison meat for sale.

➡ **Fort Bedford Museum,** Fort Bedford Dr., Bedford; (800) 259-4284 or (814) 623-8891. Hours: 10—5 daily (closed Tues. May, Sept., Oct.). Admission: $3 adults; $2.50 seniors; $1.50 ages 6—18; $7 families.

➡ **Founders Crossing,** Pitt and Juliana streets, Bedford; (814) 623-9120. Hours: 10—5 Mon.—Sat.; 12—5 Sun. 2 levels and 18,000 sq. ft. offering hand-crafted gifts, artwork, antiques and collectibles.

➡ **Graystone Galleria,** 203 E. Pitt St., Bedford; (814) 623-1768. Hours: 10—5 Mon.—Sat.; 12—5 Sun. Antiques and gift items in 1768 building listed on the National Historic Register.

➡ **Old Bedford Village,** Hwy. 220 (exit 11 off I-76), Bedford; (814) 623-1156. Hours: May —Oct., 9—5 daily. Admission: $6.95 adults; $5.95 seniors; $4.95 children; under 6, free. More than 40 original log homes and other structures in a 72-acre reincarnation of a 1790s town. Also stages holiday events.

JOHNSTOWN

➡ **Johnstown Flood Museum,** 304 Washington St., Johnstown; (814) 539-1889. Hours: May—Oct., 10—5 Sun.—Thurs., 10—7 Fri.—Sat.; Nov.—Apr., 10—5 daily. Admission: $4 adults; $3.25 seniors; $2.50 ages 6—18. Exhibits relating to the 1889 Johnstown flood housed in former Carnegie Library.

➡ **Johnstown Inclined Plane,** 711 Edgehill Dr., Johnstown; (814) 536-1816. Hours: 6:30 a.m.—10 p.m. Mon.—Thurs.; 6:30 a.m.—midnight Fri.; 7:30 a.m.—midnight Sat.; 9 a.m.—10 p.m. Sun. Admission: $3 adults; $1.75 ages 6—12. Billed by the Guinness Book of World Records as "the steepest vehicular inclined plane in the world." Restaurant and pub in the upper station.

➡ **Johnstown Flood National Memorial,** off Rt. 219 north of Johnstown; (814) 495-4643. Hours: 9—5 daily; till 6 p.m. Memorial Day—Labor Day. Admission: $2 adults; under 16 free.

ACCOMMODATIONS

Lodging is plentiful in Bedford and at the Breezewood interchange of I-70 and I-76. Chain motels in Bedford include

GO to Lincoln Highway

Econo Lodge (814-623-5174); **Hoss's Inn** (Best Western) (800-752-8592) or (814-623-9006); and **Quality Inn** (814-623-5188). At Breezewood they include **Ramada Inn** (800-535-4025 or 814-735-4005) and **Econo Lodge** (814-735-4341).

Other options listed from west to east along the route include:

➡ **Mountain View Inn,** 1001 Village Dr., Greensburg; (800) 537-8709 or (412) 834-5300. Rates: $69—$120 weekends; lower Sun.—Thurs. Individually decorated rooms range from 18th-century decor to American country. Restaurant and tavern.

➡ **Campbell House Bed & Breakfast,** 305 E. Main St., Ligonier; (412) 238-9812. Rates: $90 weekends; $80 weekdays. 3 guest rooms w/ private bath; near shops.

➡ **Ligonier Country Inn,** Rt. 30, Laughlintown (next to Compass Inn Museum); (412) 238-3651. Rates: $65—$105 weekdays; $85—$140 weekends. Lovely 1920s inn w/ country decor has 18 rooms, all w/ private bath; dining room, lounge, swimming pool.

➡ **Glades Pike Inn,** Rt. 31, Somerset (6 miles west of the I-76 Somerset exit); (814) 443-4978. Rates: $50—$60 summer; $70—$80 Christmas—mid-Mar. (2-night minimum in winter). 5 guest rooms, 3 w/ private bath; 3 w/ fireplace in 19th-century stagecoach stop.

➡ **Inn At Georgian Place,** 800 Georgian Place Dr., Somerset; (814) 443-1043. Rates: $95—$180. 11 guest rooms, all w/ private bath in restored 1918 Georgian Revival mansion. Next to Horizon Outlet Center.

➡ **Bedford's Covered Bridge Inn & Cottage,** 1 mile off Rt. 30, Schellsburg; (814) 733-4093. Rates: $75—$95 weekends; $10 lower weekdays. 6 rooms and suites, all w/ private bath; also guest house that sleeps 6. Attractive Civil War-era house on 27 acres next to Shawnee State Park.

➡ **Lincoln Motor Court,** Rt. 30 (2 miles east of Schellsburg); (814) 733-2891. Rates: $35. 1-room tourist cabins built between the '30s and the '50s evoke the days of early auto travel on the Lincoln Highway.

➡ **Bedford House Bed & Breakfast,** 203 W. Pitt St., Bedford; (814) 623-7171. Rates: $55—$85. 7 guest rooms, all w/ private bath in 1803 brick Federal-style home in heart of Bedford's historic district.

➡ **Oralee's Golden Eagle Inn,** 131 Pitt St., Bedford; (814) 624-0800. Rates: $59—$89. Late 1700s mansion and former tavern opened as B&B in 1996 w/ 16 guest rooms and suites, some w/ fireplaces and porches.

➡ **Jean Bonnet Tavern,** Rt. 30, 4 miles west of Bedford; (814) 623-2250. Rates: $49—$65. 2 rooms and 2 suites, all w/ private bath in former "public house" first licensed in 1780.

RESTAURANTS

➡ **DiSalvo's Station,** 325 McKinley Ave., Latrobe; (412) 539-0500. Hours: 11—9 Tues.—Thurs.; 11—10 Fri.; 4—10 Sat.; 10—9 Sun. Italian-American food served in restored 1902 railroad depot. Dinners, $8—$20.

➡ **Colonial Inn,** Rt. 30 (2 miles west of Ligonier); (412) 238-6604. Hours: 11:30—2:30 and 5—10 Tues.—Sat. (till 11 Fri. and Sat.); and noon—8 Sun. Pleasant lakeside setting. Lunch menu has quiche, crab cakes, burgers, $5—$9. Dinner menu features veal, chicken, seafood and some vegetarian entrees, $12—$30.

➡ **Diamond Cafe,** 109 W. Main St., Ligonier; (412) 238-3111. Hours: 7:30—4:30 Mon.—Sat. Home-style cooking. Lunch, $3—$4.

➡ **Ligonier Country Inn,** Rt. 30,

GO to Lincoln Highway

Laughlintown; (412) 238-3651. Hours: May—Dec., 5 p.m.—9 p.m. Tues.—Sat., 8 a.m.—7 p.m. Sun.; Jan.—Apr., 5 p.m.—9 p.m. Thurs.—Sat., 8 —6 Sun. Country menu has chicken pot pie, lamb casserole, pasta and seafood. Also, Sunday brunch. Entrees, $9—$18.

➡ **Green Gables Restaurant,** Rt. 985, Jennerstown (½ mile off Rt. 30); (814) 629-9412. Hours: mid-May—mid-Oct., noon—8 Tues.—Thurs. and Sun; noon—9 Fri.—Sat. Also open weekends mid-Mar.—Apr. and mid-Oct.—Dec. Attractive restaurant in rural, lakeside setting serves seafood, steaks. Lunch, about $7; dinners, $11—$25.

➡ **Jean Bonnet Tavern,** Rt. 30, 4 miles west of Bedford; (814) 623-2250. Hours: 11—9 Mon.—Thurs.; 11—10 Fri., Sat.; 8—8 Sun. Historic stone tavern. Dinner, $8—$26.

➡ **Oralee's Golden Eagle Inn,** 131 Pitt St., Bedford; (814) 624-0800. 50-seat dining room in restored 18th-century mansion. Lamb chops, fresh trout, tenderloin. Lunch, $5—$7; dinner, $11—$18.

➡ **The Baker's Loaf,** 110 E. Pitt St., Bedford; (814) 623-1108. Fresh-baked breads, sandwiches, soups, salads. $4—$7.

➡ **The Tavern,** 224 E. Pitt St., Bedford (in the Bedford Hotel); (814) 623-9021. Hours: 4—11 Mon.—Sat. All-you-can-eat seafood buffet plus a la carte menu. $7—$19.

BIG EVENTS

➡ **Bloody Run Classic,** early May, Bedford. Semi-pro bicycle race; also canoe race, chili cook-off, food, entertainment. (800) 765-3331.

➡ **Annual Antique Flea Market,** 2nd weekend in Aug., Somerset. (814) 445-6431.

➡ **Johnstown Folkfest,** Labor Day weekend, Johnstown. Popular music festival also features 50 kinds of ethnic foods and guided tours of historic buildings. (814) 539-1889.

➡ **Ligonier Highland Games,** Sat. after Labor Day, Idlewild Park, Ligonier. Scottish fair includes bagpipes, dancing, sales of woolens, shortbread and other Scottish fare, plus traditional games such as the "caber toss," in which logs are thrown end over end. (412) 851-9900.

➡ **Mountain Craft Days,** 1st Fri., Sat., Sun. after Labor Day, Somerset Historical Center, Somerset. More than 125 artisans demonstrate traditional crafts in living-history park. (814) 445-6077.

➡ **Fort Ligonier Days,** 2nd weekend in Oct., mid-town Ligonier and Fort Ligonier. Parade, music, food and crafts, plus re-enactments at the fort. (412) 238-4200.

➡ **Fall Foliage Festival,** 1st two full weekends in Oct., downtown Bedford. Crafts exhibits and entertainment. (800) 765-3331 or (814) 623-1771.

➡ **Old Fashioned Christmas Celebration,** 1st two weekends in Dec., Old Bedford Village. (814) 623-1156.

ALSO IN THE AREA

➡ From Bedford, Altoona is a quick 35-mile drive north on Rt. 220. For detailed information on attractions and lodging in the area, contact the Allegheny Mountains Convention & Visitors Bureau, Logan Valley Mall, Rt. 220 & Goods Lane, Altoona, PA 16602; (800) 842-5866 or (814) 943-4183.

Altoona was a railroad town from its founding in 1849 and although the railroad isn't the economic force it once was, the main tourist attractions in town still revolve around the rails. First is what is commonly referred to as one of the engineering marvels of the world, the **Horseshoe Curve National Historic Landmark**, a 180-degree curve of tracks about 15 minutes west of town. The loop was designed in 1854 as a means to get trains over the Allegheny Mountains.

Dozens of trains negotiate the curve every day, so your chances of seeing one from the observation deck are good. A visitors center has an orientation film and exhibits. A funicular takes visitors up to the observation deck at the curve's arc. It's open May—Oct., 9:30—7 daily and Nov.—Apr., 10—4:30 Tues.—Sun. Admission is $3.50 adults; $3 seniors; $1.50 ages 3—12.

The Altoona Railroaders Memorial Museum at 1300 9th Ave., Altoona (814-946-0834), displays reconditioned rail cars (including a mail car and the private car of steel baron Charles Schwab) and all sorts of railroad memorabilia. Hours: Apr.—Oct., 10—6 daily (last admission at 5 p.m.) It closes an hour earlier and on Mon. in winter. Admission: $6 adults; $5.50 seniors; $4 ages 3—12.

Another must-see for rail buffs is the **Allegheny Portage Railroad National Historic Site.** The visitors center is off Rt. 22 in Cresson, 12 miles west of Altoona (814-886-6150). The portage railroad was a system of 10 inclined planes constructed over 37 miles to lift rail cars over the Alleghenies. Though it was an engineering feat in its time (it opened in 1834), by the 1850s it was rendered obsolete. The U.S. Park Service maintains the site, which has a visitors center, exhibits in a former engine house and interpretive trails. Hours: 9—5 daily; till 6 Memorial Day— Labor Day. Admission: $2 adults; under 17 free.

Also in Altoona is **Lakemont Park** (Rt. 220, Frankstown Rd. exit; 800-434-8006 or 814-949-7275), an amusement park since 1894. It has more than 30 rides, a water park and other attractions. Hours: June—Aug., 11—9 daily; May and Sept., noon—8 weekends. Admission: $6.95 for an all-day ride pass.

➡ Twenty minutes southwest of Altoona in Claysburg is **Blue Knob** ski area (on Ski Gap Road, Rt. 164; 814-239-5111). The four-season resort has day and night skiing. Ask about special packages and mid-week deals.

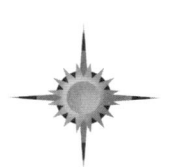

GO to Visitors Bureaus

More questions? Try these numbers

Here is a list of the visitors bureaus that can provide additional information to help you plan your trips.

MARYLAND

➡ **Maryland Office of Tourism,** 9th Floor, 217 E. Redwood St., Baltimore, MD 21202; (800) 543-1036

➡ **Allegany County Visitors Bureau,** Harrison and Mechanic Sts., Cumberland, MD 21502; (800) 508-4748 or (301) 777-5905

➡ **Deep Creek Lake-Garrett County Promotion Council,** Garrett County Courthouse, 200 S. 3rd St., Oakland, MD 21550; (301) 334-1948

OHIO

➡ **Ohio Department of Travel and Tourism,** Box 1001, Columbus, OH 43266; (800) 282-5393

➡ **Ashtabula County Convention & Visitors Bureau,** 36 W. Walnut St., Jefferson, OH 44047; (800) 337-6746 or (216) 576-4707

➡ **Amish Country Visitors Bureau,** Box 177, Berlin, OH 44610; (330) 893-3467

➡ **Cambridge/Guernsey County Visitors & Convention Bureau,** Box 427, 2250 Southgate Parkway, Cambridge, OH 43725; (800) 933-5480 or (614) 432-2022

➡ **Canton/Stark County Convention & Visitors Bureau,** 229 Wells Ave. NW, Canton, OH 44702; (800) 533-4302 or (216) 454-1439

➡ **Greater Cleveland Convention & Visitors Bureau,** 3100 Terminal Tower, Cleveland, OH 44113; (800) 321-1001 or (216) 621-4110

➡ **Coshocton County Convention & Visitors Bureau,** Box 905, Coshocton, OH 43812; (800) 338-4724 or (614) 622-4877

➡ **Holmes County Chamber of Commerce,** 5798 CR 77, Millersburg, OH 44654; (330) 674-3975

➡ **Marietta/Washington County Convention & Visitors' Bureau,** 316 Third St., Marietta, OH 45750; (800) 288-2577 or (614) 373-5178

➡ **Portage County Convention & Visitors Bureau,** 173 S. Chillicothe Rd., Aurora, OH 44202; (800) 648-6342 or (216) 562-3373

➡ **Sandusky/Erie County Convention & Visitors Bureau,** 231 W. Washington Row, Sandusky, OH 44870; (800) 255-3743 or (419) 625-2984

➡ **Steubenville Convention & Visitors Bureau,** 501 Washington St., Steubenville, OH 43952; (614) 283-4935

➡ **Sugarcreek Tourist Bureau and Information Center,** 106 W. Main St., Sugarcreek, OH 44881; (330) 852-4113

continued on next page

GO to Visitors Bureaus

➡ **Tuscarawas County Convention & Visitors Bureau,** 125 McDonald Dr. SW, New Philadelphia, OH 44663; (800) 527-3387 or (330) 339-5453

➡ **Wayne County Visitors and Convention Bureau,** 377 W. Liberty St., Wooster, OH 44691; (800) 362-6474 or (330) 264-1800

➡ **Youngstown/Mahoning County Convention & Visitors Bureau,** 101 City Center One, Youngstown, OH 44503; (800) 447-8201 or (330) 747-8200

PENNSYLVANIA

➡ **Pennsylvania Office of Travel and Tourism,** Rm. 453, Forum Bldg., Harrisburg, PA 17120; (800) 847-4872

➡ **Allegheny Mountains Convention & Visitors Bureau** (Blair County), Logan Valley Mall, Rt. 220 & Goods Lane, Altoona, PA 16602; (800) 84 ALTOONA (800-842-5866) or (814) 943-4183

➡ **Allegheny National Forest Vacation Bureau** (McKean County), 10 E. Warren Rd., Custer City, PA 16725; (814) 368-9370

➡ **Armstrong County Tourist Bureau,** 402 Market St., Kittanning, PA 16201; (412) 548-3226

➡ **Beaver County Tourist Promotion Agency,** 215B 9th St., Monaca, PA 15061; (800) 564-5009

➡ **Bedford County Conference & Visitors Bureau,** 141 S. Juliana St., Bedford, PA 15522; (800) 765-3331 or (814) 623-1771

➡ **Brookville Area Chamber of Commerce,** 70 Pickering St., Brookville, PA 15825; (814) 849-8448

➡ **Butler County Chamber of Commerce,** 100 N. Main St., Butler, PA 16003; (412) 283-2222

➡ **Cambria County Tourist Council Inc.,** 111 Market St., Johnstown, PA 15901; (800) 237-8590 or (814) 536-7993

➡ **Crawford County Tourist Association,** 242½ Chestnut St., Meadville, PA 16335; (800) 332-2338 or (814) 333-1258

➡ **Elk County Visitors Bureau,** Box 838, St. Marys, PA 15857; (814) 834-3723

➡ **Erie Tourist and Convention Bureau,** 1006 State St., Erie, PA 16501; (814) 454-7191

➡ **Greene County Tourist Promotion Agency,** 93 E. High St., Waynesburg, PA 15370; (412) 627-TOUR (8687)

➡ **Indiana County Tourist Bureau Inc.,** 1019 Philadelphia St., Indiana, PA 15701; (412) 463-7505

➡ **Greater Johnstown/Cambria County Visitors Bureau,** 111 Market St., Johnstown, PA 15901; (814) 536-7993

➡ **Laurel Highlands Visitors Bureau** (Fayette, Somerset and Westmoreland counties), 120 E. Main St., Ligonier, PA 15658; (800) 925-7669 or (412) 238-5661

➡ **Lawrence County Chamber of Commerce,** Shenango St. Station, 138 W. Washington St., New Castle, PA 16101; (412) 654-5593

➡ **Magic Forests Visitors Bureau** (Clarion, Clearfield and Jefferson counties), 175 Main St., Brookville, PA 15825; (800) 348-9393 or (814) 849-5197

continued on next page

GO to Visitors Bureaus

➡ **Mercer County Convention & Visitors Bureau,** 835 Perry Hwy., Mercer, PA 16137; (800) 637-2370 or (412) 748-5315

➡ **Northern Allegheny Vacation Region** (Forest and Warren counties), Box 608, Tionesta, PA 16353; (800) 624-7802 or (814) 354-6332

➡ **Punxsutawney Chamber of Commerce,** 124 W. Mahoning St., Punxsutawney, PA 15767; (800) 752-PHIL (7445) or (814) 938-7700

➡ **Washington County Tourism,** 1500 W. Chestnut St., Washington, PA 15301; (800) 531-4114 or (412) 228-5520

WEST VIRGINIA

➡ **West Virginia Division of Tourism,** 2101 Washington St. E., Charleston, WV 25305; (800) 225-5982

➡ **Bridgeport/Clarksburg Convention and Visitors Bureau,** 158 Thompson Dr., Bridgeport, WV 26330; (800) 368-4324 or (304) 842-7272

➡ **Buckhannon County Convention & Visitors Bureau,** Box 431, Buckhannon, WV 26201; (304) 472-1722

➡ **Harrison County Chamber of Commerce,** 348 W. Main St., Clarksburgh, WV 26302; (304) 624-6331

➡ **Lewis County Convention & Visitors Bureau,** 345 Center Ave., Weston, WV 26452; (304) 269-7328

➡ **Marion County Convention & Visitors Bureau,** 110 Adams St., Fairmont, WV 26554; (800) 834-7365 or (304) 368-1123

➡ **Potomac Highlands Travel Council** (13 counties in eastern W.Va.), 1200 Harrison Ave., Suite A, Elkins, WV 26241; (304) 636-8400

➡ **Preston County Convention & Visitors Bureau,** Box 860, Arthurdale, WV 26520; (304) 864-4601

➡ **Randolph County Convention & Visitors Bureau,** 200 Executive Plaza, Elkins, WV 26241; (800) 422-3304 or (304) 636-2717

➡ **Tucker County Convention & Visitors Bureau,** Box 565, Davis, WV 26260; (800) 782-2775 or (304) 259-5315

➡ **Wheeling Convention & Visitors Bureau,** 1310 Market St., Wheeling, WV 26003; (800) 828-3097 or (304) 233-7709

GO

WEST

GO to W. Va. Panhandle

The Mansion Museum, built about 1835, in Wheeling's Oglebay Park.
COURTESY OF WEST VIRGINIA DIVISION OF TOURISM

W.Va. Panhandle

BEAUTY CARVED BY THE OHIO RIVER

West Virginia's northern panhandle packs a wide range of attractions into the magnificent folds of its rolling landscape. In the early 1800s the Ohio River drew settlers and industry to the region, spawning towns like Wellsburg, Wheeling and nearby East Liverpool, Ohio, which became big names in the world of business and transportation. Today, reminders of those glory days remain.

It's possible to see the major sights outlined here on a leisurely two-day trip. Heading west from Pittsburgh, Route 30 leads to the northern edge of the panhandle, where the vestiges of a once-thriving pottery industry can still be seen. From there, Route 2 follows the Ohio River as it carves the West Virginia-Ohio border from north to south. The scenic byway showcases the life and times of the panhandle as it links together town and country. Along the way are splendid parklands and historic towns studded with Victorian-era gems. You

GO to W. Va. Panhandle

can view the largest prehistoric conical burial mound in the Americas and end up in the infamous West Virginia Penitentiary, though going in is purely voluntary. On Saturday nights keep the radio tuned to Wheeling's WWVA — or drop by in person — for the nationally known Country Jamboree.

RACCOON CREEK STATE PARK

Before crossing into West Virginia, a couple of spots in Pennsylvania are of interest.

Raccoon Creek State Park lies about 30 miles west of Pittsburgh off Route 18 and sports a lake, beach with bathhouse, boat rentals, 160 campsites and 10 modern cottages. Hiking trails wind through its 8,000 acres. In the 1800s, Frankfort Mineral Springs, a popular summer resort at the park's southern boundary, drew visitors from the tri-state area to its warm waters. All that remains of the resort is a dilapidated carriage house and the foundation of a once-grand hotel. But park personnel lead guided walks to the springs in summer and fall and recount its history. (No soaking or swimming allowed.)

A wildflower reserve that usually blossoms after mid-April is opposite Raccoon Creek park. Rangers lead guided walks on more than four miles of paths off Route 30.

EAST LIVERPOOL

In 1839 English immigrant James Bennet discovered that the clay in and around the northern part of West Virginia and eastern Ohio was ideal for making a kind of pottery known as yellow ware. Bennet stayed in the area only a few years, but his finding spawned an industry that would make East Liverpool, Ohio, just across the Ohio River from West Virginia, "America's Crockery City." Besides clay, two other necessary ingredients to fuel an industry existed here: coal to fire the kilns and a river to transport the finished goods to market. An influx of English immigrants arrived, including experienced potters from the Staffordshire district, and potteries rose along both sides of the river. The expansion of the railroad later in the 1800s, along with technical innovations in the potteries, further propelled the industry.

Between 1870 and 1910, more than 200 potteries in the area were cranking out 80 percent of the nation's pottery. East Liverpool's population grew from 2,000 to 20,000 residents, and 95 percent of those who worked were employed in the potteries. But when the industry began to decline in the 1920s and 1930s, mainly due to stiff competition from imports, this one-industry town lost many of its residents.

An excellent retrospective of the region's contribution to the art is in East Liverpool's Museum of Ceramics, housed in the former 1909 post office at Fifth and Broadway.

GO to W. Va. Panhandle

Prabhupada's Palace of Gold, a Hare Krishna shrine located near Moundsville.
COURTESY OF WEST VIRGINIA DIVISION OF TOURISM

The elegant building, with its solid-oak trim, ornately decorated domed ceilings and marble-and-terrazzo floor, is worth a visit, even if you don't go through all the exhibits.

The ceramic displays include an extensive array of wares produced by East Liverpool potteries in their heyday, as well as dioramas showing how ceramics were created. The collection encompasses utilitarian and art ware, including the region's famous yellow ware. Also showcased is the largest public collection of Lotus Ware, which was produced by Knowles, Taylor and Knowles for only a few years in the 1890s. Noted for its pure-white lustrous finish, graceful shapes, and fine detailing, Lotus Ware is considered by some to be the finest bone china ever produced in the United States.

HOMER LAUGHLIN

Today, only four potteries remain. The largest and best-known is Homer Laughlin China Co. in Newell, W.Va., across the river a few miles down Route 2 from East Liverpool. Laughlin is the maker of Fiesta, the brightly colored dinnerware first introduced in 1939 and sold exclusively by Woolworth's. It was reissued for the company's 1979 centennial and found a new generation of fans. Visitors can tour the plant, which claims to be the country's largest manufacturer of dinnerware. It reportedly has produced a third of all the dishes that have ever been sold in

GO to W. Va. Panhandle

The Winter Festival of Lights draws thousands of visitors to Oglebay Park in Wheeling. COURTESY OF OGLEBAY PARK

the United States. A factory outlet store is part of the Laughlin plant that stretches along the banks of the Ohio River. Some factory seconds can be had at a discount, but prices on first-quality dishware are the same as in retail stores. A slide presentation and guided tours are offered Monday through Friday.

TOMLINSON RUN STATE PARK

Twenty minutes south of Newell on Route 2 is Tomlinson Run State Park. Its 1,400 acres encompass rugged woodlands and a 29-acre lake. There's also camping, hiking, fishing, rental rowboats and a swimming pool with a water slide. Cold winter days draw skaters to the lake.

STEUBENVILLE, OHIO

South of the park, Route 2 leads to Route 22 and the turnoff to Steubenville, Ohio. A short detour back over the Ohio River into Steubenville leads to the wall paintings the city derives its "City of Murals" slogan from. These giant paintings of historical subjects were started in 1986 as an ambitious downtown revitalization project in the area of Market and Fourth streets. The scenes depict early life in this small city and include such images as an 1880s riverboat, the town's first railroad station, and a street scene circa 1890. There are now more than two dozen murals attracting hundreds of bus tours during summer months.

GO to W. Va. Panhandle

Historic sights in town include the reconstructed Old Fort Steuben, a 1787 territorial fort and the original log structure of the First Federal Land Office.

WELLSBURG

Crossing back into West Virginia, it's just a short hop south along the Ohio River on Route 2 to Wellsburg. In the early 19th century, Wellsburg rivaled Wheeling in commercial river traffic and warehousing. It's considerably sleepier today. But the riverfront still hosts high-rolling riverboats, namely, the Mississippi Queen, Delta Queen, and American Queen passenger cruise boats, which occasionally visit the downtown wharf during the sailing season. The town has a small but interesting National Historic District with a few riverfront shops, restaurants and park.

BETHANY

Just south of Wellsburg, Route 67 heads southeast to the picture-postcard college town of Bethany and its fine collection of historic buildings. The centerpiece here is Old Main on the Bethany College campus. The 1858 building, with its 122-foot tower, is one the earliest examples of collegiate Gothic architecture in the United States and is a National Historic Landmark.

Bethany College was chartered in 1840 as a liberal arts school by Scottish immigrant Alexander Campbell, a principal founder of Christian churches at the time. Campbell's 24-room mansion, ¾ mile east of the campus on Route 67, is now a museum with period rooms from the early 1800s. A smokehouse is also on the grounds and the family cemetery is nearby.

From Bethany, Route 88 is a lovely drive through hilly farmland. It leads south into Oglebay Resort Park.

OGLEBAY PARK

In the late 1800s, Earl W. Oglebay made a lot of money in Wheeling banking. Then he made tons more money in an ore-shipping company in Cleveland. But he and his family regularly returned to West Virginia, spending summers at his pied-a-terre in the hills outside Wheeling. Today, his stately yellow mansion remains a monument to the virtues of capitalism. The house is a centerpiece of Oglebay Resort Park and is open for tours. Each room has a recorded explanation of the furnishings and styles used. An interesting display of family artifacts and genealogy are also inside.

When Oglebay died in the late 1920s, he left his farm to the city. Wheeling has since added amusements that Oglebay, rich as he was, probably never considered. The park is now one of Wheeling's most elegant and amusing spots. On its 1,500 wooded acres are three golf courses, an outdoor swimming pool, tennis courts, a zoo, and fishing and boating on a small lake. There's also

GO to W. Va. Panhandle

the 204-room Wilson Lodge, with an indoor pool and a dining room overlooking the park. Some family vacation cottages are available for weekly rentals.

Also in the park is the Carriage House Glass Museum, housing a large collection of glass produced in the valley between 1817 and 1939. Glassblowing artisans are often at work.

WHEELING

From Oglebay, Route 88 winds its way into Wheeling, where one of the landmark structures is the suspension bridge spanning the Ohio River. It is considered by many to be the most important pre-Civil War engineering structure in the United States. A few blocks from downtown, the city's historic district includes two authentically restored open-market buildings that house dozens of specialty shops, an antiques mall and restaurants. The area is listed on the National Register of Historic Places.

In 1996, the Wheeling Artisan Center opened in the former Gee Electric Building at 14th and Main streets. The renovation includes a three-story atrium and skylight. A micro-brewery and the Nail City Restaurant occupy the first floor. The second floor houses craft and gift shops, historical exhibits and Wymer's General Store. The integration of historical displays and shops is meant to emphasize quality crafts produced in the Ohio River

COURTESY OF WEST VIRGINIA DIVISION OF TOURISM
The Wells Inn, built in 1894 in Sisterville.

GO to W. Va. Panhandle

Valley. One shop features crafts that have been judged as "the best of West Virginia." The general store museum offers a glimpse at a mercantile typical of the late 1800s.

In Wheeling's downtown area are more than 100 mansions and townhouses representing each decade of the Victorian era. Some are open for guided tours. Monroe Street East is a good place to begin a tour of these architectural gems.

Wheeling is also a river town, and the city's shoreline along the Ohio includes a four-mile trail popular with walkers, runners and cyclists.

But the city's attractions are aural as well as visual. On Saturday nights for the past 60 years, country music fans have flocked to the Capitol Music Hall for Jamboree USA. Radio WWVA broadcasts the weekly performances of top-name entertainers in one of the longest-running country music shows in the nation.

MOUNDSVILLE

Twelve miles south of Wheeling on Route 2 is the town of Moundsville, named after the largest and probably the most famous of the Adena Indian burial mounds. Constructed in successive stages from about 250 to 150 B.C., the mound required the movement of more than 60,000 tons of earth. Today, the seven-acre site constitutes Grave Creek Mound State Park. In 1838, excavations uncovered two burial chambers and prehistoric artifacts that are showcased adjacent to the burial mound in the Delf Norona Museum.

Surrounding the park on three sides is typical modern-day housing. On the other side, along Jefferson Avenue, is the notorious West Virginia Penitentiary. Calling the place a "horrible dungeon," the state Supreme Court in 1988 ordered the closure of the Civil-War era penitentiary on Moundsville's main street.

The stone-walled, maximum-security prison built by convicts in 1866 anchored the southern end of town like a medieval fortress. Its history was the town's history. During the 1930s townspeople watched hangings from bleachers on Eighth Street. After the prison was closed, residents who missed the pen's $8 million annual budget turned it into a tourist attraction, offering $5 tours between April and December.

On view are the unheated, double-bunk cells, no bigger than a closet, and the gallows and electric chair that took the lives of 94 inmates between 1899 and 1954.

PALACE OF GOLD

If you aspire to a higher consciousness than prison life — at least in the sightseeing realm — visit the Hare Krishna's golden palace tucked away in the hills of the panhandle. To find Prabhupada's Palace of Gold follow Route 250 out of Moundsville for eight miles over rolling pastoral hills

GO to W. Va. Panhandle

and watch for a "Palace of Gold" sign and a marker indicating Route 44 (Limestone Hill Road). The path leads into the Krishna palace built in the 1980s.

The palace is a gold and marble gem that sparkles like a diamond in a haystack amid the endless hills. It is a memorial to A.C. Bhaktivedanta Swami Prabhupada, who brought the Krishna movement to North America. The palace has 10 rooms elaborately decorated with more than 40 varieties of imported marble and onyx. Surrounding the palace are temple gardens and more than 100 fountains. Tours are offered by resident devotees.

COURTESY OF WEST VIRGINIA DIVISION OF TOURISM
The Capitol Music Hall, home of the long-running Saturday night Jamboree USA.

SISTERSVILLE

After retracing your course back to Route 2, you can extend the trip another 30 minutes south following the Ohio River past New Martinsville to Sistersville. The once rowdy turn-of-the-century oil boomtown is home to the 1894 Wells Inn, a longtime favorite gathering place for visitors and residents. It has recently undergone a restoration and facilities include 32 guest rooms, a restaurant and an indoor pool.

Maps outlining a self-guided walking tour of Sistersville are available at the city hall on Diamond Street. Also, from April to November the Sistersville car ferry transports cars and passengers across the Ohio River into Ohio.

GO to W. Va. Panhandle

West Virginia panhandle

THE ROUTE

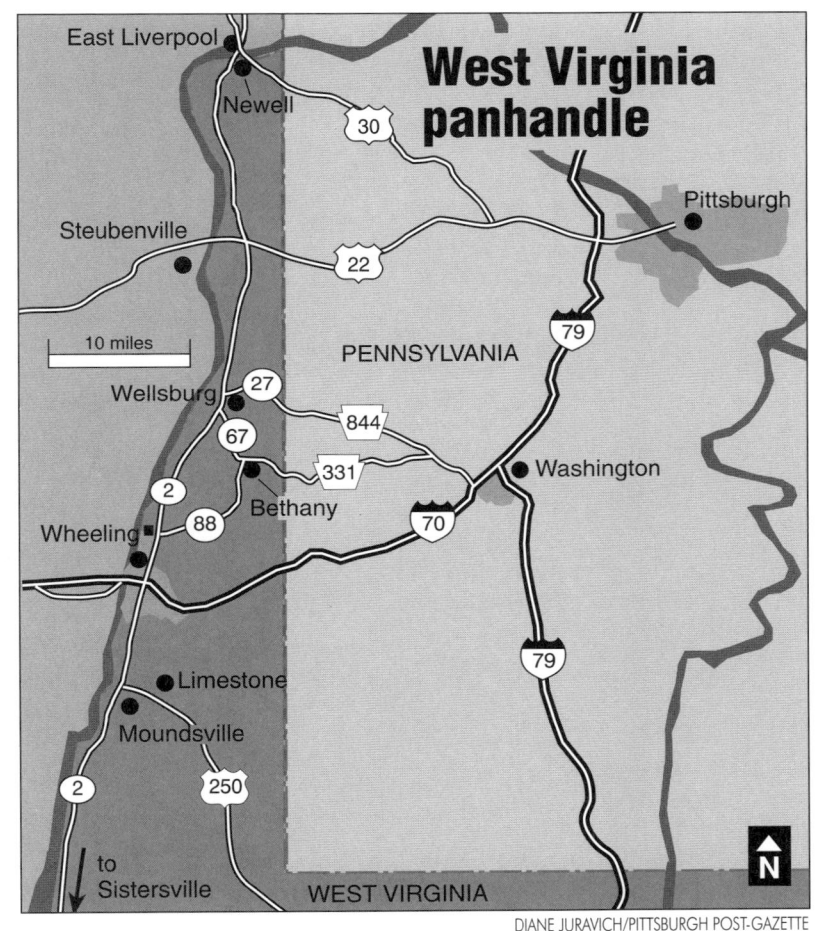

Take Rt. 22/30 west to Rt. 30 west to Newell and East Liverpool, then follow Rt. 2 south to Wellsburg. To go to Bethany, take Rt. 67 southeast, then follow Rt. 88 to Wheeling. In Wheeling pick up Rt. 40 west to I-70 west to exit 1B for Rt. 250/Rt. 2 south to Moundsville. From Moundsville, Rt. 250 and then Rt. 44 lead to the Palace of Gold. Returning to Moundsville, Rt. 2 follows the Ohio River to Sistersville. For a direct route from Pittsburgh to Wheeling that avoids the upper portion of the panhandle take I-70 west. **Round-trip mileage: 250**

GO to W. Va. Panhandle

MORE INFORMATION

→ **West Virginia Division of Tourism,** 2101 Washington St. E., Charleston, WV 25305; (800) 225-5982

→ **Wheeling Convention & Visitors Bureau,** 1310 Market St., Wheeling, WV 26003; (800) 828-3097 or (304) 233-7709

→ **Steubenville Convention & Visitors Bureau,** 501 Washington St., Steubenville, OH 43952; (614) 283-4935

THINGS TO DO, PLACES TO SEE

→ **Raccoon Creek State Park,** Rt. 18, Hookstown, PA; (412) 899-2200. Hours: office, 8—4 Mon.—Fri. Pittsburgh's closest state park has lake w/ beach, camping, 10 family cabins for rent, plus nearby wildflower reserve w/ guided walks mid-April—May.

→ **The Museum of Ceramics,** 400 E. 5th St., East Liverpool, OH; (330) 386-6001. Hours: Mar.—Nov., 9:30—5 Wed.—Sat., 12—5 Sun. and holidays. Admission: $3, adults; $2.40, seniors; $1, age 6—12. Displays of regional pottery that made the area famous in the late 1800s. Housed in a 1909 post office listed on the National Register of Historic Places.

→ **Tri-State Black Museum,** 1102 Pennsylvania Ave., East Liverpool, OH; (330) 386-5058. Hours: Memorial Day — Labor Day, 10:30—5 Thurs.—Sat. Tours by appointment. Commemorates achievements of African-Americans.

→ **Pottery City Antique Mall,** 409 Washington St., East Liverpool, OH; (800) 380-6933 or (330) 385-6933. Hours: 10—6 Mon.—Sat.; 12—6 Sun. More than 200 dealers.

→ **Wellsville River Museum,** 1032 Riverside Ave., Wellsville, OH (5 miles south of East Liverpool on Rt. 7); (330) 532-1018. Hours: Memorial Day—Sept., 1—5 Sun; also, last 2 weekends in Nov. and first 2 weekends in Dec. Admission: donation. Riverfront mansion with 10 rooms devoted to memorabilia from railroad and pottery industries, boats, also Civil War artifacts and more.

→ **Homer Laughlin China Co. Factory and Outlet,** Rt. 2, Newell; (304) 387-1300. Hours: 9:30—5 Mon.—Sat.; noon—5 Sun. Tours: 10:30 a.m. and 1 p.m. Mon.—Fri. Makers of Fiesta dinnerware. No discounts on retail prices, however, there usually are some seconds at half price and selection may be greater than in stores.

→ **Tomlinson Run State Park,** Rt. 2; (304) 564-3651 or (304) 564-3787. 50 campsites, swimming pool, rowboat rentals, fishing, hiking on 1,400 acres.

→ **Steubenville Murals,** mostly on 3rd, 4th, 5th streets, Steubenville, OH; (614) 282-0938. A series of 25 scenes painted on downtown walls.

→ **Wellsburg National Historic District,** downtown Wellsburga. Specialty shops, riverside park and restaurants. Buildings from the mid-1800s.

→ **Brooke County Historical Museum,** 600 Main St., Wellsburg. Hours: Apr.—Oct., 1—5 Fri. and Sun. and by appointment. Admission: donation.

GO to W. Va. Panhandle

Riverside museum contains artifacts from industry, education and pioneer life; housed in 1794 tavern and inn that once housed steamboat travelers.

➡ **Brooke Hills Playhouse,** Brooke Hills Park, Rt. 27, Wellsburg; (304) 737-3344. Hours: June—mid-Aug. Community theater stages productions Thurs.—Sun. Admission: varies. Reservations requested.

➡ **Brooke Glass Co.,** 6th & Yankee St., Wellsburg; (304) 737-0619. Hours: free tours 10 a.m. and 2 p.m. Mon.—Fri. See molten glass, etching and finishing processes. Gift shop, 9:30—5 Mon.—Sat.

➡ **Old Main,** Bethany College, Rt. 67, Bethany; (304) 829-7285. National Historic Landmark building is one of the earliest examples of collegiate Gothic in the United States.

➡ **Campbell Mansion and Museum,** Rt. 67, Bethany; (304) 829-7285. Hours: Apr.—Oct., 10—noon, 1—4 Tues.—Sat.; 1—4 Sun. (last tour begins 1 hour before closing); also, by reservation year-round. Admission: $4; $2 ages 6—17. Late 1700s homestead with 18 period rooms.

➡ **Oglebay Resort Park,** Rt. 88, Wheeling; (800) 624-6988 or (304) 243-4000 or (888) OGLEBAY. 15,000-acre municipal park features lodge, restaurant, cabins, 3 golf courses, tennis, swimming pool, hiking, garden center, museum and zoo.

➡ **Oglebay Institute Mansion Museum,** Rt. 88, Wheeling; (304) 242-7272. Hours: 9:30—5 Mon.—Sat.; noon—5 Sun. Admission: $4.25 adults; $3.75 seniors; $3 ages 13—18; free 12 and under. Historical material and furnishings from early days of the Ohio Valley.

➡ **Carriage House Glass Museum,** Oglebay Park, Rt. 88, Wheeling; (304) 243-4058 or (304) 242-7272. Hours: 11—5 Mon.—Fri.; 9—5 Sat., Sun. Admission: $3.25 adults; $1 ages 2—17. A history and collection of glassware produced in the valley dating from the early 1800s.

➡ **Wheeling Artisan Center at Heritage Square,** 1400 Main St., Wheeling; (304) 232-1810. Hours: 11—7 Mon.—Thurs.; 11—9 Fri.—Sat.; 12—6 Sun. Craft emporium, historical and industrial exhibits, micro-brewery and restaurant. Wymer's General Store Museum guided tour, $3 charge.

➡ **Capitol Music Hall,** 1015 Main St., Wheeling; (800) 624-5456. Box office hours: 9—4:30 Mon.—Fri.; 9—9 Sat. Saturday night performances by top names in country music. Also touring Broadway shows. Call for current schedule.

➡ **Centre Market,** 22nd and Market Sts., Wheeling; (304) 234-3878. Hours: 10—6 Mon.—Thurs.; 10—7 Fri.; 10—6 Sat. Food and crafts in century-old building, the only cast-iron columned market house in the country.

➡ **Independence Hall,** 16th and Market Sts., Wheeling; (304) 238-1300. Hours: Mar.—Dec., 10—4 daily; Jan.—Feb., 10—4 Mon.—Sat. Admission: free. Former 19th-century customs house turned state capitol now serves as an art center and a showcase for the state's history; part of the Civil War Discovery Trail.

➡ **Stifel Fine Arts Center,** 1330 National Rd., Wheeling; (304) 242-7700. Hours: 9—5 Mon.—Sat.; 12:30—5 Sun. Admission: donation. Art gallery in historic home with gardens.

➡ **Grave Creek Mound State Park,** 801 Jefferson Ave., Moundsville; (304) 843-1410. Hours: 10—4:30 Mon.—Sat.; 1—5 Sun.; closed holidays. Admission: $2 adults, $1 ages 6—18. Prehistoric grave mound built in two stages between 250—150 B.C.

➡ **West Virginia Penitentiary Tours,** Jefferson Ave., Moundsville; (304) 845-6200. Hours: Apr.—Dec., 10—5 Tues.—

GO to W. Va. Panhandle

Sun. Admission: $5; free under 3 years. Tours of the now-closed W. Va. State Penitentiary.

➡ **Prabhupada's Palace of Gold,** Rt. 250 to Rt. 44, east of Moundsville; (304) 845-7039. Hours: 9—5 daily; tours by request. Admission: $5 adults; $3 ages 5—18. Constructed by the New Vrindaban Spiritual Community, the palace has 10 rooms elaborately decorated with more than 40 varieties of imported marble and onyx.

➡ **Fenton Art Glass Factory and Museum,** Williamstown; (304) 375-7772. Hours: Apr.—Dec., 8—8 Mon.—Fri.; 8—5 Sat.; 12:15—5 Sun.; Jan.—Mar., 8—5 Mon.—Sat.; 12:15—5 Sun. Tours: Mon.—Fri. 8 times a day; call for times. Admission: free. Examples of early Ohio Valley glass and a short film.

➡ **Dalzell-Viking Glass,** off Rt. 2, New Martinsville; (304) 455-2900. Hours: 9—5 Mon.—Sat.; noon—5 Sun. Handcrafted tableware and decorative glass.

ACCOMMODATIONS

➡ Numerous chain lodgings are located along I-70 around Wheeling, including **Comfort Inn** (800-221-2222) or (304-547-1380); **Days Inn** (304-547-0610); **Hampton Inn** (304-233-0440).

➡ **Drover's Inn Lodge,** 1001 Washington Pike, Wellsburg; (304) 737-0188. Rates: $50. Restored log house built in 1790 is furnished in rustic style; 5 guest rooms w/ private baths. Continental breakfast included.

➡ **Wellsburg Inn,** 816 Main St., Wellsburg; (304) 737-2751. Rate: $65 w/ breakfast. 2 guest rooms w/ private baths in historic 1886 home w/ period furnishings. River views.

➡ **Gresham House,** Rt. 88, Bethany; (304) 829-4343. Rate: $57. Near Bethany College campus. 40 motel-style rooms.

➡ **The Eckhart House,** 810 Main St., Wheeling; (304) 232-5439. Rates: $65—$90. 1892 Queen Anne bed and breakfast. 5 rooms, 3 w/ private bath.

➡ **Elmhurst Manor,** 606 Pleasant Ave., Wellsburg; (800) 584-8718 or (304) 737-3675. Rate: $69. 3 rooms w/ private bath in restored mansion.

➡ **McLure House Hotel and Conference Center,** 1200 Market St., Wheeling; (800) 862-5873 or (304) 232-0300. Rates: $58—$82. City's largest hotel, 173 rooms; downtown location. Restaurant and lounge.

➡ **Stratford Springs,** 355 Oglebay Drive, Rt. 88, Wheeling; (800) 521-8435 or (304) 233-5100. Rates: $95—$170. Several individually decorated inn-style rooms, plus 3 rooms in a former 1906 hunting lodge.

➡ **Wells Inn,** Charles St. off Rt. 2, Sistersville; (304) 652-1312. Rates: $60—$75. 35 rooms and suites in a stately 1894 hotel a few blocks from the river and the Sistersville ferry that shuttles cars to the Ohio side. Restaurant; lunch $5—$10; dinner, $12—$25.

RESTAURANTS

➡ **Drover's Inn Restaurant,** 1001 Washington Pike, Wellsburg (3 miles east of town on Rt. 27); (304) 737-0188. Hours: 5—11 Mon.—Sat.; noon—7 Sun. Mid-19th-century inn serves dinner buffet and entrees, $7.50—$11. Also, tavern w/ lighter fare and adjoining antiques shop.

➡ **Wellsburg Inn,** 816 Main St., Wellsburg; (304) 737-2751. Hours 11—9 Mon.—Thurs.; 11—10 Fri.—Sat.; 9—3 Sun. Italian and colonial American food served in historic river inn w/ river views. Lunch, $3.50—$8; dinner $6—$15.

GO to W. Va. Panhandle

→ **Nail City Brewing Company,** 1400 Main St., Wheeling; (304) 233-5330. Hours: 11 a.m.—2 a.m. Mon.—Sat.; noon—2 a.m. Sun. Micro-brewery and restaurant serving fresh-brewed beer, steaks, seafood, salads and pasta. Dinner, $6—$16.

→ **McDonald's of Elm Grove,** National Rd. & Kruger St., Wheeling; (800) 453-7391 or (304) 242-3693. Not your average McDonald's — grand piano, live entertainment and space-age decor.

→ **Stratford Springs,** Oglebay Dr., Wheeling; (800) 521-8435 or (304) 233-5100. Hours: 11:30—2 and 5—10 Mon.—Sat.; 10—2 and 4—9 Sunday. Fine dining; dinner and luncheon specials served in former Wheeling Country Club. Dinner, $12 range.

→ **Undo's Famiglia Ristorante,** 753 Main St., Wheeling; (304) 233-0560. Hours: 11:30—10 Mon.—Thurs; 11:30—11:30 Fri., Sat.; 12—9 Sun. Italian and American cuisine. Dinner, $7—$15.

→ **Undo's 12th Street Cafe,** 1200 Market St., Wheeling; (304) 232-8817. Hours: 6 a.m.—2 a.m. Italian and American food. Dinner, about $6.

BIG EVENTS

→ **Jamboree in the Hills,** 3rd weekend in July, St. Clairsville, OH (about 15 miles west of Wheeling). Outdoor, 3-day country music festival featuring dozens of top acts attracts more than 90,000 fans. (800) 624-5456 or (304) 234-0050.

→ **Applefest,** 1st full weekend in Oct., downtown Wellsburg on Charles St. Apples and entertainment. (304) 737-0801.

→ **Winter Festival of Lights/City Festival of Lights,** early Nov.—late Jan., Oglebay Park and downtown Wheeling. More than 30 giant holiday displays and 500,000 lights in a 10-mile stretch of drive-by light displays. (800) 828-3097 or (304) 233-7709 or (888) OGLEBAY.

ALSO IN THE AREA

→ **Beaver Creek State Park,** off Rt. 7, north of East Liverpool, Ohio. Pioneer village includes a log schoolhouse, cabin, blacksmith shop, covered bridge and restored lock of the 1850s-era Sandy & Beaver Canal. Hiking, fishing, horseback trails and camping on 3,038 acres; (330) 385-3091.

GO to Ohio Amish Country

Amish carriages are common sights along the roads of northeastern Ohio.

GERRY WINGENBACH

Ohio Amish Country

QUIET PEOPLE ATTRACT A LOT OF ATTENTION

Downstairs at the Kidron Town & Country Store in the heart of Ohio's Amish country, on most any weekday you'll find the noontime crowd digging into plates of hearty comfort food. Customers in work clothes and heavy boots squeeze four to a booth or hunker down solo at the old-fashioned wraparound lunch counter.

The scene could be any rural diner in America — except the fruit pies look a lot better. And many of the regulars are dressed in broad-brimmed black felt hats and sturdy dungarees and sport graying beards

GO to Ohio Amish Country

that tumble off their chins like frothy waterfalls. In the parking lot you'll see boxy black buggies parked where you'd expect cars to be, and on the back roads the rhythmic clip clop of horseshoes on asphalt sometimes overwhelms the whoosh of traffic.

As you drive through rolling farmland and tiny towns like Charm and Mt. Hope, the notion of getting lost just might strike you as a good idea. After all, this isn't ordinary farm country.

In this slice of eastern Ohio less than three hours west of Pittsburgh, dwells the largest concentration of Amish in the world. They arrived in 1808 and today number about 35,000, centered primarily in the counties of Holmes, Wayne, Tuscarawas and Coshocton. Walking along the roadways in their plain dark clothes, or sitting behind the reins of horse-drawn buggies, or tilling their fields with old-fashioned plows, they are easy to spot.

The Amish have consciously set themselves apart in appearance and lifestyle in order to maintain a distance from the mainstream world. Visitors should respect their privacy. But changing economics are causing some Amish to turn from farming, traditionally the major source of income, to retail endeavors. And as more local Amish come out of the fields and into the shops, there are more opportunities

ROBERT J. PAVUCHAK/PITTSBURGH POST-GAZETTE
In Holmes County, Ohio, the Amish live a life of sweet simplicity.

GO to Ohio Amish Country

STORE THRIVES WITH OLD WAYS

If Lehman's hardware store had responded to the whims of technological change, it might not be in business today. But more than eight decades after it opened, the sprawling store in tiny Kidron, Ohio, is thriving.

That's because Lehman's knows its customers.

The store supplies the world's largest Amish community with the indispensable. Things like butter churns, gas refrigerators and gas lights, dozens of styles of oil lamps, cleverly designed clothes-drying racks and enough other items to fill more than an acre of floor space. The inventory runs from archaic to ingenious and is sweeping enough to give the store bragging rights to being the largest supplier anywhere of nonelectrical appliances.

The Amish lifestyle varies somewhat among congregations because, unlike most churches, the Amish are not governed by a central church hierarchy. Instead, each church (usually consisting of 20 or so families in an area) is under a bishop who sets the rules. As a result, some Amish are permitted to use solar or pneumatic power; some have access to phones. One group may use only old-fashioned, flat-bottomed sad irons, while other groups are permitted to use gas-powered irons. Lehman's carries both kinds.

continued on next page

for outsiders to have contact with them. That contact should not include taking their photographs, however. The Amish believe photographic images are a sign of vanity, which goes against their religious tenets.

Strike out west on Route 30, pass Canton, Ohio, and turn south into Holmes County and you'll encounter a wealth of buying opportunities big and small, old and new. All along the back roads and main thoroughfares of Holmes County and beyond, basket weavers, wood carvers, clock makers and others ply their trade. Handmade furniture of solid cherry and oak is for sale in rambling stores in the towns and in private workshops hidden along country lanes. Old barns and prefab storage buildings heave with pottery, glassware, paintings and other collectibles. Amish women turn out intricately stitched and appliqued quilts for sale in small shops. Blacksmiths-turned-artisans bend and shape wrought iron into useful and

GO to Ohio Amish Country

In recent years, a growing number of non-Amish have begun patronizing the store. "When we started, 80 percent of our customers were Amish, so we made it our goal to have what they needed — even if it meant manufacturing our own items," said vice president of operations Galen Lehman.

Now, with many people seeking simpler ways of doing everyday tasks (not to mention the ease of buying through the store's mail-order catalog), 80 percent of the customers are non-Amish.

The Lehmans have farmed the same land in Kidron since 1928. But they didn't get into the hardware business until 1955 when Galen Lehman's father, J.E. Lehman, bought the store. Besides increasing the inventory, including adding a number of their own designs (among them a no-springs toilet paper holder and a hand-cranked apple peeler), the Lehmans expanded the building by adding an 1830 Amish barn. It was transported from 12 miles away and reassembled notched log by notched log on the site. One item they haven't added to the everyday workings of the store is a computer. Sales are rung up the old-fashioned way, and inventory is taken by hand. It isn't a matter of tradition, Lehman insists.

"It's just a matter of Dad hates computers."

➡ Lehman's, 4779 Kidron Rd., Box 41, Kidron, OH 44636; (330) 857-5757. Hours: 7—5:30 Mon.—Sat.; Thurs. until 8.

---

decorative pieces.

Despite the booming shop trade, the hard-core commercialism and gentrification that have hit parts of Lancaster County, Pennsylvania's predominant Amish area, have so far eluded Ohio's Amish lands. That doesn't mean this territory is devoid of "shoppes" or "krafts" or other surefire signs you're deep in tourist territory, however.

WALNUT CREEK

The bulk of commerce lies along Route 39 stretching from Walnut Creek west to Berlin and into Millersburg. The short stretch between Walnut Creek and Berlin (pronounced BER-lin) has more gift emporiums and furniture stores than you could possibly comb through in a long weekend. Lodgings, restaurants and tourist attractions, such as Schrock's Amish Farm and Home, and Yoder's Amish Home, are clustered around Walnut Creek.

On Thursdays, Fridays and Saturdays from June to mid-December,

GO to Ohio Amish Country

ROBERT J. PAVUCHAK/PITTSBURGH POST-GAZETTE
The bidding has begun at the Thursday Kidron Livestock Auction.

KIDRON AUCTION IS A TRADITION

If it's Thursday in Kidron, Ohio, you can count on one thing: They'll be selling livestock at the Kidron Auction.

It's been a weekly event since 1923 in this small, Wayne County farming community. The proceedings start in the morning with hay and straw sales, then move into the main auction barn, where the animals are paraded out.

The event attracts serious buyers to the arena-style barn, but even if you aren't in the market for hogs, sheep or goats, it's fun to watch.

Nationally, livestock auctions are becoming fewer and farther between, said general manager John Sprunger, whose father founded this one. The reason: There are fewer farms.

However, Sprunger is confident the Kidron Livestock Auction will be around for some time to come.

"The farmers around here are reluctant to sell," he said. "Very few farms are being developed, because once the land is gone, it's gone."

Kidron Livestock Auction, Kidron; (330) 857-2641. Hours: 10:15—4 or later, Thurs.

GO to Ohio Amish Country

the Holmes County Amish Flea Market grinds into gear on Route 39 near Walnut Creek, with 340 vendors in two massive buildings. Stalls are crammed with woodcrafts, basketry and baked goods; craft items far outnumber antiques and collectibles.

Furniture stores are concentrated in this stretch of the route, as well. One of the stores whose styles differ from most others is Schrocks' of Walnut Creek, which specializes in Shaker designs. Prices for these clean-lined, no-frills pieces range from about $450 for a three-drawer nightstand to $1,575 for a six-drawer armoire.

BERLIN

Continuing west, Route 39 leads into Berlin. A tourist boom has brought gridlock to the one-stoplight town, so during busy times of the year, it's best to find a parking spot and walk. You'll find quilt shops, a two-story antiques mall, all-purpose country stores, Amish furniture stores and gift shops galore. One unusual establishment is the Wallpaper Place, with more than 1,000 rolls of wallpaper in stock. The shop draws customers from as far away as California and Texas.

At the Village Blacksmith, in a small converted house behind Dad's Toys in the center of town, Rebecca Schrock sells wrought-iron creations made by her husband, Emanuel. He shoed horses until back problems forced him to stop. Now he makes decorative and utilitarian items like towel racks, candle holders and shoe scrapers.

Rastetter Woolen Mill, on Route 39, a mile west of Berlin, offers brief demonstrations on how wool is processed. Amish weavers work on traditional looms in the back of the store. Rugs and throws are made and sold here, along with wool by the yard, socks and lanolin soap.

MILLERSBURG

About eight miles west of Berlin, Route 39 enters Millersburg, the Holmes County seat. It's an attractive little town with a pleasant courthouse square and a number of historic buildings. Among them is the Victorian House, a Queen Anne Victorian now owned by the county historical society and considered by many to be Ohio's finest historical house. Built by a Cleveland industrialist in 1902 for his large family, the home became a sanitarium five years later. In 1909 it sold again to a local businessman, whose offspring occupied the house until 1971. Now all 28 rooms are open for self-guided tours. Millersburg also has a number of antiques shops, many of them clustered along West Jackson Street.

DOUGHTY VALLEY

Beyond Route 39 lie small towns where decades-old businesses cater to Amish and non-Amish alike.

GO to Ohio Amish Country

Country lanes where craftsmen and farmers sell the fruits of their labor crisscross the territory. And the rolling farmland with its tidy fields, red barns, white wooden farmhouses and lines of laundry flapping in the breeze is so pastoral you'd swear you were looking at a painting.

Some of the prettiest land lies in the Doughty Valley, southeast of Millersburg and west of the village of Charm. There's also a good bit of business taking place here. Driving on and around County Road 19, you'll see signs nailed to trees indicating a staggering amount of specialization. One place sells cedar chests. Another has tarpaulins. Others offer porch swings, harnesses, pressed cider or seasonal produce.

Typical of these home-based craftsmen are Noah Raber and his daughter, Lydia, who work out of a small shop next to the family farmhouse at 5781 CR 19. Raber makes whimsical wooden toys and sells them for reasonable prices. (A large Noah's ark with 12 pairs of animals is about $60, for example; toy wagons are about $20.) He also crafts utilitarian objects like mail holders, which Lydia Raber decorates with oil-painted flowers, birds and butterflies.

In a workshop behind their house near Baltic (south of Charm), former mechanic Mose Miller and his wife, Anna, work amid the chimes and gongs and hypnotic ticktock of dozens of clocks. They are beautifully made in an adjoining workshop and sell for bargain prices. Grandfather clocks are priced from $1,250 to $1,650; wall clocks are around $205; small wooden desk clocks go for under $20.

The back roads also are home to small, independent furniture workshops operated by Amish men who build quality furniture using hydraulically powered equipment. Serious buyers are generally welcome, though the merely curious aren't always. "I need customers, but I don't want browsers," said one craftsman.

But most establishments in Amish country welcome visitors, even if they're just looking.

MT. HOPE

The homespun art of quilting is a cottage industry in these parts. And at some shops the public is welcome to watch women quilting at certain times of the month. Just north of the small community of Mt. Hope on CR 77, Lone Star Quilts sells more quilting supplies than finished quilts — a tipoff that most of the clientele is local. In Berlin, Amish quilters demonstrate their skills at the Helping Hands Quilt Shop on the first and last Tuesdays and the second Saturday of the month.

CHARM

In Charm, population 125 or so, Amanda Miller sells quilts and the supplies to make them from two buildings on Route 557 that make up Miller's Dry Goods. The merchandise ranges from quilted key chains ($1.75) to small tumbling block quilts ($165) to queen-size appliqued quilts (about $900). Amish women gather to quilt at the shop on the first and second Tuesday and the second Friday of the month.

Across the road from Miller's place is the Charm Harness Shop, which keeps local residents supplied with Red Wing shoes, sponges and broadhead horse collars in an ages-old building that smells of rich leather.

Also in the Doughty Valley is Guggisberg Cheese, one of more than a dozen cheese factories in Amish country. Historically, cheese making has been a thriving industry in the area, though the number of factories has actually decreased over the years.

Guggisberg has been run by the same Swiss family for decades. Margaret Guggisberg and her late husband, Alfred, arrived in Ohio in 1948, lured by a help-wanted ad for a cheese maker at one of the region's 32 cheese houses. They later moved to the Doughty Valley and in 1972 bought the factory that now bears the family name. The Guiggisbergs have since expanded their Doughty Valley enterprises with the

ROBERT J. PAVUCHAK/PITTSBURGH POST-GAZETTE
Flags and architecture add a European look to the Doughty Valley. These chalet-style buildings house Guggisberg Cheese.

GO to Ohio Amish Country

Swiss-styled Chalet in the Valley restaurant (featuring schnitzel, polka music and waitresses in bodice-gripping uniforms) and the Guggisberg Swiss Inn next door.

FREDERICKSBURG

North of the Doughty Valley in the little town of Fredericksburg (just over the Wayne County line), Esther Miller's homemade noodle business is growing. She started out small in 1973 making the product she knew best: old-fashioned egg noodles. More recently, Miller discovered flavored pasta and now has branched into spinach, tomato-basil and garlic-parsley flavored pasta, plus sauces and mustards. Despite expansion, the noodle factory remains a family-run operation based in a former home.

KIDRON

Another family enterprise is in Kidron, also in Wayne County, just south of Route 30. Here Lehman's hardware store does a booming business by catering to Amish needs. Though it still counts local Amish families among its best customers, an increasing number of non-Amish frequent the store. And that gives operations vice president

GERRY WINGENBACH
The beautiful scenery and the local traditions produce scenes worthy of a postcard.

GO to Ohio Amish Country

Galen Lehman some misgivings.

"I wish that we weren't as commercial as we are," he said. "In the fall, there are many more non-Amish than Amish, and I don't quite know how to make it stop. I'd hate to see what is a farming community turn into an Amish amusement park or a housing development."

SUGARCREEK

A few miles east of the heart of Amish country, the town of Sugarcreek sounds a different cultural note with its claim as the Little Switzerland of Ohio. Swiss immigrants settled here in the early 1800s and the current population, many of them descendants, are proud of that heritage. A three-block stretch of Main Street is done up like a Swiss village with chalet-style storefronts, yodeling music piped into the street and end-to-end Swiss-themed gift shops, restaurants and bakeries.

The Alpine Hills Historical Museum has tourist information on the area and interesting displays and exhibits on the town's past.

Sugarcreek also is the home of the Ohio Central Railroad, which runs excursions from May to October into Amish country. The steam railroad operated its last passenger train in 1938. The scenic rides began in 1988 with one-hour trips that reach speeds of only 15 to 20 miles per hour. The tours are narrated by knowledgeable guides like conductor Dick Marshall, a longtime schoolteacher of Ohio history. His narratives are entertaining and informative, weaving together Ohio history, railroad lore and facts on Amish traditions. Passengers have an opportunity to ask questions as the train chugs slowly through the countryside.

"A lot of the questions have to do with the Amish traditions," he said. "Those traditions are hard for us to understand because we live in a changing world."

He's right, of course, but if you pause along the rolling back roads of Ohio's Amish lands, it's easy to believe, for a while anyway, that time has stood still.

GO to Ohio Amish Country

Ohio's Amish country

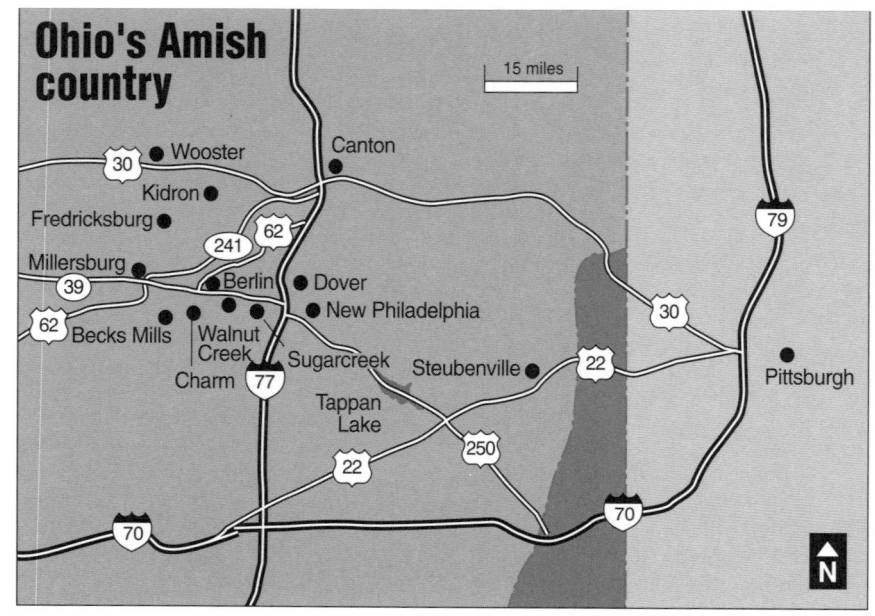

DIANE JURAVICH/PITTSBURGH POST-GAZETTE

THE ROUTE

Ohio's Amish and Mennonite population is concentrated in four northeastern counties — Holmes, Tuscarawas, Wayne and Coshocton. Rt. 30 west from Pittsburgh is the most direct (and scenic) route. However, the two-lane road can be slow until it reaches Canton, Ohio, when it opens into four lanes. To reach the heart of Amish country, drop south from Rt. 30 onto Rt. 39, either by taking I-77 to Dover, then west on Rt. 39; or via more scenic roads like Rts. 241 or 62. The best strategy for exploring this territory is to get a detailed local map (they're available at dozens of businesses in the area) and follow the roads to wherever they lead. For an alternate route back to Pittsburgh, take Rt. 39 east through Sugarcreek and into New Philadelphia, then pick up Rt. 250, which passes scenic terrain around Tappan Lake. Follow Rt. 22 east near Cadiz back into Pennsylvania. **Approximate round-trip mileage: 250**

GO to Ohio Amish Country

MORE INFORMATION

➡ **Ohio Department of Travel and Tourism,** Box 1001, Columbus, OH 43266; (800) BUCKEYE or (800) 282-5393

➡ **Holmes County Chamber of Commerce,** 5798 CR 77, Berlin, OH 44610; (330) 674-3975

➡ **Tuscarawas County Convention and Visitors Bureau,** 125 McDonald Dr. S.W., New Philadelphia, OH 44663; (800) 527-3387 or (330) 339-5453

➡ **Wayne County Visitors and Convention Bureau,** 377 W. Liberty St., Wooster, OH 44691; (800) 362-6474 or (330) 264-1800

➡ **Coshocton County Convention & Visitors Bureau,** Box 905, Coshocton, OH 43812; (800) 338-4724 or (614) 622-4877

➡ **Sugarcreek Information Center and Museum,** 106 W. Main St., Sugarcreek, OH 44681; (330) 852-4113

➡ **Amish Country Visitors Bureau,** Box 177, Berlin, OH 44610; (330) 893-3467

THINGS TO DO, PLACES TO SEE

Most shops and many other amusements in Amish country are closed Sundays. Few stay open past 5 or 6 p.m. on other days; many restaurants close by 8 p.m. Also, a number of businesses don't accept credit cards.

BERLIN

➡ **Mennonite Information Center,** 5798 CR 77, Berlin; (330) 893-3192. Hours: 9—5 Mon.—Sat. General tourist information, plus religious and historical background of the Anabaptists recounted in a 265-foot-long mural. Admission to center: free. Admission to 30-minute tour and film: $5.50 adults; $2.50 ages 6—12.

➡ **Schrock's Amish Farm and Home,** Rt. 39, 1 mile east of Berlin; (330) 893-3232. Hours: Apr.—Oct., 10—5 Mon.—Fri.; 10—6 Sat. 45-minute guided tour of house; self-guided farm tour; buggy rides. Admission: $6 adults; $4 ages 3—12.

➡ **The Village Blacksmith,** 4782 Main St., Berlin; (330) 857-3009. Hours: 10:30—5 Mon.—Sat. Decorative and functional wrought iron items for sale.

➡ **Rastetter Woolen Mill,** 5802 Rt. 39, Millersburg (just west of Berlin); (888) 262-4411 or (330) 674-2103. Hours: 10—5 Mon.—Sat. Wool rugs, throws and more, many of them woven on the premises.

➡ **Wallpaper Place and More,** 5053 Rt. 39, Berlin; (330) 893-2529. Hours: 9—5 Mon.—Sat. More than 1,000 wallpaper patterns in stock at discount prices.

WALNUT CREEK

➡ **Yoder's Amish Home,** Rt. 515 between Walnut Creek and Trail; (330) 893-2541. Hours: mid-Apr.—Oct., 10—5 Mon.—Sat. Guided tours of 100-acre working Amish farm and 10-room house. Admission: $3.50 adults; $1.50 ages 12 and under.

GO to Ohio Amish Country

➡ **German Culture Museum,** Walnut Creek (next to post office); (330) 893-2510. Hours: early June—Oct., 12:30—4:30 Tues.—Sat. German and Swiss folk culture are highlighted in changing exhibits. Admission: donation.

➡ **Holmes County Amish Flea Market,** Rt. 39 near Walnut Creek; (330) 893-2836. Hours: Apr.—May, 9—5 Fri.—Sat.; June—mid-Dec., 9—5 Thurs.—Sat. More than 300 vendors in two buildings sell crafts, baked goods and some antiques.

➡ **Rolling Ridge Ranch,** 3961 CR 168 (northwest of Walnut Creek); (330) 893-3777. Hours: 9—one hour before sunset Mon.—Sat. View exotic animals from your car. Also, wagon rides and petting zoo. Admission: $7.50 adults; $4.50 seniors and children.

➡ **Holmes Book Bindery,** Rt. 515 (3 buildings east of Der Dutchman), Walnut Creek; (888) 894-2665 or (330) 893-3466. Hours: 7—5 Mon.—Fri.; Sat. by appointment. Master bookbinder M. Leroy Chrisman meticulously restores antiquarian books using 18th-century tools.

MILLERSBURG

➡ **Victorian House,** 484 Wooster Rd., Millersburg; (330) 674-3975. Hours: May—Oct., 1:30—4 Tues.—Sun. 28-room mansion furnished in period antiques. Admission: $3 adults; $1 ages 12—18.

DOUGHTY VALLEY

➡ **Miller's Dry Goods,** Rt. 557, Charm. Hours: 8—5 Mon.—Sat. Finished quilts and quilting supplies. Watch Amish quilters at work on the 1st and 2nd Tues. and 2nd Fri. of the month.

➡ **Hershberger Antique Mall,** Rt. 557, 3 miles east of Charm. Hours: 9—8 Mon.—Sat. Armoires, dressers, trunks and small items in two well-maintained buildings.

➡ **New Bedford Clocks,** 1439 TR 183, Baltic (south of Charm). Hours: 9—5 Mon.—Sat. Amish-made clocks in walnut, oak or cherry.

SUGAR CREEK

➡ **Ohio Central Railroad,** 111 Factory St., Sugarcreek; (330) 852-4676. Informative 1-hour narrated train rides through Amish country depart 4 times daily Mon.—Sat. May—Oct. Fare: $7 adults; $4 ages 3—12.

➡ **Alpine Hills Historical Museum,** 106 Main St., Sugarcreek; (330) 852-4113. Hours: Apr.—Nov., 10—4:30 Mon.—Sat.; July—Sept., 9—4:30 Mon.—Sat. Admission: donation. Household artifacts, a replica of a cheese house and more, show why Sugarcreek dubs itself the Little Switzerland of Ohio.

AMISH-MADE FURNITURE

Dozens of area shops sell Amish-made furniture mainly crafted in cherry and oak. Also, watch for small workshops on back roads where craftsmen take individual orders. Amish-owned stores may not have telephones; those that don't can't accept credit cards. Among the stores:

➡ **Schrocks' of Walnut Creek,** 3360 Rt. 39, Walnut Creek; (330) 893-2141. Hours: 7—5 Mon.—Fri.; 8—4 Sat. Specializes in Shaker designs.

➡ **Brookside Furniture and Woodcrafts,** 2949 Rt. 93, Sugarcreek; (330) 852-4528. Hours: summer, 9:30—6 Mon.—Sat.; closes at 5 in winter.

➡ **Ole Mill Furniture,** Rt. 557, Charm. Hours: 9—5 Mon., Tues. and Sat.; 9—8 Wed. and Fri.; 9—noon Thurs.

➡ **Farmerstown Furniture,** 3155 Rt. 557, Baltic. Hours: 10—5 Mon.—Sat. Amish-owned furniture store also sells antique hardware, caning supplies and

GO to Ohio Amish Country

cabriolet legs in a variety of sizes.

➥ **Homestead Furniture,** CR 77, Mt. Hope. Hours: 8—5 Mon.—Sat.

➥ **Eastwood Furniture,** Kidron Road, Kidron. Hours: 9—5 Mon.—Sat.

EDIBLES

Amish bakeries and cheese factories also abound in the area. Among the edible buys:

➥ **Mrs. Miller's Homemade Noodles,** 110 Crawford St., Fredericksburg; (330) 695-2393. Hours: 9—4 Mon.—Fri. Old-fashioned and flavored noodles, plus sauces.

➥ **Coblentz Chocolate,** Rt. 515, Walnut Creek; (800) 338-9341 or (330) 893-2995. Hours: June—Oct., 9—6 Mon.—Sat.; closes at 5 p.m. Nov.—May. Hand-dipped chocolates and other sweet things, including exotic fudge flavors like apple pie and blueberry cheesecake.

➥ **Guggisberg Cheese,** Rt. 557 (between Berlin and Charm); (330) 893-2500. Hours: Jan.—Mar., 8—5 Mon.—Sat.; Apr.—Dec., 8—6 Mon.—Sat.; 11—4 Sun. Claims fame as the first to develop baby Swiss cheese; plus 30 other varieties for sale.

➥ **Heini's Cheese Chalet,** CR 77 off Rt. 62, 1 mile north of Berlin; (330) 893-2131. Hours: Apr.—Nov., 8—6:30 Mon.—Sat.; Dec.—Mar., 8—5 Mon.—Sat. More than 50 varieties of cheese include all the usual kinds, plus chocolate, peanut butter and an unearthly green "moon cheese."

ACCOMMODATIONS

A number of new full-service inns and B&Bs have popped up in the past few years in the area. However, lodging can be difficult to find on summer and fall weekends; it's also wise to reserve ahead during special events. If you can't find a place in Amish country, try New Philadelphia, about 15 miles east, which has an abundance of chain motels. Closer in are:

➥ **Carlisle Village Inn,** Rt. 515, Walnut Creek; (330) 893-3636. Rates: May—Oct. $84—$167; lower other times of year. 52-room, Victorian-style inn is furnished with Amish-made pieces.

➥ **The Inn at Honey Run,** 6920 CR 203, Millersburg; (330) 674-0011. Rates: in-season, $85—$140 Sun.—Thurs. and $90—$150 weekends.; off-season, $65—$120 Mon.—Thurs. and $85—$140 weekends. (Rates higher mid-Sept.—Oct.) Contemporary country inn has accommodations in main building and in second earth-sheltered building, plus 2 guest houses in pleasant wooded setting. Some rooms w/ fireplaces, whirlpool tubs, VCRs. Restaurant on premises. Continental breakfast included in room rate.

➥ **Hotel Millersburg,** 35 W. Jackson St., Millersburg; (330) 674-1457. May—Oct., $52—$85; less other times of year. 24-room hotel in downtown Millersburg, whose oldest section dates to 1847. Suites sleep 4 or more and are a good choice for families. No elevator.

➥ **Guggisberg Swiss Inn,** Rt. 557, Charm; (330) 893-3600. Rates: $79—$84 (includes breakfast) June—Oct. Lower other times of year. Beautiful location in large, open meadow w/ swan-filled pond. 24 rooms.

➥ **Amish Country Inn,** Rts. 39 and 62, Berlin (1 mile west of Berlin); (330) 893-3000. Rates: $75—$113 weekends; $67—$105 weekdays, July—Oct.; lower other times of year. Motel-style rooms w/ nice rocker-lined porch.

Among bed and breakfasts are:

➥ **Charm Country View Inn,** Rt. 557, Charm; (330) 893-3003. Rates: $75—$110. Attractive inn set in rolling farm-

GO to Ohio Amish Country

land has 15 rooms, all w/ private bath.

➨ **Gilead's Balm Manor,** 8690 CR 201, Fredericksburg; (330) 695-3881. Rates: $125 weekdays; $165 weekends. New Tudor-style house on 5 acres w/ small private lake. 4 suites w/ Biblical names have private bath, gas fireplaces, Jacuzzi tubs and small kitchen areas.

➨ **Fields of Home Guest House,** 7278 CR 201, Millersburg (5 miles northwest of Berlin); (330) 674-7152. Rates: $65—$125. Modern log house has 4 guest rooms w/ whirlpool baths; 2 w/ gas fireplace.

RESTAURANTS

This is "Dutch" style buffet country with hearty meat-and-potatoes and dumplings fare. A sampling includes:

➨ **Homestead Restaurant,** Rt. 557, Charm; (330) 893-2717. Hours: 7 a.m.—8 p.m. Mon.—Sat. From-scratch offerings include Amish-style roast beef and country ham dinners. Daily specials, $6.

➨ **Chalet in the Valley,** Rt. 557, south of Rt. 62; (330) 893-2550. Hours: 11—7 Tues.—Thurs.; 11—8 Fri.—Sat.; 11—3 Sun. Swiss-owned restaurant specializes in Swiss and Austrian food. Menu features 4 kinds of schnitzel, plus Amish specialties. Dinner specials, $6—$8.

➨ **Boyd & Wurthmann Restaurant,** E. Main St., Berlin; (330) 893-3287. Hours: 6 a.m.—8 p.m. Mon.—Sat. Local favorite serves fresh pies and other rich desserts. Dinners, $4—$6.

➨ **Dutch Harvest Restaurant,** Rts. 39 & 62, Berlin; (330) 893-3333. Hours: 7 a.m.—8 p.m. Mon.—Sat.; 8—3 Sun. Amish-style cooking includes pan-fried chicken, ham and roast beef; meals w/ lots of fixin's, $7—$11.

➨ **Der Dutchman of Walnut Creek,** Rt. 515, just off Rt. 39; (330) 893-2981. Hours: 7 a.m.—8 p.m. Mon.—Sat. Typical Amish-style food. Dinners, $6—$8.

➨ **Dutch Valley of Sugarcreek,** Rt. 39, Sugarcreek; (330) 852-4627. Hours: 7 a.m.— 8 p.m. Mon.—Sat. Amish food in a commercial complex that includes a bakery, market and antiques mall. Dinners, $6—$9.

➨ **Beachys' Country Chalet Restaurant,** Andreas Dr. (off Main St.), Sugarcreek; (330) 852-4644. Hours: 11—10 Mon.—Sat. Amish home cooking and Swiss specialties, plus 15 kinds of pies. Dinners, $6.

BIG EVENTS

➨ **Ohio Mennonite Relief Sale,** 1st Sat. in Aug., Central Christian High School, Kidron. Pancake breakfast followed by quilt auction. Preview on Fri. night. (330) 682-4843.

➨ **Ohio Swiss Festival,** 4th Fri.—Sat. after Labor Day in Sugarcreek. Polka bands, yodeling, Swiss costume contest, schwingfest (Swiss wrestling) and the crowning of a Grand Champion Cheese Maker.

➨ **Holmes County Antique Festival,** usually the 1st weekend in Oct., Holmes County Fairgrounds, Millersburg. Antiques market, horse show, tractor pull and other contests.

ALSO IN THE AREA

➨ **Warther Carvings,** 331 Karl Ave., Dover; (330) 343-7513. Hours: Mar.—Nov. 9—5 daily; Dec.—Feb., 10—4 daily. Amazing and intricate creations by master carver Ernest Warther are displayed in museum surrounded by Swiss gardens.

➨ **Dover Antique Mall,** 416 W. 8th St., Dover; (330) 343-3336. Hours: 10—

GO to Ohio Amish Country

5 Mon.—Sat. 35 stalls housed in an old street car building. 18th- and 19th-century furniture; more antiques than collectibles.

➡ **Zoar Village,** Rt. 212, Zoar (3 miles east of I-77 off exit 93); (330) 874-3011. Hours: Memorial Day—Labor Day, 9:30—5 Wed.—Sat. and noon—5 Sun.; Apr.—Memorial Day and Oct., 9:30—5 Sat. and noon—5 Sun. Admission: $4 adults; $1 children under 12. German separatist settlement from the early 1800s is now home to 75 families, some of whom live in the original early 19th-century homes; 12-block historic district has 10 museums.

➡ **Roscoe Village,** 381 Hill St., Coshocton (19 miles west of I-77); (800) 877-1830. Hours: Apr.—June, 10—5 Sun.—Thurs. and 10—6 Fri.—Sat.; July—Labor Day, 10—8 Mon.—Sat. and 10—6 Sun.; Labor Day—Mar., 11—5 Sun.—Thurs. and 11—6 Fri.—Sat. Admission: $7.95 adults; $3.95 ages 5—12. Six-museum complex includes 19th-century houses, a blacksmith shop and 1840s canal toll house with costumed interpreters in former milling center. Admission: free to village; charge for living history tour.

➡ **Schoenbrunn Village,** 1984 E. High Ave., New Philadelphia (exit 81 off I-77); (330) 339-3636. Hours: Memorial Day—Labor Day, 9:30—5 Mon.—Sat.; noon—5 Sun. Admission: $4 adults; $1 ages 6—12. Restored 18th-century Moravian mission consists of log buildings, original cemetery and cultivated fields.

➡ **The House of Baskets,** 1202 E. High Ave., New Philadelphia (exit 81 off I-77 to 3 miles east on Bus. Rt. 250); (330) 339-2461. Hours: summer, 9—5 Mon.—Sat.; noon—5 Sun.; opens at 10 other times of year. Baskets from 39 countries and 8 states; claims largest inventory in the nation.

➡ **Riverfront Antique Mall,** 1203 Front St., New Philadelphia,; (800) 926-9806 or (330) 339-4448. Hours: 10—8 Mon.—Sat.; 10—6 Sun.; Memorial Day—Labor Day, opens 9 a.m. Ohio's largest antiques mall has 80,000 square feet of space.

➡ **Pro Football Hall of Fame,** 2121 George Halas Dr. N.W., Canton; (330) 456-8207. Hours: Memorial Day—Labor Day, 9—8 daily; 9—5 rest of year. Admission: $9 adults; $4 ages 6—14; $6 ages 62 and up. History and legends of the gridiron are enshrined in 5-building complex.

GO to Marietta, Ohio

Harmar Village, the oldest section of Marietta, was settled by Revolutionary War officers.

Marietta, Ohio

CHARMING TOWN GOES WITH THE FLOW

The days when stern-wheelers churned the muddy waters of the Ohio River delivering everything from mail to settlers ended more than a century ago. But strolling along the river on a sultry summer evening in this classic old river town is bound to conjure up images of life as it used to be.

The air has a heavy, somnolent quality. Loafers languish on the benches along the cobblestone path that meanders above the Ohio River's banks. On warm summer evenings it seems even the power boats operate in low gear.

Marietta is a river town that puts its waterways to good use. Three blocks of park land stretch along the Muskingum River, which divides Marietta in two before joining the Ohio. The original cobblestone levee on the Ohio River is a gather-

GO to Marietta, Ohio

ing spot with places to sit and watch the river roll by.

On some evenings, you'll hear live music being performed on the levee. Locals relax in lawn chairs they've toted along for the occasion, or lean back on the grass. It's a scene that brings lyrical cliches buzzing around your head like flies on a glass of lemonade. Lazy, hazy days of summer ... Summertime and the livin' is easy.

HISTORIC MARIETTA

But other, more active, diversions make Marietta an ideal spot for a quick getaway. History buffs can explore the origins of the first permanent settlement in the Northwest Territory. The city's Mound Cemetery (named for the substantial hill left by early Indian inhabitants known as the Mound Builders) claims more graves of Revolutionary War officers than any other.

The Ohio River Museum charts the ebb and flow of the golden era of river transport. A replica of a flatboat used by early settlers to haul their goods downriver is moored behind the museum. So is the original W.P. Snyder Jr., the only surviving steam-powered stern-wheel towboat, which pushed coal barges from West Virginia to Pittsburgh's steel mills.

HARMAR VILLAGE

A walkway along an old railroad bridge crosses high over the Muskingum River to Harmar Village, Marietta's oldest section. A fort was built here in 1785 at the confluence of the two rivers. Marietta was settled three years later by Revolutionary War officers who took advantage of land grants offered as payment for their wartime service.

On the original bricked streets of Harmar Village are several antiques shops and restaurants, along with a few kid-pleasing museums. One is crammed with Coca-Cola memorabilia. The newest, Harmar Station, is a model railroad museum, where more than a dozen model trains buzz around 2,000 feet of track at once. This well-regarded collection of 275 trains belongs to retired Latrobe, Pa., dentist Jack Moberg.

ROLLING ON THE RIVER

Out on the rivers, a mix of commerce and leisure pushes a steady wake shoreward. The Valley Gem stern-wheeler, a replica of an 1898 riverboat, carries sightseers along the Ohio River. On lengthier fall foliage tours, the boat cruises the Muskingum, passing through the only hand-operated lock system still operating in this country.

Marietta is an easy 2½- to three-hour drive from Pittsburgh. Heading west on I-70 you cross through West Virginia's northern panhandle in an eye blink. Ohio beckons with rolling farmland, few exits and fewer towns.

CAMBRIDGE GLASS

Fifty miles north of Marietta, where I-70 meets I-77, lies the straight-laced

GO to Marietta, Ohio

Like so many colossal collections, Butch Badgett's Coca-Cola empire began innocently enough. His family owned a carryout restaurant with a 1950s Coke cooler inside. When the place closed, Badgett salvaged the machine.

And in the words of countless collectors, "From there, it just kept going."

That was in 1981, and today, the old Coke cooler sits near the entrance of Butch's Cola Museum in Marietta's historic Harmar Village.

Over the past 1½ decades, Badgett has amassed cans, bottles, signs, trays, toys and just about every sort of Coke memorabilia there is, including products that flopped, like plastic cans and TAB Root Beer. Enough to fill a one-room museum, a seven-car garage, a carriage house and part of his own house. Badgett admits he lost track a long time ago of how many individual items he's amassed.

The collection remained under wraps for a decade. "But I had a dream that some day I would have a museum," he said, indicating the one-room exhibit space that was once a grocery store. "That it's only this size is basically a matter of resources."

In Badgett's view, Coke memorabilia is more than just packaging and paraphernalia meant to sell a simple product. Chart the history of Coke from its inception in 1886 as a cocaine-laced "elixir" to its more recent claim of being "The Real Thing," and you'll witness a parade of advertising and fashion history, not to mention a chronicle of American sensibilities.

Take the wire rack that was designed to hold two Coke bottles and hook onto a grocery cart. "Enjoy Coca-Cola while you shop," reads the sign attached to the 1940s holder. "You do that now, they'll arrest you," Badgett said.

Not at Butch's Cola Museum, they won't. Customers can help themselves to a cold drink (a Coke product, naturally) from the 1950s cooler that originally sparked Badgett's cola fervor. Payment is strictly on the honor system.

"We trust you until we know you," Badgett quipped.

➡ **Butch's Cola Museum,** 118 Maple St. (614) 376-2653. Hours: July—Aug., 10—5 Tues.—Sat.; noon—5 Sun. Call for hours during other months. Admission: 50 cents per person; $1 per family.

GO to Marietta, Ohio

little town of Cambridge, home of tidy churches, neat frame houses and a stately 1881 courthouse.

The town was a hub of glass manufacturing when Cambridge Glass Co., one of the largest glassmakers of its day, churned out decorative objects from 1902 to 1958.

In an old barn-turned-antique-shop just east of Cambridge on Route 22, owner Shirlee Bistor will gladly provide a brief history of the local glass industry by making a single circuit of the barn's dusty interior, where bottles and glasses and gewgaws are crowded onto every inch of flat surface.

"Cambridge was the first to color glass," she said. "See the flowing waves? The shell feet? Motion and color, that's what they were known for."

There were other glass companies, of course. The riverfront was full of them until competition from less-expensive imports drove them out of business.

Today, just two small enterprises, Mosser Glass and Boyd's Crystal Art Glass, operate in Cambridge. Both allow visitors a free look at the manufacturing process and a chance to buy from the factory. In addition, two museums chronicle the industry's heyday. The Cambridge Glass Museum has 5,000 pieces on display. A later company, Degenhart Paperweight & Glass, which operated from 1947 to 1978, has a museum tucked behind a BP gas station just off I-77. On display are paperweights, perfume bottles, novelties and even personalized glass gearshift knobs.

CAMBRIDGE ANTIQUES MALLS

Cambridge, population about 12,000, is thus far untouched by shopping malls, but it does have three antiques malls. Not surprisingly, they're stocked with a wealth of regional glass and pottery. They also sport a lot of cowboy memorabilia, which seems curious, until you learn this is the hometown of William Boyd, better known as '40s cowboy star Hopalong Cassidy. His image doesn't come cheap. A life-size papier-mache statue of Hopalong at one of the malls on Cambridge's main drag sold for $7,900. The town pays homage to Boyd the first weekend of May with a Hopalong Cassidy festival.

SALT FORK STATE PARK

About six miles east of the I-77 interchange on Route 22 is the entrance to Salt Fork State Park, Ohio's largest. It's a resort-style park with boating, beaches, golfing, campsites and cabins. The park also sports a handsome stone and timber lodge with cavernous fireplaces and comfortable seating ideal for settling into on chilly nights. On hot summer days most guests are content to oil up and lie around the outdoor pool.

MARIETTA RIVERFRONT

A fast 50-mile trek south on I-77

GO to Marietta, Ohio

The Valley Gem stern-wheeler, a replica of an 1898 riverboat, plies the Ohio River.
TONY TYE/PITTSBURGH POST-GAZETTE

leads to Marietta. The rambling development on the outskirts of downtown includes a number of budget lodgings. But a good choice for overnighters who want to soak up the river town ambience is to stay at one of several B&Bs, or at the Lafayette Hotel on the Ohio River.

The 1918 hotel has weathered several devastating floods, including one during Prohibition in which six pints of moonshine floated into the lobby. The bootleg whiskey was traced to an enterprising bellhop named "Skinny" who'd been selling the stuff at huge profits. (The discovery did explain how he was able to afford a new Ford coupe on a bellhop's salary.) The Lafayette got its liquor license — Marietta's first — in 1934, and Skinny reportedly went on to become a merchandising executive.

The hotel's public areas have undergone renovations that bring new luster to the Victorian finery. On Friday and Saturday nights in summer, a horse-drawn carriage stands ready at the entrance to take passengers on half-hour jaunts around town. Or you could opt for the hour-long narrated trolley tour that runs from April through October and cruises the tree-lined streets of the historic town.

Marietta's founders planned their town carefully. They built wide, cobbled streets, left undeveloped park land along the Muskingum River and respected the ancient Indian mounds that dot what is now Camp Tupper Park off Warren Street.

The Ohio riverfront wasn't as pleasant. Until 15 years ago or so it was a rundown area that attracted little life, said longtime resident Ethel May Noland. Now, park space, condominiums, a restaurant and several other enterprises have brought new vitality to this section of riverfront.

ANTIQUING IN MARIETTA

Downtown Marietta also has a number of good antiques shops. Among the more unusual is the aptly named Old Tool Shop at 208 Front St., where owner John Walter claims the largest collection of antique tools in the Midwest. Treasures include a $3,000 boxwood ruler, an 1875 scraper plane priced at $2,200 and lots of other functional items so valuable you wouldn't dream of actually using them.

STATELY HOMES

Architecturally, Marietta is a gem, with dozens of lovingly restored houses. The trolley tour is not only a good way to get the lay of the land, but also to hear the stories behind some of those grand old beauties. For example, Larchmont, a stately white pillared home at 524 Second St., was built for Waldo Putnam, grandson of Civil War Gen. Rufus Putnam. He planned to move here with his bride, the daughter of Tennessee's first governor. But, as the historical marker outside the house explains, Putnam's bride "couldn't give up her Southern heritage," and so the couple never moved north to Marietta. Noland puts a different spin on the story: Ohio was free territory and rather than give up her slaves, the Memphis belle stayed home.

"You had to have a dream to come here or you wouldn't have come. And those dreams are reflected in the houses," Noland said. "There are so many stories in this town. You could spend the whole day on one block."

GO to Marietta, Ohio

Map: Marietta, Ohio and surrounding area, including Salt Fork State Park, Cambridge, Bridgeport, Wheeling, Steubenville, Pittsburgh, and Parkersburg. Interstates 22, 70, 77, 79, and Route 7 are shown. Scale: 20 miles.

DIANE JURAVICH/PITTSBURGH POST-GAZETTE

THE ROUTE

Take I-79 south to I-70 west to I-77. To get to Cambridge and/or Salt Fork State Park, head north on I-77, 2 miles to Rt. 22. The park entrance is 6 miles east off Rt. 22. Turn west on Rt. 22 to get to downtown Cambridge. To go directly to Marietta, take I-77 south 50 miles to Rt. 7. For an alternate view on the way back, take Ohio Rt. 7 north from Marietta. The two-lane road hugs the Ohio River until it meets I-70 near Wheeling, W.Va.
Approximate round-trip mileage: 309.

MORE INFORMATION

➡ **Marietta Area/Washington County Tourist and Convention Bureau,** 316 3rd St., Marietta, OH, 45750; (800) 288-2577

➡ **Cambridge/Guernsey County Visitors & Convention Bureau,** Box 427, 2250 Southgate Pkwy., Cambridge, OH 43725; (800) 933-5480

GO to Marietta, Ohio

THINGS TO DO, PLACES TO SEE

MARIETTA

➡ **Ohio River Museum,** Front and St. Clair Sts.; (800) 860-0145. Hours: May—Sept., 9:30—5 Mon.—Sat. and noon—5 Sun; Mar.—Apr., 9:30—5 Wed.—Sat. and noon—5 Sun. Call for winter hours. Admission: $4 adults; $1 ages 6-12. Chronicles life in the 1800s along the Ohio River. Displays of cabin furniture, nautical gear and a 24-foot model of a sternwheel packet are inside. Moored behind the building on the Muskingum River is the W.P. Snyder Jr., the last surviving steam-powered stern-wheel towboat, and a full-sized replica of a flatboat.

➡ **Campus Martius: The Museum of the Northwest Territory,** 2nd and Washington Sts.; (800) 860-0145. Hours: same as Ohio River Museum. Admission: $4 adults; $1 ages 6—12. Highlights the 18th-century origins of Marietta and the westward settlement.

➡ **Trolley Tours of Marietta,** 127 Ohio St.; (614) 374-2233. Apr.—Oct. Call for times. Fare: $7.50 adults; $7 seniors; $5 children. Informative hour-long narrated tours of town.

➡ **The Showboat Becky Thatcher Theater and Restaurant,** 237 Front St.; (614) 373-6033. Professional summer season runs June—Aug. (daily shows beginning in July), except Sun. Call for times. Restaurant hours: 11—11 Mon.—Sat. Melodramas staged in revamped 1926 U.S. Army work boat.

➡ **The Castle,** 418 4th St.; (614) 373-4180. Hours: June—Aug., 10—4 Mon.—Fri.; 1—4 weekends. Apr.—May and Sept.—Dec., closed Tues.—Wed. Closed Jan.—Mar. except for group tours. Admission: $3.50 adults; $3 seniors; $2 students; children under 5 free. Splendid 1855 Gothic Revival house furnished w/ historical accuracy.

➡ **The Valley Gem Sternwheeler,** Washington Street Bridge and Front St.; (614) 373-7862. Sails hourly June—Aug., 1—5 Tues.—Sun. except Sat., when there's a 5:30 dinner cruise. In May and Sept., cruises depart hourly 1—4 on weekends and holidays only. Special 3-hour fall foliage tours depart on weekends in Oct. Fare: $5 adults; $3 children.

➡ **Harmar Station Historical Model Railroad Museum,** 220 Gilman St.; (614) 374-9995. Hours: 11—5 daily. Admission: $5 adults; children under 4th grade free w/ adult.

➡ Marietta boasts enough **antiques shops** to keep avid shoppers happy for a day or more. Several are located on Front St. near the river.

➡ **The Old Tool Shop,** 208 Front St., (614) 373-9973. Hours: 9—5 Mon.—Sat. Specializes in hard-to-find and antique tools.

➡ **Rossi Pasta,** 114 Greene St.; (800) 227-6774. Hours: 9—7 Mon.—Sat.; noon—5 Sun. Designer pastas, like calamari fettuccini and wild mushroom linguini made on the premises.

➡ **Fenton Art Glass Co.,** Elizabeth and Caroline Sts., Williamstown, W.Va. (across the river from Marietta); (304) 375-7772. Hours: Apr.—Dec., 8—8 Mon.—Fri.; 8—5 Sat.; noon—5 Sun. Jan.—Mar., 8—5 Mon.—Fri. Factory outlet sells seconds and discontinued designs at a discount.

CAMBRIDGE

➡ **Salt Fork State Park,** 14755 Cadiz Rd., Lore City; (800) 282-7275 or (614) 439-3521. Resort park sports large

GO to Marietta, Ohio

beach. Also, boating on the Salt Fork Reservoir (and guided boat trips if you don't have your own sails); 18-hole golf course and hiking trails. Handsome lodge has indoor and outdoor pools, tennis courts and restaurant. 212-site campground has electricity, heated showers and flush toilets; some sites wheelchair accessible. Snowmobiling in winter and horseback riding facilities nearby in summer.

➡ **Degenhart Paperweight & Glass Museum,** Highland Hill Rd. at I-77 and Rt. 22; (614) 432-2626. Hours: Apr.—Dec., 10—5 Mon.—Sat.; 1—5 Sun. Jan.—Mar., 10—5 Mon.—Fri.

➡ **Cambridge Glass Museum,** 812 Jefferson Ave.; (614) 432-3045. Hours: June—Oct., 1—4 Mon.—Sat. (closed holidays). Admission: $2.

➡ **Mosser Glass,** Rt. 22, ½ mile west of I-77; (614) 439-1827. Hours: 8—4 weekdays. One of two working glass factories in town; free tours 8:15—3 Mon.—Fri. (No tours 2nd and 3rd weeks of July and last week of Dec.)

➡ **Boyd's Crystal Art Glass,** 1203 Morton Ave.; (614) 439-2077. Hours: free tours June—Aug., 7—3:30 weekdays; 9—1 Sat. Call for hours at other times of year.

➡ Three antiques malls in town are: **Penny Court,** 637 Wheeling Ave., (614) 432-4369. Hours: 10—6 Mon.—Sat.; noon—5 Sun. **Guernsey Antique Mall,** 617 Wheeling Ave.; (614) 432-2570. Hours: 10—5 Mon.—Sat. **10th Street Antique Mall,** 127 S. 10th St.; (614) 432-3364. Hours: 10—5 Mon.—Sat.

➡ **Mouse House Antiques,** Rt. 22, 1 mile east of I-77. Open by chance.

ACCOMMODATIONS

MARIETTA

➡ Chain motels on the outskirts of downtown include **Best Western** (800-528-1234); **Econo Lodge** (800-424-4777); **Holiday Inn** (800-465-4329); and **Knights Inn** (800-526-5947).

➡ **The Lafayette Hotel,** 101 Front St.; (800) 331-9336. Rates: $65-$100. Historic lodging bills itself as a "grand riverboat era hotel." Excellent location facing the Ohio River, within walking distance of major attractions. Some rooms are a bit worn; ask for an updated one.

➡ **Larchmont B&B,** 524 2nd St.; (800) 376-9001 or (764) 376-9000. Rates: $85—$125. Greek Revival beauty built in 1824 has 4 guest rooms, including 1 suite; 2 w/ private bath; 2 others share an adjoining bath. Some rooms enter onto spacious 2nd-story porch overlooking garden.

➡ **The Buckley House B&B,** 332 Front St.; (614) 373-3080. Rates: $70—$85. An 1879 Victorian facing the Muskingum River has 3 guest rooms, all w/ private bath.

➡ **The Claire E,** 900 Gilman Ave. at Noland's Landing; (614) 374-2233. Rates: $80 per room; $120 for 3-bed suite. 115-foot stern-wheeler w/ 3 staterooms, main salon and 2 decks.

CAMBRIDGE

➡ Lodging chains in the Cambridge area include the **Best Western Cambridge** (800-528-1234); **Holiday Inn** (800-465-4329); and **Days Inn** (800-329-7466). Other options include:

➡ **Salt Fork Resort & Conference Center,** Salt Fork State Park; (614) 439-2751. Rates: May—Oct., $103. Nov.—Apr., $89 weekdays, $99 weekends. Resort amenities in a handsome stone lodge. 148 motel-style guest rooms; 54 4-room cabins sleep 6. Year-round daily rates, $125—$140; weekly rates, $625—$725.

➡ **Bogart's Bed & Breakfast,** 62 W. Main St., New Concord (8 miles west of

Cambridge); (614) 826-7439. Rates: $65 Sun.—Thurs.; $75 weekends. 1830s house has screened-in porch, deck and 4 guest rooms w/ private baths.

→ **Timberline Cabins,** 65744 Endley Rd. (about 1 mile west of Salt Fork Park off Rt. 22); (614) 432-9662. Rates: $80 a night Sun.—Thurs. w/ 2-night minimum; $85 a night weekends; $425 a week. 3 aluminum-sided cabins each sleep 8. Modern and fully equipped, including fireplace in kitchen. Guests also have use of "party barn" w/ picnic tables and fireplace.

RESTAURANTS

MARIETTA

→ **Levee House Cafe,** 127 Ohio St.; (614) 374-2233. Hours: 11:30—9:30 Mon.—Thurs.; 11:30—10 Fri.—Sat. On the Ohio River with indoor and outdoor dining. Pasta, salads and daily specials. A la carte pasta, about $7; full dinners, about $12—$14.

→ **The Gun Room Restaurant,** 1010 Front St. (in the Lafayette Hotel); (800) 331-9336. Hours: 6—2 and 5—10 Mon.—Fri.; 7:30—2 and 5—10 Sat.; 7:30 a.m.—9 p.m. Sun. "Steamboat Gothic" room decorated with a collection of 18th- and 19th-century long rifles. Traditional American food. Full dinners, $8—$19.

→ **Betsey Mills Club Dining Room,** 300 4th St., (614) 373-3804. Hours: 11—9 Mon.—Sat. Homestyle dinners in the $9 range.

CAMBRIDGE

→ **Salt Fork Resort Dining Room,** Salt Fork State Park; (614) 439-2751. Hours: 7—11 a.m.; noon—2 p.m.; 5—9 p.m. Sun.—Thurs.; 5—10 Fri.—Sat. Great views through floor-to-ceiling windows. Lunch, $4—$7; dinner, $7—$19.

→ **Hondros Restaurant and Lounge,** 828 Wheeling Ave.; (614) 439-4907. Hours: 6 a.m.—9 p.m. Mon.—Thurs.; 7 a.m.—11 p.m. Fri.—Sat.; 7—3 Sun. American food and some Greek specialties. Lunch from $4; dinner, $4—$13.

BIG EVENTS

→ **River City Blues Festival,** mid-Mar., Marietta. Music fest.

→ **Hopalong Cassidy Festival,** 1st weekend in May, Cambridge. Town pays homage to cowboy actor and native son William Boyd.

→ **Salt Fork Arts & Crafts Festival,** 2nd weekend in Aug., Salt Fork State Park. Arts and crafts sales and demonstrations.

→ **Ohio River Sternwheel Festival,** starts Fri. after Labor Day, Marietta. Weekend riverboat races.

→ **Oktoberfest,** 1st weekend in Oct., Cambridge. Traditional fall festival.

→ **Little Muskingum Fall Foliage Tour,** 2nd or 3rd weekend in Oct., depending on the foliage. Driving tour along scenic Rt. 26; small towns along the way put out the welcome mat.

ALSO IN THE AREA

→ **Blennerhassett Historical State Park** lies on an island in the Ohio River near Parkersburg, W.Va., 7 miles south of Marietta. A 20-minute ride on a sternwheeler ferries visitors from Point Park in Parkersburg to the island, site of a mansion built around 1800 by wealthy Irishman Harman Blennerhassett. Though the house burned in 1811, it has been

GO to Marietta, Ohio

rebuilt and is open for tours. Also on the island are a crafts village, an 18th-century flatboat, picnic areas and bicycle rentals. The park is open from Apr. to the last weekend in Oct. The schedule varies, so call before you go. Contact: Blennerhassett Historical State Park, 137 Juliana St., Parkersburg, WV, 26101; (800) 225-5982 or (304) 420-4800.

➥ **Lee Middleton Original Dolls,** 1301 Washington Blvd., Belpre, OH (across the river from Parkersburg); (800) 233-7479 or (614) 423-1717. Weekday tours of doll factory from Mar.—Dec.; by appointment Jan. and Feb. Call for times and availability. There's also an outlet store open 9—5 Mon.—Sat.

➥ **U.S. Forest Service 35-mile covered bridge scenic tour.** Self-guided auto tour from Marietta takes 4 to 5 hours, or break into shorter segments. For a map contact: Wayne National Forest, RR 1, Box 132, Marietta, OH, 45750; (614) 373-9055 or the Marietta CVB, 316 3rd St., Marietta, OH 45750; (800) 288-2577.

GO to State Parks

Plenty of parks for outdoor fun

State parks not only encompass some of the best of nature, they also can offer excellent travel values. Besides having day facilities, a number of parks in Pennsylvania, West Virginia, Maryland and Ohio operate cabins and lodges. Some even have resort amenities such as swimming pools, tennis and golf; others have more rustic lodgings where guests supply their own necessities. If you're up for roughing it, pitching a tent in a state park campground is an inexpensive way to get away from it all.

Following is a list of state parks that fall roughly within a 175-mile radius in the four-state area surrounding Pittsburgh. The parks are listed in alphabetical order by state with a brief description of amenities.

PENNSYLVANIA

For general information on Pennsylvania's state parks, call **(800) 63-PARKS (800-637-2757)**. (The state was to have instituted a toll-free, statewide reservations number by the fall of 1997 for all state parks facilities.)

NORTHWEST

➡ **Bendigo** (Elk County), Box A, Glen Hazel Rd., Johnsonburg 15845; (814) 965-2646. 100-acre park w/ lake, fishing, swimming pool, picnic area.

➡ **Chapman** (Warren County), RR2, Box 1610, Clarendon 16313; (814) 723-0250. 68-acre lake, beach, boat rentals, camping, fishing on 805 acres.

➡ **Clear Creek** (Jefferson County), RD1, Box 82, Sigel 15860; (814) 752-2368. River, beach and visitors center on 1,600 acres.

➡ **Cook Forest** (Forest, Clarion and Jefferson counties), Box 120, River Rd., Cooksburg 16217; (814) 744-8407. Rustic cabins, camping, horseback riding, swimming pool, visitors center, hiking, cross-country skiing on 6,600 acres.

➡ **Elk** (Elk County), c/o Bendigo State Park, Box A, Glen Hazel Rd., Johnsonburg 15845; (814) 965-2646. 3,000-acre park w/ fishing and boat launch.

➡ **Jennings** (Butler County), 2951 Prospect Rd., Slippery Rock 16057; (412) 794-6011. Environmental education center on 300 acres.

➡ **Kinzua Bridge** (McKean County), c/o Bendigo State Park, Box A, Glen Hazel Rd., Johnsonburg 15845; (814) 965-2646. Hiking, picnic, scenic railroad bridge on 300 acres.

➡ **Maurice K. Goddard** (Mercer County), 684 Lake Wilhelm Rd.,

continued on next page

GO to State Parks

Sandy Lake 16145; (412) 253-4833. 2,800-acre park (half of it lake), marina, fishing, boat rental.

➡ **Oil Creek** (Venango County), RR1, Box 207, Oil City 16301; (814) 676-5915. 7,000-acre park w/ visitors center, trails, bicycle rentals, canoeing.

➡ **Parker Dam** (Clearfield County), RD1, Box 165, Penfield 15849; (814) 765-0630. 16 rustic cabins sleep 4 to 8 w/ nearby showers and toilets, camping, beach, visitors center, boat rentals, cross-country skiing, skating on 900 acres.

➡ **Presque Isle** (Erie County), Box 8510, Erie 16505; (814) 833-7424. Popular 3,200-acre park on Lake Erie, visitors centers, beaches, marina, boat rentals, biking.

➡ **Pymatuning** (Crawford County), Box 425, Jamestown 16134; (412) 932-3141. 20 modern cabins w/ showers and toilets, camping, interpretive center, beach, marina, boat rentals on 21,000 acres.

➡ **S.B. Elliott** (Clearfield County), c/o Parker Dam State Park, RD1, Box 165, Penfield 15849; (814) 765-0630. 6 rustic cabins, visitors center on 318 acres.

SOUTHWESTERN PENNSYLVANIA

➡ **Blue Knob** (Bedford County), RD1, Box 449, Imler 16655; (814) 276-3576. Downhill skiing, horseback riding, interpretive center, swimming pool on 5,600 acres.

➡ **Canoe Creek State Park** (Blair County), RR2, Box 560, Hollidaysburg 16648; (814) 695-6807. 8 modern cabins w/ showers and toilets, visitors center, boating, fishing, beach, horseback riding on 900 acres.

➡ **Keystone** (Westmoreland County), RD2, Box 101, Derry 15627; (412) 668-2939. Modern cabins, visitors center, beach, boat rentals, fishing on 1,200 acres.

➡ **Kooser** (Somerset County), 943 Glades Pike, Somerset 15501; (814) 445-8673. Rustic cabins, interpretive center, beach, fishing on 250 acres.

➡ **Laurel Hill** (Somerset County), 1454 Laurel Hill Park Rd., Somerset 15501; (814) 445-7725. 3,900-acre park w/ interpretive center, horseback riding, beach.

➡ **Laurel Mountain** (Westmoreland County), c/o Linn Run State Park, Box 50, Rector 15677; (412) 238-6623. Downhill skiing on 493 acres; picnicking.

➡ **Laurel Ridge** (Cambria, Fayette, Westmoreland and Somerset counties), RD3, Box 246, Rockwood 15557; (412) 455-3744. Cross-country skiing, camping, hiking, fishing in 15,000-acre park.

➡ **Laurel Summit** (Westmoreland County), c/o Linn Run State Park, Box 50, Rector 15677; (412) 238-6623. Cross-country skiing on 15 acres.

➡ **Linn Run State Park** (Westmoreland County), Box 50, Rector 15677; (412) 238-6623. 10 rustic cabins, hiking on 570 acres.

➡ **McConnell's Mill** (Lawrence County), RD2, Box 16, Portersville 16051; (412) 368-8091. Historic mill, hiking on 2,550 acres.

➡ **Moraine** (Butler County), 225 Pleasant Valley Rd., Portersville 16051; (412) 368-8811. 11 modern cabins, beach, boat rentals, horseback riding, large lake set in 16,700-acre park.

➡ **Ohiopyle** (Fayette County), Box 105, Ohiopyle 15470; (412) 329-8591. River-rafting, biking, hiking, visitors center on 19,000 acres.

continued on next page

GO to State Parks

➡ **Prince Gallitzin** (Cambria County), 966 Marina Rd., Patton 16668; (814) 674-1000. 10 modern cabins sleep 6 to 8, fishing, boat rentals, lake on 6,250 acres.

➡ **Raccoon Creek** (Beaver County), 3000 Rt. 18, Hookstown 15050; (412) 899-2200. 10 modern cabins sleep 6 to 8, camping, lake, beach, boat rentals, fishing, horseback riding, visitors center on 7,570 acres.

➡ **Ryerson Station** (Greene County), RR1, Box 77, Wind Ridge 15380; (412) 428-4254. Camping, fishing, boat rentals, swimming pool on 1,160 acres.

➡ **Shawnee** (Bedford County), RR 2, Box 142B Schellsburg 15559; (814) 733-4218. Camping, interpretive center, fishing, boat rentals, beach on 3,980 acres; modern house w/ 4 bedrooms sleeps up to 8.

➡ **Yellow Creek** (Indiana County), RD1, Box 145D, Penn Run 15765; (412) 357-7913. Lake, beach, visitors center, boat rentals, fishing, cross-country skiing on 2,900 acres.

MARYLAND

Rangers from the Maryland Department of Natural Resources State Forest and Park Service offer guided hiking, canoeing, biking, wildflower and forest walks in many state parks. For information, call **(410) 974-3771**. Rental cabins are available at some state parks (reservations can be made up to a year in advance).

➡ **Big Run** (Garrett County), c/o New Germany State Park, 349 Headquarters Lane, Grantsville, 21536; (301) 895-5453. Camping, canoeing, fishing, boat launch, hiking on 300 acres.

➡ **Casselman River Bridge** (Garrett County), c/o New Germany State Park, 349 Headquarters Lane, Grantsville, 21536; (301) 895-5453. Historic stone bridge, picnicking on 4 acres.

➡ **Dans Mountain** (Allegany County), Water Station Run, Lonaconing 21539; (301) 463-5564. Hiking, fishing, Olympic-size swimming pool on 481 acres.

➡ **Deep Creek Lake Recreational Area** (Garrett County), 849 State Park Rd., Swanton 21561; (301) 387-5563. Lake, camping, boat rentals, fishing, hiking, swimming on 1,818 acres.

➡ **Fort Frederick** (Washington County), 11100 Fort Frederick Rd., Big Pool 21711; (301) 842-2155. Stone fort, camping, boat rentals, hiking on C&O canal, visitors center on 561 acres.

➡ **Greenbrier** (Washington County), 21843 National Pike, Boonsboro 21713; (301) 791-4767. Lake, beach, camping, visitors center on 1,288 acres.

➡ **Herrington Manor** (Garrett County), 222 Herrington Lane, Oakland 21550; (301) 334-9180. 20 modern cabins, boat rentals, cross-country ski rentals, hiking on 365 acres.

➡ **New Germany** (Garrett County), 349 Headquarters Lane, Grantsville 21536; (301) 895-5453. 11 modern cabins, boat rentals, swimming, hiking, cross-country skiing, visitors center on 455 acres.

➡ **Rocky Gap** (Allegany County), 12500 Pleasant Valley Rd. NE, Flintstone 21530; (301) 777-2139. 3-bedroom chalet, lake, camping, beaches, boat rental, hiking, scuba diving on 2,983 acres.

➡ **Swallow Falls** (Garrett County), 22 Herrington Lane, Oakland 21550; (301) 334-9180. Scenic waterfall, camping, fishing, hiking, cross-country skiing on 257 acres.

continued on next page

GO to State Parks

OHIO

Some Ohio state parks offer weekly cabin rentals. Most cabins have some kitchen facilities and bathrooms with showers, and include a supply of blankets, linens and towels, in addition to other amenities such as microwaves and televisions. For lodge and cabin information, call **(800) 282-7275**.

Following are a list of state parks located in eastern Ohio.

➟ **Beaver Creek** (Columbiana County), 12021 Echo Dell Rd., East Liverpool 43920; (330) 385-3091. Hiking, fishing, river, bridle trails, camping on 3,038 acres.

➟ **Cleveland Lakefront** (Cuyahoga County), 8701 Lakeshore Blvd. NE, Cleveland 44108; (216) 881-8141. Swimming, fishing, boat rentals on 617 acres on Lake Erie.

➟ **Findley** (Lorain County), 25381 Rt. 58, Wellington 44090; (216) 647-4490. Lake, swimming, camping, boat rentals, fishing, hiking on 931 acres.

➟ **Geneva** (Ashtabula County), Box 429, Padanarum Rd., Geneva 44041; (216) 466-8400. Swimming, camping, hiking on 696 acres on Lake Erie.

➟ **Guilford Lake** (Columbiana County), 6835 E. Lake Rd., Lisbon 44432; (330) 222-1712. Swimming, hiking, fishing, camping on 488 acres.

➟ **Headlands Beach** (Lake County), 9601 Headlands Rd., Mentor 44060; (216) 881-8141. Swimming, fishing, hiking on 126 acres on Lake Erie.

➟ **Jefferson Lake** (Jefferson County), RD1, Box 140, Richmond 45656; (614) 765-4459. Swimming, camping, hiking, fishing, bridle trails on 961 acres.

➟ **Lake Milton** (Mahoning County), 16801 Mahoning Ave., Lake Milton 44429; (330) 654-4989. Swimming, hiking, fishing on 2,685 acres.

➟ **Malabar Farm** (Richland County), 4050 Bromfield Rd., Lucas 44843; (419) 892-2784. Camping, lake, restaurant, fishing, hiking on 917 acres.

➟ **Mohican** (Ashland and Richland counties), 3116 Rt. 3, Loudonville, 44842; (419) 994-4290. River, camping, fishing, hiking on 1,294 acres.

➟ **Mosquito Lake** (Trumbull County), 1439 SR 305, Cortland 44410; (330) 637-2856. Swimming, camping, hiking, fishing on 11,811 acres.

➟ **Nelson Kennedy** (Portage County), c/o Punderson State Park, Box 338, Newbury 44065; (216) 564-2279. Hiking on 167 acres.

➟ **Portage Lakes** (Summit County), 5031 Manchester Rd., Akron 44319; (330) 644-2220. Camping, swimming, hiking on 3,520 acres.

➟ **Pymatuning** (Ashtabula County), Box 1000, Andover 44003; (216) 293-6329. Cabins, camping, boating, swimming, hiking, fishing on 17,500 acres.

➟ **Quail Hollow** (Stark County), 13340 Congress Lake Ave., Hartville 44632; (330) 877-6652. Hiking, bridle trails on 700 acres.

➟ **Salt Fork** (Guernsey County), 14755 Cadiz Rd., Lore City 43755; (614) 439-3121. Resort park w/ lodge, cabins, camping, lake, boat rentals, swimming, hiking, fishing on 17,229 acres.

➟ **Tinkers Creek** (Portage County), 5708 Esworthy Rd., Ravenna 44266; (330) 296-3239. Hiking, swimming, fishing on 369 acres.

➟ **West Branch** (Portage County), 5708 Esworthy Rd., Ravenna 44266; (330) 296-3239. Camping, swimming, fishing hiking, bridle trails on 8,502 acres.

continued on next page

WEST VIRGINIA

West Virginia's state park system includes a number of "resort parks" with extensive amenities such as swimming pools, spa facilities and meeting rooms for groups. For lodging information and reservations, including campground reservations statewide, phone **(800) CALL WVA (800-225-5982)**.

➡ **Audra** (Upshur County), Rt. 4, Box 564, Buckhannon 26201; (304) 457-1162. Camping, swimming (bathhouse), hiking on 355 acres.

➡ **Blackwater Falls** (Tucker County), Box 490, Davis 26260; (304) 259-5216. 55-room lodge, 25 cabins, camping, nature programs, horseback riding, river, beach on 1,688 acres.

➡ **Canaan Valley Resort** (Tucker County), HC 70, Box 330, Davis 26260; (304) 866-4121. 250-room lodge, 23 cabins, camping, downhill and cross-country skiing, golf, swimming pool, hiking in 6,015-acre National Wildlife Refuge.

➡ **Cathedral** (Preston County), Rt. 7, Box 370, Aurora 26705; (304) 735-3771. 132-acre virgin hemlock and hardwood grove w/ hiking, cross-country skiing.

➡ **Cass Scenic Railroad** (Pocahontas County), Box 107, Cass 24927; (304) 456-4300. Antique steam train tour, museum, picnicking, hiking on 1,089 acres.

➡ **Coopers Rock** (Preston County), Rt. 1, Box 270, Bruceton Mills 26525; (304) 594-1561. State's largest forest encompasses 12,713 acres w/ camping, hiking, cross-country skiing.

➡ **Grave Creek Mound** (Marshall County), Box 527, Moundsville 26041; (304) 843-1410. Museum and cultural center at site of 2,000-year-old burial mound; 7 acres.

➡ **Lost River** (Hardy County), Hwy. 67, Box 24, Mathias; (304) 897-5372. 24 cabins, horseback riding, swimming pool, hiking on 3,712 acres.

➡ **Prickett's Fort** (Marion County), Rt. 3, Box 407, Fairmont 26554; (304) 363-3030. Historic fort, living-history demonstrations, museum, boat launch on 188 acres.

➡ **Stonewall Jackson Lake** (Lewis County), Rt. 1, Box 0, Roanoke, 26423; (304) 269-0523. Camping, nature center, boat rentals, fishing, marina on 3,000 acres.

➡ **Tomlinson Run** (Hancock County), Box 97, New Manchester 26056; (304) 564-3651. Camping, boating, fishing, swimming pool on 1,398 acres.

➡ **Tygart Lake** (Taylor County), Rt. 1, Box 260, Grafton 26354; (304) 265-2320. 20-room lodge, 10 cabins, camping, 11-mile-long lake, swimming, scuba diving, boat rentals, hiking on 2,134 acres.

➡ **Valley Falls** (Marion County), Rt. 6, Box 244, Fairmont 26554; (304) 367-2719. Hiking, white-water rafting on 1,145 acres.

INDEX

A

African American Heritage Trail (Cleveland OH), **41**
Allegheny National Forest (PA), **16-17, 23, 25, 28, 146**
Allegheny Portage Railroad National Historic Site (Altoona PA), **144**
Allegheny Reservoir (Warren PA), **16-17, 21**
Allegheny River (PA), **21**
  favorite fall foliage sites, **81-82**
  riverfront greenbelt (Emlenton PA), **44**
Allegheny River Trail (Franklin PA), **50**
Altoona PA, **143-144**
  Allegheny Portage Railroad National Historic Site, **144**
  Altoona Railroaders Memorial Museum, **144**
  Horseshoe Curve National Historic Landmark, **144**
  Lakemont Park, **144**
  visitor information, **143, 146**
American Golf Hall of Fame (Foxburg PA), **45, 50**

AMISH COMMUNITIES & CULTURAL SITES
  Berlin OH, **167**
  Charm OH, **168-170**
  Coshocton County OH, **163**
  Doughty Valley (Charm OH), **167-170**
  Grantsville MD, **101-102**
  Kidron OH, **170-171**
  Mennonite Information Center (Berlin OH), **173**
  Millersburg OH, **167**
  Mount Hope OH, **168**
  New Wilmington PA, **68-69**
  Smicksburg PA, **55-56**
  Sugarcreek OH, **171**
  Walnut Creek OH, **165-167, 173-174**
  Wayne County OH, **163, 170-172**

AMUSEMENT, THEME & WATER PARKS
  Conneaut Lake Park & Hotel (Conneaut Lake PA), **9, 13**
  Geauga Lake Park (Aurora OH), **39, 41**
  Idlewild Park (Ligonier PA), **130, 140**
  Lakemont Park (Altoona PA), **144**
  Sea World of Ohio (Aurora OH), **39, 41**
  Waldameer Park (Erie PA), **4, 13**

ANTIQUES
  10th St. Antique Mall (Cambridge OH), **186**
  1806 Antiques (Jennerstown PA), **132**
  Annual Antique Flea Market (Somerset PA), **143**
  Antiques & Collectibles (Buckhannon WV), **95**
  Buckhannon Antique Mall (Buckhannon WV), **95**
  Clarion Antique Mall (Clarion PA), **65**
  Coleman House (Smicksburg PA), **55, 58, 63**
  Davis Avenue (Elkins WV), **88**
  Dover Antique Mall (Dover OH), **176-177**
  Founders Crossing (Bedford PA), **137, 141**
  Graham's Antique Mall (Ligonier PA), **140**
  Graystone Galleria (Bedford PA), **137, 141**
  Guernsey Antique Mall (Cambridge OH), **186**
  Guide to Antiques Shops in Western Pa., **77**
  Harmar Village (Marietta OH), **179**
  Hershberger Antique Mall (Charm OH), **174**
  Historic Cumberland Antique Mall (Cumberland MD), **108**
  historic district (Wheeling WV), **154-155**
  Holmes County Antique Festival (Millersburg OH), **176**
  Hotel Lincoln (Schellsburg PA), **136**
  Main Street (Schellsburg PA), **135**
  My Mother's Treasures Antique Mall (Brookville PA), **64**
  Old Tool Shop (Marietta OH), **183, 185**
  Patrick Henry Antiques (New Wilmington PA), **76**
  Penny Court (Cambridge OH), **186**
  Pottery City Antique Mall (East Liverpool OH), **158**
  Riverfront Antique Mall (New Philadelphia OH), **177**
  West Jackson Street (Millersburg OH), **167**
Armstrong County PA

GO to Find information

favorite fall foliage sites, **81-82**
visitor information, **63, 146**
Arthurdale WV **91-92**
　historic district, **91-92, 95**
　visitor information, **147**
Audra State Park (Buckhannon WV), **193**

B

Bedford County PA
　favorite fall foliage sites, **81-82**
　visitor information, **139, 146**
Bedford PA, **136-137**
　accommodations, **136, 141-142**
　downtown historic district, **137**
　Fall Foliage Festival, **80, 143**
　Fort Bedford Museum, **137, 141**
　Old Bedford Village, **137, 141**
　restaurants, **143**
　visitor information, **139, 146**
Bendigo State Park (Johnsonburg PA), **189**
Berlin OH, **167**
　accommodations, **175**
　Mennonite Information Center, **173**
　restaurants, **176**
　shops, **167**
　visitor information, **145, 173**
Bethany WV **153**
　accommodations, **160**
　Campbell Mansion and Museum, **153, 159**
　Old Main, Bethany College, **153**
Blackwater Falls State Park (Davis WV), **89, 96, 193**
Blennerhassett Historical Site (Parkersburg WV), **187-188**
Blue Knob State Park (Imler PA), **144, 190**
Bradford PA, **20**
　accommodations, **27**
　Crook Farm, **20, 26**
　Penn-Brad Historical Oil Well Park, **20, 26**
　visitor information, **25, 146**
　Zippo Family Store & Museum, **20, 26**
Brady's Bend (East Brady PA), **82**
Breezewood PA
　accommodations, **141-142**
　favorite fall foliage sites, **82**
Bridgeport WV
　visitor information, **94, 147**
Brookville PA, **58**
　accommodations, **65**
　downtown historic district, **58**
　Magic Forests Visitors Bureau, **63, 146**
　restaurants, **66**

visitor information, **63, 146**
Brownsville PA
　Nemacolin Castle, **122-123, 125**
Brush Mountain Tunnel (Frostburg MD), **104**
Buckhannon WV, **87-88**
　Audra State Park, **193**
　accommodations, **95**
　restaurants, **96**
　visitor information, **147**
Buckstown PA, **133**
Butler County
　visitor information, **76, 146**

C

C&O Canal National Historical Park (Cumberland MD), **103, 105, 108**
C&O Canal Visitors Center (Cumberland MD), **105-106, 108**
Cambridge OH, **179-181**
　accommodations, **186-187**
　Boyd's Crystal Art Glass, **181, 186**
　Cambridge Glass Museum, **181, 186**
　Degenhart Paperweight & Glass, **181, 186**
　Mosser Glass, **181, 186**
　restaurants, **187**
　visitor information, **145, 184**
Campus Martius: The Museum of the Northwest Territory (Marietta OH), **185**
Canaan Valley WV, **88-89**
　accommodations, **95**
　Canaan Valley Ski Resort, **95**
　Canaan Valley Resort State Park, **88-89, 96, 193**
　Deerfield Village, **96**
　restaurants, **96**
Canoe Creek State Park (Hollidaysburg PA), **190**
Canton OH
　Pro Football Hall of Fame, **36-37, 177**
　visitor information, **145**
Chalk Hill PA, **120-121**
　accommodations, **126**
　Farm Implement Museum, **120-121**
　Kentuck Knob, **121, 125**
　restaurants, **126**
　shops and historic buildings, **120**
　visitor information, **124, 146**
Chapman State Park (Clarendon PA), **189**
Charm OH, **167-170**
　accommodations, **175**
　Doughty Valley, **167-170**

195

GO to Find information

Cheat Lake (Morgantown WV), **99**
Cheat River (WV), **88, 90**
Clarion County PA
  favorite fall foliage sites, **81-82**
Clarion PA, **61**
  accommodations, **65**
  Clarion County Courthouse, **61**
  Main Street, **61**
  restaurants, **66**
  Sutton-Ditz House Museum and Library, **65**
  walking tour, **61, 65**
Clarion River (PA), **53, 59**
Clarksburg WV, **86-87**
  Jackson's Mill Historic Area, **87, 94**
  Stonewall Jackson Jubilee, **97**
  visitor information, **94, 147**
  Waldomore, **86, 94**
Clear Creek State Park (Sigel PA), **59, 64, 189**
Cleveland OH, **30-42**
  accommodations, **41-42**
  African American Heritage Trail, **41**
  Cleveland Lakefront State Park, **192**
  Cleveland Metroparks Zoo and RainForest, **39, 41**
  Cleveland Museum of Art, **38, 41**
  Cleveland Museum of Natural History, **38, 41**
  Cleveland Public Library, **32**
  Cuyahoga River, **30-31, 33-34**
  Flats, **34-35**
  Great Lakes Science Center, **33, 41**
  Lake View Cemetery, **39**
  Little Italy, **39**
  North Coast Harbor, **33**
  Ohio City Restoration Area, **36**
  Old Stone Church, **32**
  Public Square, **32**
  restaurants, **34-35, 39, 42**
  Rock and Roll Hall of Fame and Museum, **31, 34-35, 41**
  Severance Hall, **39**
  shopping, **32, 39**
  Steamship William G. Mather Maritime Museum, **33**
  Terminal Tower & City Center, **32**
  University Circle, **38-39**
  visitor information, **41, 145**
  Western Reserve Historical Society, **38-39**
Colton Point State Park (Wellsboro PA), **81**
Compass Inn Museum (Laughlintown PA), **131, 140**
Conemaugh River (Johnstown PA), **138**

Confluence PA
  restaurants, **126**
Conneaut Lake, PA, **9-10**
  Barbara J Stern-wheeler, **9, 13-14**
  Conneaut Lake Park & Hotel, **9, 13**
Cook Forest State Park (Cooksburg PA), **53, 59-61, 63, 189**
Cooksburg PA, **59-61**
  accommodations, **65-66**
  Cathedral National Natural Landmark, **59**
  Knox & Kane Railroad (Marienville PA), **17-18, 26, 65**
  Longfellow Trail, **59**
  restaurants, **66**
  Sawmill Center for the Arts I & II, **60, 64**
  Seneca Point, **59**
  Verna Leith Sawmill Theatre, **60**
  visitor information, **63**
Cool Springs Park (Aurora WV), **90**
Coolspring PA, **58-59**
  Coolspring General Store, **58, 64**
  Coolspring Power Museum, **58-59, 64**
Coopers Rock State Park (Morgantown WV), **99, 107, 193**
Coshocton County OH
  Amish community, **163**
  visitor information, **145, 173**
Covered Bridges (Schellsburg PA), **135**
Crawford County PA
  visitor information, **12, 146**
Cumberland MD, **104-105**
  accommodations, **109**
  Artist Co-op Gallery, **108**
  C&O Canal Boat Replica, **108**
  C&O Canal National Historical Park, **103, 105, 108**
  C&O Canal Visitors Center, **105-106, 108**
  Cumberland Theatre, **108**
  downtown walking trail, **105**
  Emmanuel Episcopal Church, **105**
  Historic Cumberland Antique Mall, **108**
  History House, **108**
  Paw Paw Tunnel, **105, 108**
  Transportation and Industrial Museum, **108**
  visitor information, **105-106, 108, 145**
  Washington Street Historic District, **105, 108**
  Western Maryland Scenic Railroad, **104-105, 108**
Custer City PA
  visitor information, **25, 146**

GO to Find information

Cuyahoga River (Cleveland OH), **30-31, 33-34**

D

Dans Mountain State Park (Lonaconing MD), **191**
Davis WV
  accommodations, **95**
  Art Company of Davis, **95**
  Blackwater Falls State Park, **89, 96, 193**
  restaurants, **96**
  Timberline Four-Seasons Resort, **95**
  visitor information, **94, 147**
  White Grass Cross Country Ski Area, **95**
Dayton PA, **56**
  Mahoning Creek Lake, **56**
  restaurants, **66**
Deep Creek Lake MD
  accommodations, **109**
  Deep Creek Lake (Garrett County MD), **99-101, 107**
  Deep Creek Lake Recreational Area (Swanton MD), **101, 107, 191**
  visitor information, **106, 145**

DISABLED, ACCESSIBLE ATTRACTIONS
  Presque Isle State Park (Erie PA), **4-5, 12-13, 190**
  Pymatuning Visitors Center (Linesville PA), **10**
  Salt Fork State Park (Lore City OH), **181, 185-186, 192**
  Shawnee State Park (Schellsburg PA), **135, 141, 191**
Dolly Sods Scenic Area (Seneca Rocks WV), **97**
Donegal PA
  accommodations, **126**
  favorite fall foliage sites, **81-82**
Doughty Valley (Charm OH), **167-170**
Dover OH
  Dover Antique Mall, **176-177**
  Warther Carvings, **176**
Drake Well Park & Museum (Titusville, PA), **47-48, 50**

E

East Brady PA
  Brady's Bend, **82**
  favorite fall foliage sites, **81-82**

East Liverpool OH **150-151**
  Museum of Ceramics, **150-151, 158**
  Tri-State Black Museum, **158**
Elk County PA
  visitor information, **25, 146**
Elk State Park (Johnsonburg PA), **189**
Elkins WV, **88**
  accommodations, **95**
  Cheat River, **88**
  Civil War auto tour, **97**
  Davis and Elkins College, **88**
  Monongahela National Forest, **88, 94, 97**
  restaurants, **96**
  visitor information, **94, 147**
  walking tour, **88, 95**
Emlenton PA, **44**
  accommodations, **51**
  visitor information, **49**
Erie PA, **2-15**
  accommodations, **14**
  Best of All Tours, **12-13**
  Bicentennial Tower, **2, 4, 12**
  Dickson Tavern, **3**
  Discovery Square, **3**
  Dobbins Landing, **2, 4**
  Erie Art Museum, **3, 12**
  Erie Civic Center, **3**
  Erie Historical Museum & Planetarium, **3, 12**
  Erie History Center, **3**
  Erie Maritime Museum, **2**
  ExpERIEnce Children's Museum, **3, 12**
  Flagship Niagara, **2, 12**
  Old Customs House, **3**
  Perry Memorial House, **3**
  Perry Monument, **12**
  Presque Isle State Park, **4-5, 12-13, 190**
  restaurants, **14-15**
  visitor information, **12, 146**
  Waldameer Park, **4, 13**
  Zoological Park and Botanical Gardens of Northwestern Pennsylvania, **4**

F

Fairmont WV
  Prickett's Fort State Park, **85-86, 94, 193**
  Valley Falls State Park, **94, 193**
  visitor information, **94, 147**
Fall Fling (Portersville PA), **78**
FALL FOLIAGE
  fall festivals, **80-81**
  favorite fall foliage sites, **81-82**

197

GO to Find information

Pennsylvania Fall Foliage Hotline, **27**, **79**
  peak times by Pennsylvania region, **79**
Fallingwater (Mill Run PA), **114-117**, **125**
Farmington PA, **118-120**
  accommodations, **125-126**
  Braddock's (Gen. John) tomb, **121**
  Fort Necessity National Battlefield, **119-120**
  Laurel Caverns, **121**, **125**
  Mount Washington Tavern, **120**
  Nemacolin Woodlands Resort, **118**, **125**
  restaurants, **119**
  visitor information, **139**, **146**
Findley State Park (Wellington OH), **192**
Flintstone MD
  Rocky Gap State Park, **108**, **191**
Fort Frederick State Park (Big Pool MD), **191**
Fort Ligonier (Ligonier PA), **130**, **140**
Fort Necessity National Battlefield (Farmington PA), **119-120**
Foxburg PA, **44-45**
  American Golf Hall of Fame, **45**, **50**
  restaurants, **52**
Franklin PA, **45-47**
  accommodations, **51**
  Allegheny River Trail, **50**
  DeBence Antique Music World, **46**, **50**
  restaurants, **52**
  Samuel Justus Recreational Trail, **50**
  visitor information, **49**
  Wild West Museum, **46-47**, **50**
Fredericksburg OH, **170**
  accommodations, **176**
Freeport PA
  favorite fall foliage sites, **81-82**
Frostburg MD, **102-104**
  accommodations, **109**
  Frostburg Depot, **104-107**
  Frostburg Museum, **107-108**
  restaurants, **110**
  Thrasher Carriage Museum, **107**

G

Garrett County MD
  visitor information, **106**, **145**
Geauga Lake Park (Aurora OH), **39**, **41**
Geneva State Park (Geneva OH), **192**
German Culture Museum (Walnut Creek OH), **174**
Grafton WV, **90-91**
  restaurants, **94**
  Tygart Lake State Park, **90-91**, **94**, **193**

Grantsville MD, **101-102**
  Amish country, **101-102**
  Big Run State Park, **101**, **191**
  Casselman River Bridge State Park, **102**, **191**
  Farmers' Market & Springs Museum, **107**
  maple sugar camps, **102**
  New Germany State Park, **101**, **107**, **191**
  Penn Alps, **102**
  Savage Reservoir, **101**
  Savage River, **101**
  Spruce Forest Artisan Village, **100**, **102**
  visitor information, **106**, **145**
Grave Creek Mound State Park (Moundsville WV), **155**, **159**, **193**
Greenbrier State Park (Boonsboro MD), **191**
Greene County PA
  visitor information, **146**
Greensburg PA, **129**
  accommodations, **142**
  Hanna's Town, **129**, **140**
  visitor information, **139**, **146**
  Westmoreland Museum of American Art, **129**, **140**
Grove City PA, **69-71**
  Grove City Factory Shops, **69-70**, **76**
  restaurants, **78**
  Wendell August Forge, **71**, **72-73**, **76**
Guilford Lake State Park (Lisbon OH), **192**

H

Harlansburg Station Transportation Museum (Harlansburg PA), **76**
Harmar Station Historical Model Railroad Museum (Marietta OH), **179**, **185**
Harmar Village (Marietta OH), **179**
Harmony PA, **73**
  Historic Harmony House Tour, **78**
  Historic Harmony Museum, **73**, **77**
  restaurants, **78**
Harrison County WV
  visitor information, **94**, **147**
Headlands Beach State Park (Mentor OH), **192**
Heart's Content National Scenic Area (Warren PA), **17**, **23**
Herrington Manor State Park (Oakland MD), **101**, **107**, **191**
Hickory Creek Wilderness (Warren PA), **23**
Hidden Valley Resort (Hidden Valley PA), **127**

Holmes County OH, **162-170**
  Amish community, **162-170**
  Holmes County Amish Flea Market (Walnut Creek OH), **167**, **174**
  shops, **164**
  visitor information, **145**, **173**
Hopwood PA, **121-122**
  restaurants, **126**
  visitor information, **139**, **146**
Horseshoe Curve National Historic Landmark (Altoona PA), **144**

Idlewild Park (Ligonier PA), **130**, **140**
Indiana PA
  favorite fall foliage sites, **81-82**
  Jimmy Stewart Museum, **81**
  visitor information, **146**

J

Jackson's Mill Historic Area (Clarksburg WV), **87**, **94**
Jamestown NY
  Jamestown Audubon Nature Center, **29**
  Lucy-Desi Museum, **22-24**
Jefferson Lake State Park (Richmond OH), **192**
Jefferson OH
  Covered Bridge Festival, **80-81**
  visitor information, **145**
Jennerstown PA, **132**
  1806 Antiques, **132**
  Green Gables Restaurant, **141**
  Jennerstown Speedway, **132**
  Mountain Playhouse, **133**, **141**
  restaurants, **143**
  Somerset Historical Center, **132-133**, **140-141**
Jennings Environmental Education Center (Slippery Rock PA), **71**, **77**
Jennings State Park (Slippery Rock PA), **189**
John G. Smick Memorial Museum (Smicksburg PA), **63**
Johnstown PA, **137-138**
  Johnstown Flood Museum, **138**, **141**
  Johnstown Flood National Memorial, **138**, **141**
  Johnstown Inclined Plane, **138**, **141**
  visitor information, **139**, **146**

K

Kane, PA, **19**
  Holgate Factory Toy Store & Museum, **19**, **26**
  Thomas L. Kane Memorial Chapel, **19**
Kentuck Knob (Chalk Hill PA), **121**, **125**
Keystone State Park (Derry PA), **190**
Kidron OH, **170-171**
  Kidron Livestock Auction, **166**
  Lehman's hardware store, **164-165**, **170-171**
  Ohio Mennonite Relief Sale, **176**
Kinzua Bridge State Park (Johnsonburg PA), **19-20**, **26**, **189**
Kittanning PA
  Armstrong County Historical Society Museum, **63**
  favorite fall foliage sites, **81-82**
  visitor information, **146**
Knox & Kane Railroad (Marienville PA), **17-18**, **26**, **65**
Knox PA
  accommodations, **66**
  restaurants, **66-67**
Kooser State Park (Somerset PA), **190**

L

Lake Arthur (Portersville PA), **72**
Lake Erie (NY, OH, PA), **2-5**, **31**, **33-34**
Lake Milton State Park (Lake Milton OH), **192**
Lake Shore Railway Museum (North East PA), **13**
Latrobe PA, **129-130**
  Latrobe Brewing Company Store, **129**, **140**
  Loyalhanna Creek, **120**
  Loyalhanna Gorge Scenic Recreation Area, **130**
  restaurants, **142**
  Saint Vincent College, **129**, **140**
  visitor information, **139**, **146**
Laughlintown PA
  Compass Inn Museum, **131**, **140**
  Laurel Ridge State Park (Rockwood PA), **132**, **190**
  visitor information, **139**, **146**
Laurel Caverns (Farmington PA), **121**, **125**
Laurel Highlands Hiking Trail (Ohiopyle PA), **118**
Laurel Highlands Railroad (Scottdale PA), **140**

Laurel Hill State Park (Somerset PA), **190**
Laurel Mountain State Park (Rector PA), **190**
Laurel Ridge State Park (Rockwood PA), **132**, **190**
Laurel Summit State Park (Rector PA), **190**
LaVale MD
 restaurants, **110**
Leonard Harrison State Park (Wellsboro PA), **81**
Ligonier PA, **130**
 accommodations, **142**
 favorite fall foliage sites, **81-82**
 Fort Ligonier, **130**, **140**
 Graham's Antique Mall, **140**
 Idlewild Park, **130**, **140**
 Linn Run State Park (Rector PA), **130-131**, **140**, **190**
 Powdermill Nature Reserve, **131**, **140**
 restaurants, **142-143**
 visitor information, **139**, **146**
Lincoln Highway (U.S. 30) (PA), **128-139**
Linesville, PA **10**
 Linesville Fish Culture Station, **10**, **14**
 Pymatuning Reservoir & Spillway, **10-11**
 Pymatuning State Park (Jamestown PA), **11**, **14**, **190**
 visitor information, **10**
Linn Run State Park (Rector PA), **130-131**, **140**, **190**
Little Orleans MD
 accommodations, **109**
 Bill's Place, **103**
Longhouse National Scenic Byway (Warren PA), **21**
Lost River State Park (Mathias WV), **193**
Loyalhanna Gorge Scenic Recreation Area (Latrobe PA), **130**
Lucy-Desi Museum (Jamestown NY), **22-24**

M

Mahoning Creek Lake (Dayton PA), **56**
Malabar Farm State Park (Lucas OH), **192**
Marienville, PA, **17-18**
 Allegheny National Forest (PA), **17**
 Kinzua Viaduct, **17-18**, **26**
 Knox & Kane Railroad, **17-18**, **26**, **65**
 Pioneer Lodge, **27**
Marietta OH, **178-179**, **181-183**
 accommodations, **186**
 antique shops, **183**, **185**
 Butch's Cola Museum, **179-180**

Campus Martius: The Museum of the Northwest Territory, **185**
 covered bridge tour, **188**
 Fenton Art Glass Co., **185**
 Harmar Village, **179**
 Lafayette Hotel, **182**, **186**
 Larchmont B&B, **183**, **186**
 Mound Cemetery, **179**
 Ohio River Museum, **179**, **185**
 restaurants, **187**
 Rossi Pasta, **185**
 Showboat Becky Thatcher Theater and Restaurant, **185**
 Trolley Tours of Marietta, **183**, **185**
 Valley Gem riverboat, **179**, **185**
 visitor information, **145**, **184**, **188**
Maryland Office of Tourism (MD), **145**
Maryland State Parks information, **191**
Maurice K. Goddard State Park (Sandy Lake PA), **189-190**
McConnell's Mill State Park (Portersville PA), **72**, **77**, **190**
McHenry MD
 accommodations, **109**
 restaurants, **110**
 visitor information, **106**, **145**
 Wisp Ski Resort, **100**, **107**
McKean County PA
 visitor information, **25**, **146**
Meadville PA, **9**
 visitor information, **12**, **146**
Meyersdale PA
 maple sugar camps, **102**, **116-118**
Mill Run PA
 Fallingwater, **114-117**, **125**
 restaurants, **125**
 visitor information, **139**, **146**
Millersburg OH, **167**
 accommodations, **175-176**
 antiques, **167**
 Victorian House, **167**
 visitor information, **145**
Mohican State Park (Loudonville OH), **192**
Monongahela National Forest (Elkins WV), **88**, **94**, **97**
Moraine State Park (Portersville PA), **71-72**, **77**, **190**
Morgantown WV
 accommodations, **109**
 Cheat Lake, **99**
 Coopers Rock State Park, **99**, **107**, **193**
 Edgewater Marina, **107**

GO to Find information

restaurants, 110
Mosquito Lake State Park (Cortland OH), 192
Moundsville WV
  Grave Creek Mound State Park, 155, 159, 193
  Prabhupada's Palace of Gold, 155-156, 160
  West Virginia Penitentiary, 155, 159-160

N

National Highway (U.S. 40), 98, 102, 114, 118-120, 122-123, 126-127
Nemacolin Woodlands Resort (Farmington PA), 118, 125
New Castle PA
  accommodations, 77
  restaurants, 77
  visitor information, 76, 146
New Germany State Park (Grantsville MD), 101, 107, 191
New Manchester WV
  Tomlinson Run State Park, 152, 158, 193
New Philadelphia OH
  House of Baskets, 177
  Riverfront Antique Mall, 177
  Schoenbrunn Village, 177
  visitor information, 146
New Wilmington PA, 68-69
  accommodations, 77
  Amish community, 69
  restaurants, 77-78
  shops, 69
  Westminster College, 69
Newell WV
  Homer Laughlin China Co. Factory and
North East PA, 6-9
  Grape Arbor Inn, 14
  Heritage Wine Cellars, 8, 13
  Lake Country Bike, 13
  Lake Shore Railway Museum, 13
  Mazza Vineyards, 8, 13
  Penn Shore Vineyards, 8-9, 13
  Presque Isle Wine Cellars, 9, 13
  visitor information, 12

O

Oakland MD
  accommodations, 109
  Garrett County Historical Museum, 107
  Herrington Manor State Park, 101, 107, 191
  Swallow Falls State Park, 101, 107, 191
  visitor information, 106, 145
Oglebay Resort Park (Wheeling WV), 153-154, 159
Ohio B&Bs, 112
Ohio Central Railroad (Sugarcreek OH), 171, 174
Ohio Department of Travel and Tourism (OH), 145, 173
Ohio River (OH & WV), 81-82, 150-155, 178-179, 182
Ohio State Parks information, 192
Ohiopyle PA, 117-118
  accommodations, 126
  favorite fall foliage sites, 81-82
  visitor information, 139, 146
Oil City PA, 47-48
  accommodations, 51
  Oil Creek State Park, 47, 50, 190
  restaurants, 52
  visitor information, 49
Oil Creek and Titusville Railroad (Titusville PA), 48
Old Bedford Village (Bedford PA), 137, 141
Old Stone House (Slippery Rock PA), 71, 76-77

P

Parker Dam State Park (Penfield PA), 190
Passavant and Buhl Houses (Zelienople PA), 74, 77
Paw Paw Tunnel (Cumberland MD), 105, 108
Penn Alps (Grantsville MD), 102
Penn-Brad Historical Oil Well Park (Bradford PA), 20, 26
Pennsylvania Office of Travel and Tourism (Harrisburg PA), 146
Pennsylvania State Parks information, 189
Pennsylvania Travel Council, 112
Perry Memorial House (Erie PA), 3
Perry Monument (Erie PA), 12
Portage Lakes State Park (Akron OH), 192
Portersville PA
  accommodations, 77
  Lake Arthur, 72
  McConnell's Mill State Park, 72, 77
  Moraine State Park, 71-72, 77, 190
  shops, 73
  Slippery Rock Creek Gorge, 72
Potomac Eagle Scenic Railroad (Romney

GO to Find information

WV), **97**
Potomac Highlands Travel Council (Elkins WV), **147**
Powdermill Nature Reserve (Ligonier PA), **131, 140**
Prabhupada's Palace of Gold (Moundsville WV), **155-156, 160**
Presque Isle State Park (Erie PA), **4-5, 12-13, 190**
Preston County WV
 visitor information, **147**
Prickett's Fort State Park (Fairmont WV), **85-86, 94, 193**
Prince Gallitzin State Park (Patton PA), **191**
Pro Football Hall of Fame (Canton OH), **36-37, 177**
Punxsutawney PA, **56-58**
 accommodations, **65**
 Groundhog Day, **56-57, 67**
 Punxsutawney Area Historical & Genealogical Museum, **57, 64**
 restaurants, **66**
 Silverbrook Farms, **58, 64**
 visitor information, **63, 147**
Pymatuning Reservoir & Spillway (Linesville PA), **10-11**
Pymatuning State Park (Andover OH), **192**
Pymatuning State Park (Jamestown PA), **11, 14, 190**
Pymatuning Visitors Center (Linesville PA), **10**

Q

Quail Hollow State Park (Hartville OH), **192**

R

Rocky Gap State Park (Flintstone MD), **108, 191**
Russell City, PA, **19**
Ryerson Station State Park (Wind Ridge PA), **191**

S

S.B. Elliott State Park (Penfield PA), **190**
Saint Marys PA
 visitor information, **25, 146**
 wild Elk herd, **29**
Saint Vincent College (Latrobe PA), **129, 140**
Salisbury PA
 maple sugar camps, **102, 116-118**
Salt Fork State Park (Lore City OH), **181, 185-186, 192**
Samuel Justus Recreational Trail (Franklin PA), **50**
Sandusky OH
 visitor information, **145**
Savage Reservoir (Grantsville MD), **101**
Savage River (Grantsville MD), **101**
Sawmill Center for the Arts I & II (Cooksburg PA), **60, 64**
Scenery Hill PA, **123**
 accommodations, **126**
 Century Inn, **123, 126**
 restaurants, **123, 126**
 shops and historic buildings, **123**
 visitor information, **139, 146**
Schellsburg PA, **134-136**
 accommodations, **135-136, 142**
 backroads bicycling routes, **135**
 Cedarrow's Bison Farm, **134, 141**
 covered bridges, **135**
 farm markets and orchards, **135**
 Hotel Lincoln, **136**
 Jean Bonnet Tavern, **136, 142-143**
 Lincoln Motor Court, **135-136, 142**
 restaurants, **136, 143**
 Schellsburg Cemetery & Chapel, **134, 136**
 Shawnee State Park, **135, 141, 191**
Schoenbrunn Village (New Philadelphia OH), **177**
Seneca Caverns (Riverton WV), **97**
Seneca Point (Cooksburg PA), **59**
Seneca Rocks WV
 Dolly Sods Scenic Area, **97**
 Seneca Rocks, **97**
Seven Springs Mountain Resort (Champion PA), **127**
Shawnee State Park (Schellsburg PA), **135, 141, 191**
Sigel PA
 Belltown Canoe Rental, **64**
 Clear Creek State Park, **59, 64, 189**
 Farmer's Inn, **64**
Silver Lake WV
 Our Lady of the Pines, **90**
Sisterville WV, **156**
 self-guided walking tour, **156**
 Sisterville Ferry, **156**
 Wells Inn, **156, 160**

SKIING, CROSS-COUNTRY OR DOWN-HILL
Blue Knob State Park (Imler PA), **144, 190**
Canaan Valley Ski Resort (Canaan Valley WV), **95**
Cathedral State Park (Aurora WV), **89-90, 95, 193**
Cook Forest State Park (Cooksburg PA), **53, 59-61, 63, 189**
Coopers Rock State Park (Morgantown WV), **99, 107, 193**
Deerfield Village (Canaan Valley WV), **96**
Herrington Manor State Park (Oakland MD), **101, 107, 191**
Hidden Valley Resort (Hidden Valley PA), **127**
Laurel Mountain State Park (Rector PA), **190**
Laurel Ridge State Park (Rockwood PA), **132, 190**
Laurel Summit State Park (Rector PA), **190**
New Germany State Park (Grantsville MD), **101, 107, 191**
Ohiopyle State Park (Ohiopyle PA), **82, 118, 125, 190**
Presque Isle State Park (Erie PA), **4-5, 12-13, 190**
Pymatuning State Park (Jamestown PA), **11, 14, 190**
Seven Springs Mountain Resort (Champion PA), **127**
Swallow Falls State Park (Oakland MD), **101, 107, 191**
Timberline Four-Seasons Resort (Davis WV), **95**
White Grass Cross Country Ski Area (Davis WV), **95**
Wisp Ski Resort (McHenry MD), **100, 107**
Yellow Creek State Park (Penn Run PA), **191**

Slippery Rock PA, **71**
  accommodations, **77**
  Jennings Environmental Education Center, **71, 77**
  Jennings State Park, **189**
  Old Stone House, **71, 76-77**
  restaurants, **78**
  Slippery Rock Heritage Festival, **78**
Smicksburg PA, **55-56**
  Amish community, **55-56**
  John G. Smick Memorial Museum, **63**
  shopping, **55-56, 63**
  Windgate Vineyards, **56, 63**
Somerset County, PA
  favorite fall foliage sites, **81-82**
  maple sugar camps, **102, 116-118**
Somerset Historical Center (Jennerstown PA), **132-133, 140-141**
Somerset PA
  accommodations, **142**
  Annual Antique Flea Market, **143**
  Glades Pike Winery, **141**
  Horizon Outlet Center, **127**
  Kooser State Park (Somerset PA), **190**
  Laurel Hill State Park (Somerset PA), **190**
STATE PARKS, complete listings **189-193**
Steubenville OH, **152-153**
  visitor information, **145, 158**
Stonewall Jackson Lake State Park (Roanoke WV), **193**
Sugarcreek OH, **171-172**
  Alpine Hills Historical Museum, **171, 174**
  Ohio Central Railroad, **171, 174**
  restaurants, **171, 176**
  visitor information, **145, 173**
Swallow Falls State Park (Oakland MD), **101, 107, 191**

T

Tidioute PA
  Hickory Creek Wilderness Ranch (Tidioute PA), **27-28**
  Indian Waters Canoe Rentals (Tidioute PA), **27**
Timberline Four-Seasons Resort (Davis WV), **95**
Tinkers Creek State Park (Ravenna OH), **192**
Tionesta PA
  Tionesta Scenic Area (Sheffield PA), **17**
  visitor information, **25, 147**
Titusville PA
  accommodations, **51**
  Drake Well Park & Museum, **47-48, 50**
  Oil Creek and Titusville Railroad, **48**
  Oil Creek State Park (Oil City PA), **47, 50, 190**
  restaurants, **52**
  visitor information, **49**
Tomlinson Run State Park (New Manchester WV), **152, 158, 193**
Tucker County WV
  visitor information, **94, 147**

GO to Find information

Tuscarawas County OH
  visitor information, **146, 173**
Tygart Lake State Park (Grafton WV), **90-91, 94, 193**

U

Uniontown PA
  accommodations, **126**
  Searight's Tollhouse, **122, 125**
  visitor information, **139, 146**

V

Valley Falls State Park (Fairmont WV), **94, 193**
Venango County PA
  visitor information, **49**
Volant PA
  Neshannock Creek, **69**
  shopping, **69, 76**

W

Waldameer Park (Erie PA), **4, 13**
Walnut Creek OH, **165, 167**
  accommodations, **175**
  German Culture Museum, **174**
  restaurants, **176**
  Rolling Ridge Ranch, **174**
  Schrock's Amish Farm and Home, **165, 173**
  shops, **165, 167, 173-174**
  visitor information, **145, 173**
  Yoder's Amish Home, **165, 173**
Warren PA, **22-23**
  accommodations, **27**
  Allegheny River, **22**
  Heart's Content National Scenic Area, **17, 23**
  Hickory Creek Wilderness, **23**
  Jakes Rocks (Warren PA), **21**
  Kinzua Beach (Warren PA), **21**
  Kinzua Dam (Warren PA), **21**
  Longhouse National Scenic Byway (Warren PA), **21**
  Rimrock Overlook (Warren PA), **21**
  visitor information, **25, 147**
Washington County PA
  visitor information, **147**
Wayne County OH, **163, 170-172**
  Amish community, **163, 170-172**
  visitor information, **146, 173**
Wayne National Forest (Marietta OH), **188**
Waynesburg PA
  visitor information, **146**
Wellsburg WV **153**
  accommodations, **160**
  Brooke County Historical Museum, **158-159**
  Brooke Hills Playhouse, **159**
  restaurants, **160-161**
Wendell August Forge (Grove City PA), **71,72-73, 76**
West Branch State Park (Ravenna OH), **192-193**
West Virginia B&B Directory, **112**
West Virginia Division of Tourism (Charleston WV), **94, 147, 158**
West Virginia Penitentiary (Moundsville WV), **155, 159-160**
Western Maryland Scenic Railroad (Cumberland & Frostburg MD), **104-105, 108**
Western Maryland Station Center (Cumberland MD), **105**
Westminster College (New Wilmington PA), **69**
Westmoreland County, PA
  favorite fall foliage sites, **81-82**
  visitor information, **139, 146**
Westmoreland Museum of American Art (Greensburg PA), **129, 140**
Weston WV
  visitor information, **147**
Wheeling WV **153-155**
  accommodations, **160**
  Capitol Music Hall, **155-156, 159**
  Carriage House Glass Museum, **154, 159**
  Centre Market, **159**
  historic district, **154-155**
  Independence Hall, **159**
  Jamboree in the Hills, **161**
  Oglebay Resort Park, **153-154, 159**
  restaurants, **154-155, 161**
  riverfront trail, **155**
  Stifel Fine Arts Center, **159**
  suspension bridge, **154**
  visitor information, **147, 158**
  Wheeling Artisan Center at Heritage Square, **154-155, 159**
  Wymer's General Store Museum, **154-155, 159**
White Grass Cross Country Ski Area (Davis WV), **95**

Wisp Ski Resort (McHenry MD), **100**, **107**
Woodcarving Competition & All-Wood Crafts Festival (Cooksburg PA), **67**
Wooster OH
  visitor information, **146**, **173**

Y

Yellow Creek State Park (Penn Run PA), **191**
Youghiogheny River (Ohiopyle PA), **118**, **125**
Youngstown OH
  visitor information, **146**

Z

Zelienople PA, **73-74**
  accommodations, **77**
  Passavant and Buhl Houses, **74**, **77**
  restaurants, **78**
  Zelienople-Harmony Chamber of Commerce, **76**
Zippo Family Store & Museum (Bradford PA), **20**, **26**
Zoar Village (Zoar OH), **177**

GO to Order more copies

GIVE A LITTLE GIFT TO HELP OTHERS GO!

Send your order to:
THE GO GUIDE
c/o Pittsburgh Post-Gazette
P.O. Box 476
Pittsburgh, PA 15230

Please send me _____ copies of at $16 per copy ....$ _____
(Price includes tax, shipping and handling)   **TOTAL**

Make check payable to "Pittsburgh Post-Gazette"

For order via credit card, call (412) 263-1741

NAME: ....

ADDRESS ....

CITY ....STATE ....ZIP ....

Send your order to:
THE GO GUIDE
c/o Pittsburgh Post-Gazette
P.O. Box 476
Pittsburgh, PA 15230

Please send me _____ copies of at $16 per copy ....$ _____
(Price includes tax, shipping and handling)   **TOTAL**

Make check payable to "Pittsburgh Post-Gazette"

For order via credit card, call (412) 263-1741

NAME: ....

ADDRESS ....

CITY ....STATE ....ZIP ....

GO to Order more copies

GIVE A LITTLE GIFT TO HELP OTHERS GO!

Send your order to:
THE GO GUIDE
c/o Pittsburgh Post-Gazette
P.O. Box 476
Pittsburgh, PA 15230

Please send me ____ copies of at $16 per copy .... $ _____
(Price includes tax, shipping and handling)   **TOTAL**

Make check payable to "Pittsburgh Post-Gazette"

For order via credit card, call (412) 263-1741

NAME: ....

ADDRESS ....

CITY ....STATE ....ZIP ....

Send your order to:
THE GO GUIDE
c/o Pittsburgh Post-Gazette
P.O. Box 476
Pittsburgh, PA 15230

Please send me ____ copies of at $16 per copy .... $ _____
(Price includes tax, shipping and handling)   **TOTAL**

Make check payable to "Pittsburgh Post-Gazette"

For order via credit card, call (412) 263-1741

NAME: ....

ADDRESS ....

CITY ....STATE ....ZIP ....

GO to Order more copies

GIVE A LITTLE GIFT TO HELP OTHERS GO!

Send your order to:

THE GO GUIDE
c/o Pittsburgh Post-Gazette
P.O. Box 476
Pittsburgh, PA 15230

Please send me ____ copies of at $16 per copy ....$ _____
(Price includes tax, shipping and handling)   TOTAL

Make check payable to "Pittsburgh Post-Gazette"

For order via credit card, call (412) 263-1741

NAME: ....

ADDRESS ....

CITY ....STATE ....ZIP ....

Send your order to:

THE GO GUIDE
c/o Pittsburgh Post-Gazette
P.O. Box 476
Pittsburgh, PA 15230

Please send me ____ copies of at $16 per copy ....$ _____
(Price includes tax, shipping and handling)   TOTAL

Make check payable to "Pittsburgh Post-Gazette"

For order via credit card, call (412) 263-1741

NAME: ....

ADDRESS ....

CITY ....STATE ....ZIP ....

THE ALL NEW GO GUIDE

Pittsburgh Post-Gazette